Handmade Electronic Music

Disclaimer

Despite stringent efforts by all concerned in the publishing process, some errors or omissions in content may occur. Readers are encouraged to bring these items to our attention where they represent errors of substance. The publisher and author disclaim any liability for damages, in whole or in part, arising from information contained in this publication.

This book contains references to electrical safety that must be observed. *Do not use AC power for any projects discussed herein.*

The publisher and the author disclaim any liability for injury that may result from the use, proper or improper, of the information contained in this book. We do not guarantee that the information contained herein is complete, safe, or accurate, nor should it be considered a substitute for your good judgment and common sense.

Handmade Electronic Music

THE ART OF HARDWARE HACKING

Nicolas Collins

Illustrated by Simon Lonergan

Routledge
Taylor & Francis Group
New York   London

Routledge is an imprint of the
Taylor & Francis Group, an informa business

Published in 2006 by
Routledge
Taylor & Francis Group
270 Madison Avenue
New York, NY 10016

Published in Great Britain by
Routledge
Taylor & Francis Group
2 Park Square
Milton Park, Abingdon
Oxon OX14 4RN

Printed in the United States of America on acid-free paper
10 9 8 7 6 5 4 3 2 1

International Standard Book Number-10: 0-415-97591-3 (Hardcover) 0-415-97592-1 (Softcover)
International Standard Book Number-13: 978-0-415-97591-9 (Hardcover) 978-0-415-97592-6 (Softcover)
Library of Congress Card Number 2005030693

Library of Congress Cataloging-in-Publication Data

Collins, Nicolas.
  Handmade electronic music : the art of hardware hacking / by Nicolas Collins ; illustrated by Simon Lonergan.
    p. cm.
  Includes bibliographical references and index.
  ISBN 0-415-97591-3 (hardcover) -- ISBN 0-415-97592-1 (pbk.)
  1. Electronic apparatus and appliances-Design and construction-Amateurs' manuals. 2. Electronic musical instruments-Construction. I. Title.

TK9965.C59 2006
786.7'1923--dc22   2005030693

informa
Taylor & Francis Group
is the Academic Division of Informa plc.

Visit the Taylor & Francis Web site at
http://www.taylorandfrancis.com

and the Routledge Web site at
http://www.routledge-ny.com

CONTENTS

FOREWORD

DAVID BEHRMAN

The appearance of Nic Collins' *Handmade Electronic Music* has made me feel nostalgia for the sixties, when I was young and first heated up a soldering iron.

There was a mixture of exhilaration and wonder that my generation felt, those of us who worked on a grass-roots level with new technology in music in the sixties and seventies, as we taught ourselves about the fresh marvels then made available for the first time ever: the transistor, a little later the integrated circuit, then the microcomputer.

Most musicians in the sixties and seventies didn't make their own circuitry. They had other things to do. The few of us who did were aligning ourselves into the tinkerer-inventor tradition handed down from earlier artists who had built things, questioned the establishment, and found new sounds or tuning systems: artists like the Futurists, like Henry Cowell, Conlon Nancarrow, and Harry Partch.

Nic, the talented author of this manual, is roughly a generation away from me—he started building circuits as a way to make music in 1972. When I started around 1965—learning mostly from two artists who were friends and mentors—David Tudor and Gordon Mumma—there were no music synths for sale; when Nic started, synths existed but were out of reach unless you had a fat budget from a university or a record company.

In the sixties, I learned from Tudor and Mumma that you didn't have to have an engineering degree to build transistorized music circuits. David Tudor's amazing music was based partly on circuits he didn't even understand. He liked the sounds they made, and that was enough.

In the old days there wasn't any distinction between high tech and low tech. The early analog synths were made by creative individuals like Bob Moog and Don Buchla; even the early microcomputers were mostly made by garage start-ups and there wasn't so much difference between these and the craft shops that had made lutes, guitars, or violins for centuries. There had always been a good relationship between performing musicians and the craftspeople who made instruments—whether those were mbiras, clarinets, or gamelans. That relationship was comfortable—it was on a human scale and almost personal.

Only in recent decades have music instruments and software become corporate, mostly mass-produced and mass-marketed, and only recently are the computers used for music generally the same ones found in tens of millions of business establishments.

It isn't surprising that there had to be a reaction among artists to this corporate stain, if one could put it that way, that has spread into the fabric of music.

It's been interesting for me to learn that some independent-minded young artists won't even go near a computer when they think about doing their music. Their instincts tell them to rebel against this "obedient" mode in which artists—like everyone else—are pushed into continually buying, from ever-growing corporations, the latest computer and the latest software packages and then spending a vast number of hours learning how to use them.

There's an inescapable love–hate ambivalence about working as an artist with high-technology tools. On the one hand, computers and digital music-making devices have never been as miraculously powerful and reliable as they are today. They've gotten much cheaper than they used to be. Some software packages like Max/MSP are not really corporate products in the bad sense and they are infinitely personable and endlessly fascinating. I'm amazed when I compare audio recording or post-production work today with the way it was in the sixties when I worked on the night shift at Columbia Records. It used to take three burly professional engineers an hour to accomplish with bulky fifty-thousand-dollar machines what one can do today alone with a laptop in ten seconds.

But on the other hand, if you think about the "laptop music" style of performance which is currently in vogue, you might notice that there could be a problem, even if the music sounds good, with watching a person sitting in front of a computer and operating the mouse and keyboard. It is just too depressingly similar to what hundreds of millions of workers have to do from nine to five at the office. When evening comes and we go to the concert, we might like to experience something different, something visceral, something that is a direct result of muscular energy. We might like the relief of something zany and crazy. As Antonin Artaud said, there are plenty of people in the real world with two arms and two legs; in the theater we would like to see creatures with three.

Nic Collins' book helps us create creatures with three arms and three legs. It carries the maverick, inventor-tinkerer tradition of Harry Partch, Henry Cowell, and David Tudor into the twenty-first century. And it does so in a light, deft way—its charmingly simple, casual instructions hide the fact that its author is a sophisticated fellow who has done a lot of thinking, conversing, and music-making in the course of his travels and explorations.

Now that we're all stuck in the twenty-first century whether we want to be or not, we have amazing new high-tech devices to work with, but we have to accept our ambivalent relationship with these products of our corporate world. From the past we have the universe of acoustic instruments as well as the tinkerer's arsenal which is explored in this manual. The reassuring smell of heated solder remains. The vise-grip is still with us. So is the alligator clip. The good old soldering iron, the resistor and capacitor, the voltmeter, the color-coded wires—these remain. The fingers that Nic tells us how to use to coax the hidden treasures out of unknown circuit boards—they're still with us. The finger isn't obsolete. The ear isn't obsolete.

ACKNOWLEDGMENTS

This book began as a series of handouts for a course I offered in the summer of 2002 at The School of the Art Institute of Chicago. Over the next few years, after four sessions of the course at SAIC and a dozen workshops elsewhere in the United States and Europe, those handouts gradually evolved into the book you are holding. I owe a great debt to all those students who unwittingly served as guinea pigs while I struggled to clarify my prose and develop projects that would appeal to a diverse group, and be within the reach of would-be-hackers from a wide range of technical backgrounds.

There would have been no course and no book without the support of my colleagues at SAIC, especially Anna Yu, facilities manager of the Department of Art and Technology Studies, who generously made lab space, tools, and parts available to a class that was not at its best when it came to tidy up time; and Robb Drinkwater, the sound facilities manager, who repeatedly hunted down oddball supplies and offered constant support to puzzled students. Professor Frank DeBose of the Department of Visual Communication kindly gave accesss to his department's computer lab for work on the illustrations. The School's Dean of Faculty, Carol Becker, patiently tolerated my absences when I traveled for the workshops that helped hone this text.

I greatly appreciate the enthusiasm and support of those who risked their budgets (and possibly their reputations) producing my workshops in Hardware Hacking: Phil Hallet of Sonic Arts UK initiated and helped organize the first of these in January 2004 in cooperation with Gill Haworth and Dani Landau at The Watershed in Bristol, Simon Waters of the Music Department of the University of East Anglia in Norwich, and Pedro Rebelo of the Sonic Arts Research Center at Queens University in Belfast. Daniel Schorno, René Wassenburg, Nico Bes, and Michel Waisvisz brought my workshop to STEIM (the Vatican of Hacking) in Amsterdam, in a truly coals-to-Newcastle gesture. Other intrepid producers were Annemie Maes, Ferdinand Du Bois, and Guy van Belle at x-med-k in Brussels, Belgium; Chris Brown and John Bischoff at Mills College in Oakland, CA; Mark Trayle and Lorin Parker at the California Institute of the Arts, in Valencia, CA; Roland Roos and Monya Pletsch at Hochschule für Gestaltung und Kunst and Dorkbot in Zurich, Switzerland; Hans Tammen, Carol Parkinson, and Martin Baumgartner at Harvestworks in New York City; and Ulrich Müller and Christof Hoefig at T-U-B-E in Munich, Germany. The feedback I received from these workshops was invaluable.

Most of the technology and aesthetics in this book, as well as many of the circuit designs and artists highlighted, date from the 1970s—the early days of homemade electronic music.

I was fortunate to have started in the field at that time, and this text basically chronicles my evolution as a self-serving luthier during the heyday of "chipetry." There are many composers, artists, engineers, teachers, and colleagues who helped me on my way, by providing information, schematics, bench space, parts, and encouragement. Wherever possible I have tried to credit individuals in the text, but for their vital, ongoing support over the years I would like to single out David Behrman, Bob Bielecki, Ralph Burhans, Sukandar Kartadinata, Ron Kuivila, Alvin Lucier, Paul De Marinis, Bob Sakayama, David Tudor, and Bob White. I am greatly in debt to all the artists who contributed information, images and sound files to the book and CD, and who took the time to answer my questions.

Richard Carlin at Routledge not only took on this project enthusiastically, but made suggestions for changes and additions that make the book much more useful and enjoyable. The manuscript got into his hands through the spirited support of Thom Holmes. David Behrman, Chris Brown, Jonathan Impett, and Robert Poss gave me useful criticism on the text and the projects it covered. Finally, Devon Sherman at Taylor & Francis/Routledge provided editorial assistance, and Lynn Goeller and her able crew at EvS Communication Networx did a wonderful job of turning digital files into an analog book.

The early drafts of this book were filled with clumsy scribbles that elicited head scratching and laughter from my students and my children alike. Fortunately one student, Simon Lonergan, came to my rescue. Simon spent countless hours patiently translating my doodles and suggestions into the illustrations and photos in this book. I am full of awe and gratitude.

My wife, Susan Tallman, and my children Ted and Charlotte, put up with too many physical absences as I conducted workshops around the world, and tolerated my frequent mental absences while I revised this text—they are far more accommodating and supportive than I deserve. Finally, if I can write clearly enough to be understood it is entirely the result of the years of patient advice and editing by Susan. For this gift I owe her my greatest thanks, and a fresh red pen.

INTRODUCTION

This book teaches you how to tickle electronics. It is a guide to the creative transformation of consumer electronic technology for alternative use. We live in a cut-and-paste world: CMD-X and CMD-V give us the freedom to rearrange words, pictures, video and sound to transform any old thing into our new thing with tremendous ease. But, by and large, this is also an "off-line" world, whose digital tools, as powerful as they might be, are more suitable to preparing texts, photo albums, movies and CDs in private, rather than on stage. These days "live electronic music" seems to be hibernating, its tranquil countenance only disturbed from time to time by the occasional, discrete click of a mouse.

My generation of composers came of age before the personal computer, at a time when electronic instruments were far too expensive for anyone but rock stars or universities, but whose building blocks (integrated circuits) were pretty cheap and *almost* understandable. A small, merry (if masochistic) band, we presumed to Do-It-Ourselves. We delved into the arcane argot of engineering magazines, scratched our heads, swapped schematics, drank another beer, and cobbled together homemade circuits—most of them eccentric and sloppy enough to give a "real" engineer dyspepsia. These folk electronic instruments became the calling cards of a loose coalition of composers that emerged in the mid-1970s, after John Cage, David Tudor, and David Behrman, and before Oval, Moby, and Matmos. By the end of the 1970s the microcomputers that would eventually evolve into Apples and PCs had emerged from the primordial ooze of Silicon Valley, and most of us hung up our soldering irons and started coding, but the odd circuit popped up from time to time, adding analog spice to the increasingly digital musical meal.

Computers are wonderful, don't get me wrong, but the usual interface—an ASCII keyboard and a mouse—is awkward, and makes the act of *performing* a pretty indirect activity, like trying to hug a baby in an incubator. "Alternative controllers" (such as those made by Donald Buchla and artists working at STEIM) are a step in the right direction, but sometimes it's nice to reach out and *touch* a sound. This book lifts the baby out of the basinet and drops her, naked and gurgling, into your waiting arms, begging to be tickled.

The focus is on sound—making performable instruments, aids to recording, and unusual noisemakers—though some projects have a strong visual component as well. No previous electronic experience is assumed, and the aim is to get you making sounds as soon as possible.

After learning basic soldering skills, you will make a variety of listening devices: acoustic microphones, contact mikes, coils for picking up stray electromagnetic fields, tape heads. Then you will lay hands upon, and modify, cheap electronic toys and other found circuitry—the heart and soul of hacking. You'll build some circuits from scratch: simple, robust oscillators that can be controlled through a variety of means (light, touch, knobs, switches), and combined to create rich electronic textures at minimum cost and difficulty. With the confidence instilled by such a delicious din you will proceed with circuits to amplify, distort, chop, and otherwise mangle any sounds, be they electronic in origin or not: electric guitars, amplified voice, CDs, radio, environmental ambience, etc. You will then move on to designs for linking sound with visual material, and some convenient "glue" circuits, useful for putting disparate parts together for performance, recording, or interfacing to computers. There are several appendices that direct you to sources of supplies and further resources for information. Finally, tucked into the back cover is a CD, included not as an audio illustration for specific projects in the book (that would be giving away too many endings), but rather to show "real music" that some two dozen artists have made with the same kind of instruments you will be building.

In selecting the specific projects to include in this book I was guided by a handful of fundamental assumptions and goals:

1. To keep you alive. All the projects in this book are battery powered; none plug into the potentially lethal voltage running through your walls. This makes the early stages of unsupervised electronic play activity considerably safer, and less daunting for the beginner.
2. To keep things simple. We work with a small number of very simple "axiomatic" circuits and concepts that can be combined with great permutational richness as you proceed and gain experience, but are easy to understand and quick to get running at the beginning. The point is to make cool sounds as quickly as possible.
3. To keep things cheap. By limiting ourselves to a few core designs we minimize the quantity and cost of supplies needed to complete this book. You don't need a full electronics lab, just a soldering iron, a few hand tools, and about $50 worth of parts that you can easily obtain online. By focusing on toys and other simple consumer electronics we also minimize the threat of "catastrophic loss" in the early, unpredictable days of freestyle hacking: a Microjammer sets you back considerably less than a vintage Bass Balls.
4. To keep it stupid. You will find here an absolute minimum of theory. We learn to design by ear, not by eye, gazing at sophisticated test instruments or engineering texts. Ignorance is bliss, so enjoy it.
5. To forgive and forget. There's no "right way" to hack. I will try to steer you away from meltdowns, but have included designs that are robust, forgiving of wiring errors, and accept a wide range of component substitutions if you don't have the preferred part. Most of these circuits are starting points from which you can design many variations with no further help from me—if you love a hack, let it run free.

As a result of these axioms, this is a distinctly nonstandard introduction to electronic engineering. Many of the typical subjects of a basic electronics course, such as the worrisomely vague transistor and the admittedly useful little thing called an op-amp, are left unmentioned. After turning over the last page, you will emerge smarter, if weirder, than when you first opened the book. You will have acquired some rare skills, and ones that are exceedingly useful in the pursuit of unusual sounds. You will have significant gaps in your knowledge, but these gaps can be filled by a less structured stroll through resources easily available in books and online (as described in Appendix A). And everything electronic you choose to do after this book will be easy, I promise. Why? Because you will be fearless. You will have the confidence to survey those presumptuous "No user serviceable parts inside!" labels and laugh. You will be a hacker.

PART I

STARTING

Chapter 1

GETTING STARTED:
TOOLS AND MATERIALS NEEDED

You will need certain tools and materials to undertake the projects in this book. I have kept the supplies to an absolute minimum—none of the fancy test equipment and drawers full of teeny parts found in a typical electronics lab; a few basic hand tools, and a modest collection of easily obtainable components will see you through.

Listening

Whereas electronic engineering is typically taught with *visual* reinforcement—staring at an oscilloscope, meters, or a computer screen—we will work by *ear*, as befits the development of sonic circuitry. A *monitor amplifier* thus becomes your primary tool. Whereas it would be nice to listen to our boops and beeps through a 250 watt Bryston amplifier and a pair of Altec 604E loudspeakers, I advocate the use of a small, battery-powered amplifier (see figure 1.1). It is cheaper, but more importantly it is *safer*: many of our experiments entail touching electronic circuitry with damp fingers, and those fingers should be kept far, far away from the 120 (or 240) volts streaming into any device with a power cord.

We need a fair amount of *gain* at the input to our amplifier, especially at the beginning of this book, where we start out making a variety of microphones with pretty low output levels. Therefore a typical pair of battery-power speakers intended for amplifying a portable CD player, MP3 player, computer or other *line level device* will not do. Better to use one of those wee bitty guitar amps by Fender, Marshall, Dan Electro, etc.—they look like little lunchboxes, or the guitarist's equivalent of a shrunken head. The cheapest one I've found is from Radio Shack (#277-1008, $12.99). It also has a very useful jack for an external speaker, which comes in handy in chapter 8. The more expensive ones pitched at guitarists, on the other hand, have the advantages of a bigger speaker, a tone control, overdrive/distortion, and a more robust and useful 1/4 inch input jack (the Radio Shack amp uses 1/8 inch inputs).

If you are feeling slightly adventurous, the cheapest (and most flexible) solution is to buy a low power (< 1 watt) amplifier kit from any of a number of online retailers (see figure 1.2). These kits include all components, a tidy little printed circuit board, and instructions

Figure 1.1 Some battery-powered mini-amplifiers.

on where to place which component. This is an excellent way to bootstrap your soldering skills, while saving some money. See Appendices A and C for suggestions on kits and where to find them, then jump ahead to chapter 6 for advice on how to solder. Besides the economic and pedagogic advantages of building your own tool, you can connect to these amplifiers using clip leads instead patch cords, so it's faster and cheaper to test out your projects.

Tools

You'll need some basic tools. Many will already be in your collection if you've ever had to change a washer, wire up a lamp, or serve in the Swiss Army. None are expensive—the only place you might want to splurge a little is on a better-than-terrible soldering iron.

- A soldering iron, with a very fine point, 25–60 watts. Not a soldering gun—that's for VoTech classes. Don't get a cheap iron—it makes it very frustrating to learn soldering. Weller makes good ones that are reasonably priced and have replaceable, interchangeable tips.

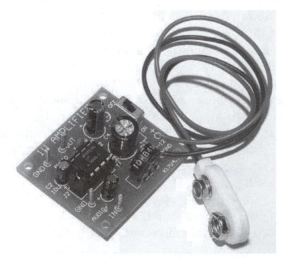

Figure 1.2 A low-power amplifier kit.

- Solder—fine, rosin core—not "acid-core" solder, that's for plumbers.
- Diagonal cutters, small, for cutting wire and component leads down by the circuit board.
- Wire strippers (unless you have the perfect gap between your front teeth)—simple, adjustable manual kind for light-gauge wire.
- A set of jeweler's screwdrivers (flat & Philips)—for opening toys with tiny screws.
- A Swiss Army Knife.
- A pair of scissors.
- A cheap digital multimeter, capable of reading resistance, voltage, and current.
- Plastic electrical tape.
- Mini jumper cables with small alligator clips at each end, at least 20 of them—you can never have too many.
- A "Sharpie"-style fine-tipped permanent marker.
- Some small spring clamps or clothespins.
- A small vise or "3rd Hand" device for holding things while you solder them.
- Basic shop tools—such as a small saw for metal and plastic, files, and an electric drill—are useful when you start to work on packaging.

Parts

At the head of each chapter you'll find a list of the specific parts needed to complete the projects covered, and complete inventory of parts for all projects is included in Appendix C. But here are the supplies you'll need for almost everything, so you might as well pick them up early. Appendix C also lists online retail sources for most of this stuff.

- Lightweight insulated hookup wire, 22–24 gauge, one roll stranded, one roll solid.
- Lightweight shielded audio hookup cable, single conductor plus shield.
- Assortment of standard value resistors, 1/8 or 1/4 watt. (Sets are easily and inexpensively available from Radio Shack or mail order/Web retailers.)
- Assortment of capacitors, in the range of 10pf to .1 uf monolithic ceramic or metal film, and 1uf to 47uf electrolytic. These can be bought in assortments, or you can purchase a handful of each of a few different values from across the full range, then replace or supplement them as needed.
- Nine-volt battery clips—the things that snap onto the nipples at the end of a battery and terminate in lengths of wire. Get five or more.
- Assorted audio jacks and plugs to mate with other devices, i.e., your amplifier, CD player, radio, toys, etc.

Batteries

Because of our core philosophy of avoiding unnecessary electrocution, we will be working exclusively with battery-powered devices. This means we will need a lot of batteries, for your amplifier, toys, radio, and the circuits you make. Please be *milieu vriendelijk* (a friend of the environment) as the Dutch say, and invest in some rechargeable ones if at all possible. Your groundwater will thank you.

Architecture

You'll need a clean, well-lighted place. It should also be well ventilated—soldering throws up some pretty unhealthy fumes. You'll also want a fair amount of table space, since hacking has an unfortunate tendency to sprawl (see figure 1.3). The table surface can be damaged by soldering, drilling and filing, so no Boule inlay please. You'll need electrical power at the table for your soldering iron and a good strong desk light.

Ok, are you feeling ready to hack? First, a few rules to live by…

Figure 1.3 A typical worktable, before and during hacking.

Chapter 2

THE SEVEN BASIC RULES OF HACKING: GENERAL ADVICE

Like boot camp or Candyland, this book is almost devoid of theory, but heavy on rules. Here are a few guidelines for keeping you healthy and happy:

Rule #1: Fear not!
Ignorance *is* bliss, anything worth doing is worth doing *wrong*, and two wrongs *can* make a right.

Rule #2: Don't take apart anything that plugs directly into the wall.
We will work almost exclusively with battery-powered circuitry. AC-powered things can kill you. AC adapters (wall-warts) may be used *only* after you have displayed proper understanding of the difference between insulation and electrocution.

Rule #3: It is easier to take something apart than put it back together.
Objects taken apart are unlikely to function normally after they are put back together, no matter how careful you are. Consider replacement cost before you open.

Rule #4: Make notes of what you are doing as you go along, not after.
Most wires look pretty much alike. As you take things apart make notes on which color wire goes to where on the circuit board, to what jack, etc. Especially important are the wires that go to the battery. Likewise, note what you add as you add it, what you change as you change it.

Rule #5: Avoid connecting the battery backwards.
This can damage a circuit.

Rule #6: Many hacks are like butterflies: beautiful but short-lived.
Many hacks you perform, especially early in your career, may destroy the circuit eventually. Accept this. If it sounds great, record it as soon as possible, and make note of what you've done to the circuit so you can try to recreate it later (see Rule #4).

Rule #7: In general, try to avoid short circuits.

Try to avoid making random connections between locations on a circuit board using plain wire or a screwdriver blade. This can damage a circuit—not *always*, but inevitably at the most inconvenient time.

Additional rules will emerge from time to time throughout the book, and are reiterated in Appendix D.

PART II

LISTENING

Chapter 3

CIRCUIT SNIFFING:
USING RADIOS AND COILS TO EAVESDROP ON HIDDEN
ELECTROMAGNETIC MUSIC

You will need:

- A battery-powered AM radio or two.
- A battery-powered amplifier.
- An inductive telephone pickup coil or a loose electric guitar pickup.
- Optional: 100 feet of light-gauge insulated wire, an audio plug and two pieces of wood, approximately 1 inch × 2 inches × 5 feet.

Radios

Radios make the inaudible audible. Unlike microphones and amplifiers, which merely make very quiet *acoustic* sounds much louder, radios pick up electromagnetic waves that have no acoustic presence whatsoever and translate them into signals that can be heard through a loudspeaker. Radios are manufactured for listening to intentionally transmitted electromagnetic waves (i.e., those sent from radio stations) from which they extract music and speech through a process of *demodulation*—multiple stages of amplification, filtering, and frequency shifting. But radios can also be used to sniff out other types of waves, such as those emitted by lightning, sunspots, Aurora Borealis, meteorites, subway trains, and a gaggle of household appliances (see "Mortal Coils"). Generally speaking, AM radios (the cheaper the better) do a better job of picking up these "spurious" noises than FM radios.

Put batteries in the radio and turn it on; if it has a *band select switch* set it initially to AM. Tune it to a dead spot. Try moving it around various electrical appliances: fluorescent lights, electric motors, computers, portable CD players, cell phones, MP3 players, infrared remote controls, and controllers for RC planes and cars are especially noisy. Fire off a camera flash next to it. Experiment with tuning the radio to different stations, in-between stations, and to the dead bands at either end of the dial.

As the FCC often warns you, certain electrical appliances can cause "radio interference." What this means is that, as a byproduct of whatever useful thing the appliances are doing,

Mortal Coils

In addition to constituting the basic mechanism of radios, microphones, and speakers, electromagnetic fields have spookier aspects that have been central to instrument design and artists' works for almost one hundred years. The siren song of the Theremin (the earliest commercial electronic instrument, invented by Leon Theremin in 1924) resulted from two high frequency radio signals beating like out-of-tune strings on a piano. Seventy years later Gert-Jan Prins (Netherlands) and David First (USA) (see track 3 on the CD) created music out of Theremin-like interference and feedback between radio receivers and transmitters. Some of the earliest realizations of computer music were heard through radios placed on top of the central processing units of mainframes: engineers would run programs with instruction cycles whose lengths were calculated to emit a composed sequence of radio frequencies, which were duly demodulated by the radios.

Alvin Lucier's (USA) "Sferics" (1980) is a recording of electromagnetic "tweaks," "bonks," and "swishes" originating in the ionosphere, the result of self-immolating meteorites, the dawn chorus, and the Aurora Borealis. The squeal and chatter of mistuned shortwave receivers has been an inspiration to composers from Karlheinz Stockhausen (Germany), whose 1968 composition "Kurzwellen" used four receivers in live performance, to Disinformation (UK), who has made a career of recording and performing with radio signals from across the spectrum,

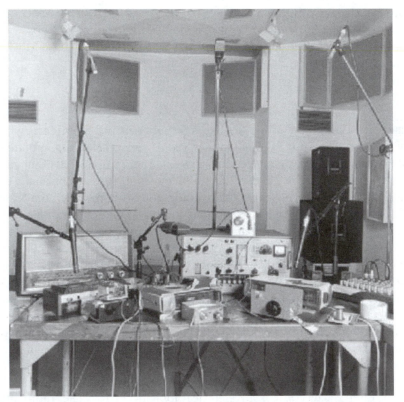

Gert-Jan Prins, installation for *Sub V* at STEIM, Amsterdam, The Netherlands, March 1996.

emanating from both human activities (power stations, navigation satellites, submarine communication, camera flashes) and natural sources (sun spots, thunderstorms). Australian artist Joyce Hinterding has worked with enormous coils both in gallery settings and in the wild. Recently telephone taps have been used to pick up stray radio emissions from laptops, CD players, subway trains, and a host of other unexpected objects by artists such as Nathan Davis (USA), Haco (Japan), Andy Keep (UK) (see track 1 on the CD), Jérôme Noetinger (France), Lorin Parker (USA), and Sonia Yoon (USA). And the electric guitar pickup just might be the single most important musical discovery of the twentieth century.

they emit lots of spurious electromagnetic radiation in the same frequency region as radio and TV broadcasts—they whistle while they work. As you tune the radio it becomes sensitive to specific frequency ranges (mostly very high) of electromagnetic waves, shifts them down into the range of our hearing and amplifies them. Compared to radio stations, these appliances put out very weak signals—the noise from a computer drops off rapidly as you move the radio a few feet away (hence the FCC advice).

If your radio has a FM band, try it as well. The technique of FM radio transmission and reception is designed to minimize interference, but strong periodic signals (like the clock frequency of a computer) can sometimes be tuned in.

Coils

An alternate approach to picking up electromagnetic signals is to use a simple coil of wire and an amplifier. A *telephone pickup* consists of yards of thin copper wire wrapped around an iron slug (see figure 3.1). Plugged into an amp, this coil acts like a radio antenna for low frequencies. Stuck on a telephone receiver (or held against any other loudspeaker), it picks up the electromagnetic field generated by the voice coil of the speaker, allowing you to record your landlord making unsavory threats.

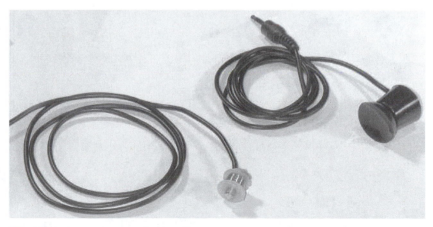

Figure 3.1 A telephone coil pickup, showing internal coil construction (left) and packaging (right).

Plug the tap coil into your portable amp and repeat the experiments we did with the radio. Sometimes you will hear different sounds from the same appliance. The coil is small enough that you can move it close in to precise locations, like a stethoscope. Boot your laptop, and note the change in sound as you move the coil across the surface, from the CPU area to the RAM to the battery to the CDROM drive to the screen (see track 1 on the CD). Stick it onto a portable CD player and notice the racket as you press "play", ">>|" and "|<<"—you're hearing the frantic electromagnetic fields of all those little motors and servos that spin the disk and move and focus the laser. Eavesdrop on a cell phone as you initiate a call. Listen to small motors in fans, vibrators, and toys; notice the change in pitch as you change the motor speed. Take a ride on the subway and listen to the motors and doors as you come in and out of stations (see track 2 on the CD). Cozy up to a neon sign.

The stethoscope-like accuracy of the coil moving over a circuit board makes it a useful, nondestructive device for pinpointing the location of interesting sounds that we can later tap off directly with a wires soldered to the board (see chapter 17.)

If you move the coil near the speaker of your amplifier it will begin to feed back with the coil that moves the speaker cone (see chapter 4). As with feedback between a microphone and speaker, the pitch is a function of the distance between the two parts, but here the pitch changes smoothly and linearly, without the odd jumps caused by the vagaries of acoustics, giving you a Theremin-like instrument. Try this with a full-size guitar amplifier for greater range.

Speaking of guitars, you can use a guitar pickup in place of a telephone tap—a guitar pickup is just a coil of wire, wrapped around a magnet, inside an expensive package (see figure 3.2). You can repeat the above experiments with a whole guitar in your hands, but a loose pickup is handier. At repair shops you can sometimes buy cheap the low-end pickups removed when better ones are installed. Jump ahead to chapter 6 if you need advice on wiring the pickup to a cord and plug. As most guitarists know, "single coil" pickups

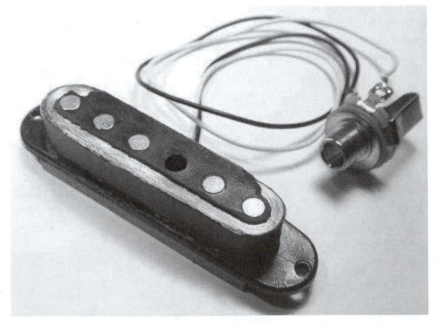

Figure 3.2 A guitar pickup with case broken away to reveal internal coil.

are better at picking up hum and weird electromagnetic noise, while "humbuckers" are so called because they tend to be less sensitive to exactly the kind of garbage we want to hear here.

Finally, any chunk of ferric metal (a magnet or piece of metal that is attracted to a magnet) with enough wire wrapped around it will pick up magnetic fields. You can solder a plug onto the wires coming out of any transformer (such as a wall-wart external power supply), relay coil, solenoid, or electric motor; connect it to your amp and listen. You can also wrap your own coils, which brings us to…

Cults

The *length* of wire used in the coil affects its sensitivity to different frequencies (like the tuning dial on a radio.) Fans of what is know as VLF (Very Low Frequency) radio make big coils by wrapping yards of wire around big wooden crosses and then camp out on remote hilltops like hermit Klansmen. Get far enough from civilization's ubiquitous 60/50 Hz hum and you may be lucky enough to pick up the Aurora Borealis, "whistlers" induced by meteorites self-immolating as they enter the earth's atmosphere, the pipping of GPS satellites, or top-secret submarine radio communication.

If you want to experiment, take a hundred feet or so of ordinary insulated wire and wrap it around a wooden armature (nail two 5 foot pieces of 1 inch x 2 inch lumber together and notch the ends to keep the wire from slipping off). Solder one end of the wire to the *tip* of a plug that fits into your amp or tape recorder, and solder the other end to the *sleeve*. Plug in, turn on, drop out.

Dueling Radios

In the process of receiving and demodulating transmissions, radios actually generate and send back out intermediary electromagnetic signals. These transmissions aren't very powerful, but evidently are strong enough that airline passengers are warned not to turn on radios in flight for fear of disrupting the navigation system (knowing just how weak these signals really are further diminishes one's faith in air travel safety). What one radio transmits another will receive: turn on two AM radios, tune them to the dead band at the end of the tuning range, and set them close together; by moving the radios and varying the tuning you should be able to produce Theremin-like whistling and interference patterns (see track 3 on the CD).

Chapter 4

IN/OUT (THE EIGHTH RULE OF HACKING): SPEAKER AS MICROPHONE, MICROPHONE AS SPEAKER— THE SYMMETRY OF IT ALL

You will need:

- A battery-powered amplifier.
- A pair of headphones or a small speaker.
- A pair of jumper leads with alligator clips and a plug to fit the input jack of your amplifier.

Electromagnetism

There is a beautiful symmetry to the principles of electricity that are most commonly used to translate acoustic sound into an electrical signal and then back into sound again. Inside every dynamic microphone (such as a typical PA mike) is a lightweight plastic membrane affixed to a coil of fine wire encircling a cylindrical magnet. Madonna sings, and her sound waves jiggle the membrane, which moves the coil in the field of the magnet, generating a very small electrical current. This current is amplified, equalized, flanged, reverberated, compressed, and finally amplified even more before being sent back out to a bigger coil wrapped around an even bigger magnet. Now this shimmering electromagnetic field pushes and pulls against the big magnet (think of the two magnetic Scotty dogs, forever trying to align themselves nose to tail), moving a paper cone back and forth, producing sound waves of…a louder, possibly improved, Madonna.

A record player cartridge is basically a microphone with a needle where the diaphragm should be; and record cutting heads are beefy backwards phonograph cartridges. Head-phones are tiny speakers. The telephone tap coils we used earlier are electromagnets with no moving parts, receiving or emitting electromagnetic waves rather than acoustical sound waves.

Not only is the same electromagnetic force used for both input and output devices (microphones and speakers), but sometimes the gizmos themselves are interchangeable. Try plugging a pair of headphones into the input jack on your amp or cassette recorder;

speak into it and listen—more than one band's demo tape was recorded this way. Plug any small speaker into the input of the amp. According to legend, Motown engineers recorded kick drum with a large speaker placed in front of the drumhead—a sort of a subwoofer mike. These alternative microphones don't sound as generically "good" as a $5,000 Neumann tube mike, but (as Motown's sales have shown) for special applications they can be very useful.

Likewise any dynamic (i.e., coil and magnet) microphone can be used as a very quiet speaker or headphone, but microphones have very delicate coil windings and can be easily blown out, so BE CAREFUL. Also, condenser mikes (like the "plug-and-power" mikes for cassette recorders, or expensive studio mikes) use a different, not-so-easily reversible principle of translation, so:

IF THE MIKE USES A BATTERY OR PHANTOM POWER OR
IS REALLY, REALLY EXPENSIVE, DON'T USE IT BACKWARDS.

Rule #8: In electronics some things are reversible with interesting results, but some things are reversible only with irreversible results.

Some of you may recognize that the 8th Rule of Hacking is a pragmatic offshoot of the First Law of the Avant-Garde:

Do it backwards.

Chapter 5

THE CELEBRATED JUMPING SPEAKER OF BOWERS COUNTY: TWITCHING LOUDSPEAKERS WITH BATTERIES

You will need:

- A few dispensable raw loudspeakers of any size (salvage them from old TVs, cast-off boom-boxes or stereos, answering machines, etc.)
- A 9-volt battery and a few C or D batteries.
- Some jumper leads with alligator clips.
- Some hookup wire.
- Electrical tape or gaffing tape.
- A medium size nail.
- A file.
- A sheet of copper, steel or iron, or a chunk of some conductive metal, the more corroded or scratched the better.
- Pop-tabs from soda cans, paper clips, loose change, nuts and bolts, assorted scrap metal.
- A can whose diameter is slightly less than that of one of your speakers.
- Some rice, beans, or gravel.
- Plastic or metal bowls, larger than your speaker, or a toilet plunger.

Creative mistreatment of loudspeakers goes beyond Motown, and even precedes amplification as we now know it. British computer scientist and musician John Bowers has developed a beautiful electric instrument, evoking the spirit of nineteenth-century electrical experimentation (think twitching frogs legs and early telephones) out of nothing more than a speaker, some batteries, wire, and scrap metal.

Hook up the circuit shown in figure 5.1. Clip one end of a test lead to one terminal of the speaker (it doesn't matter which). Clip the other end to the "+" or "−" terminal of the battery (again, it doesn't matter which one). Now tap the loose end of the second clip lead to the open terminal of the battery. The speaker should pop in or out from its position of repose. If it doesn't, the battery is dead, speaker is blown, or/and one or both of the clip leads is faulty; replace suspect elements until you hear and see the speaker jump. Disconnect the clip and the cone should pop back to its original position. Reversing the

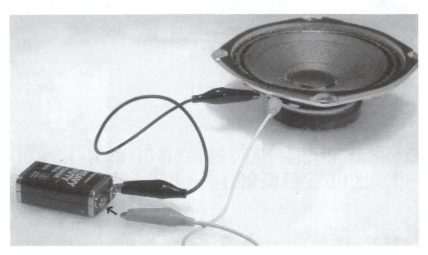

Figure 5.1 Twitching a speaker.

polarity of the battery will change an inny to an outy or vice versa: the cone that popped out should now suck in.

What's happening? Passing the battery current through the speaker coil (which is attached to the paper cone) creates an electromagnet that interacts with the speaker's fixed magnet (attached to the metal framework) and moves the cone in or out, depending on the polarity of the battery and resultant magnetic field (remember our Scotty dogs from the last chapter). Incidentally, the racetrack-like path of the current from the positive terminal of the battery, though the leads and speaker cone, to the minus terminal of the battery neatly demonstrates the etymological root of the electronic usage of the term "circuit."

Tapping the alligator clip against the battery terminal will produce a nice little percussive accent, at one and the same time drum-like and "speaker-ish," acoustic and electronic. But that's just the start. Connect one lead from a battery terminal to a speaker terminal. But this time, instead of connecting the second lead directly from the battery to the other speaker terminal, clip it between the speaker and a metal file or a chunk of some conductive metal: a pie tin, a cookie sheet, scrap copper flashing, an anvil, a piece of girder, a brake drum, a frying pan, etc.—the rougher or more corroded the metal surface, the better. Clip one end of a third jumper lead to the other terminal of the battery and the other end to a nail, bent paperclip, knife, or other pointed piece of conductive metal (see figure 5.2).

Touch the nail to the metal. When it contacts the metal, the nail completes the circuit, sending current through the speaker coil, and making the cone jump, as before. Now scrape the nail across the metal: as the contact is broken by irregularity of the surface, the speaker emits scratchy, percussive sounds whose character is quasi-controllable through hand gesture. Drawing the nail across a file yields sounds curiously like those of turntable scratching.

You may notice sparks as the contact is made and broken, and the battery will probably get warm—the speaker coil is almost a short circuit, and sucks a lot current from the battery. Avoid holding the nail on the metal for an extended period of time—loudspeakers get hot and bothered when presented with a steady DC voltage, so it's better to send them shorter pulses. Don't try this with your roommate's Bang & Olufsen, and don't plug a speaker directly into the wall. A 9-volt battery won't last very long under such treatment (see chapter 17 for a little bit of battery science)—try substituting one or more C or D cells. You can buy holders for multiple batteries at Radio Shack or online retailers if you're

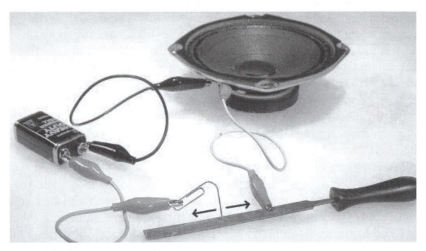

Figure 5.2 Scratching a speaker.

fussy, or you can just tape them together with a bit of bare wire held against each end, onto which you then clip the leads previously attached to the 9-volt battery terminals.

Instead of using the nail and file, you can clip the leads to two paperclips, washers, coins, aluminum pop-tabs, or loops of copper wire that you place inside the speaker cone. The cone jumps when contact is made, breaking the contact for a moment, then the metal bits fall against each other and the process starts all over—a mechanical oscillator and the beginning of what Bowers calls "The Victorian Synthesizer" (see figure 5.3 and track 4 of the CD).

Hold two contacts (like flip-tabs) close together against the speaker cone: by varying your touch and the location on the cone, you can change the pitch and rhythm of the buzzing sounds.

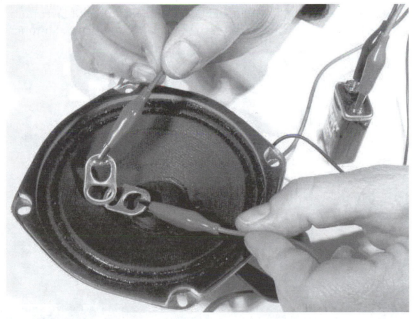

Figure 5.3 The Victorian Synthesizer.

You can line the cone with aluminum foil or apply metal tape (such as the kind sold in hardware stores or Radio Shack for preparing windows for home burglar alarms), connect one lead to the foil or tape and the other to a flip-tab or other light metal fragment. The tab gets thrown up from the foil or tape, breaking and making contact as before. Multiple speakers can be wired in series (like those frustrating Christmas lights from our childhood) or parallel, with contacts resting in each cone, so they interact to produce more complex rhythms. You can substitute a tilt-switch (see chapter 16) for the aluminum tabs as another way of using the speaker's own movement to turn on and off the current.

Sound doesn't end at the loudspeaker, it starts there. You can use your hands, bowls, or toilet plungers to mute and resonate the sound further. Put gravel, loose change, or dried lentils inside the cone for additional rhythmic accents. Place a can on the cone, open end down; clip one lead to the can and one to a metal washer placed on top of the can (see figure 5.4). The speaker cone will jump, breaking and remaking the contact as before, but in addition, as the can jiggles it changes resonance like a trumpet mute; additional loose coins or beans place on top of the can produce additional percussive accents. Alternatively, put some jangly things inside a small glass bottle/vial and place it inside a cone—*maracas de cristal*.

You'll notice that different speakers sound different, even if in similar configurations. It's mostly a function of size, as with drums, but if you try these experiments with a speaker in an enclosure (such as one from a home stereo) you'll hear that it has considerably more bass presence—the box gives a woofer its woof.

You can further extend the sound world of the jumping speaker by placing a telephone tap (see chapter 3) in the cone and connecting it to an amplifier. The sound will change as the signal is amplified into a second ("normal") speaker, and the bouncing of the coil inside the cone produces variations in the speaker's percussive snap.

Finally, there's a visual element: you can fill the speaker cone with talcum powder or light sand and watch it make patterns as the cone jumps. For a touch of the old Fillmore light show, waterproof the speaker cone by painting it with enamel or rubber cement. Fill the cone with water or oil and turn down the lights; reflect a flashlight or laser pointer off the surface, and watch the resulting patterns on the wall or ceiling. Think Summer of Love.

Figure 5.4 A "prepared speaker."

Chapter 6

HOW TO SOLDER:
AN ESSENTIAL SKILL

You will need:

- A soldering iron with a fine tip.
- A small damp sponge (or, in a pinch, a folded wet paper towel).
- Rosin-core solder.
- Diagonal wire cutters.
- Wire strippers.
- Some light gauge insulated wire, solid or stranded.
- An audio jack or plug of some kind.

Soldering is one of the fundamental skills of hardware hacking. It is almost impossible to hack hardware *without* knowing how to solder. As a skill it commands a lower hourly wage than Java or C++, but your friends and parents will be very impressed at your acquisition of such arcane knowledge (as if you had learned fire eating or Linear B).

Successful soldering, like fundamentalist Christian comedy performed in mid-winter by an L-Dopa patient, depends on cleanliness, heat, steady hands, and...timing!

Soldering is not a question of dropping melted solder onto a joint. Rather, one must first melt a thin layer of solder onto each surface, then let them cuddle up to one another while you heat both surfaces to re-melt the solder until it commingles to form a strong bond. The process is similar to gluing wood: the strongest bond comes from permeating the surfaces of both pieces of wood with a layer of glue before assembly, rather than just squeezing out a blob of glue and slapping them together.

We will begin by practicing soldering wires together—high temperature knitting.

1. Plug in the iron and place it somewhere where the tip will not make contact with flammable, meltable or scorchable surfaces, or its own power cord (cute little wire rests are sold for this purpose). Wait a long time for it to warm up. The iron is hot enough to use when solder touched to the tip melts.
2. Wipe the tip of the hot iron across a damp sponge. The tip must be smooth and clean enough that the solder flows evenly, leaving a shiny silver coating. If blobs of solder fall off and the tip remains grey and crusty even after sponging, unplug the iron and,

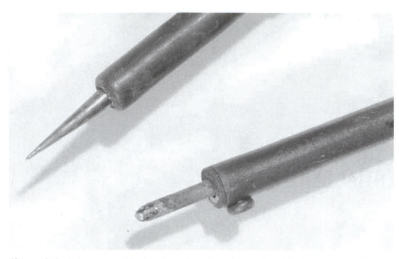

Figure 6.1 A happy soldering iron (top) and a sad soldering iron (bottom).

after it has cooled down, polish the tip with steel wool, fine sandpaper, or a file, and try again (see figure 6.1). If the tip of the iron is seriously pitted you will need to replace the tip (or, if it is a cheap iron with nonreplaceable tip, the whole iron).

3. Strip about 1 inch of insulation from the ends of two pieces of wire. Use the adjustments on the strippers (or a fine sense of touch) to avoid cutting through the wire. If the wire is stranded, twist the strands to eliminate frazzling. Hold the wires in something so that the tips are up in the air but don't wiggle. You can use a fancy "third hand" gizmo (two articulated arms with alligator clips, affixed to a weighted metal base,) or a vise, or just weight the coil of wire down under a book or something.

4. "Tin" the wires. Melt a small blob of solder on the tip of the iron. Hold this blob against one of the wires. Hold the tip of the solder roll against the *wire*, not the iron. After about two to five seconds the wire should be hot enough that the solder will melt, flowing around the wire to coat it evenly in a smooth layer; if not, apply a *tiny* bit more solder to the tip of the iron and try again (see figure 6.2).

    Remove the iron from the wire. The solder should cool to a smooth, shiny silver; if it is rough and grey you did not get the wire hot enough—try again. Then go ahead and tin the second wire.

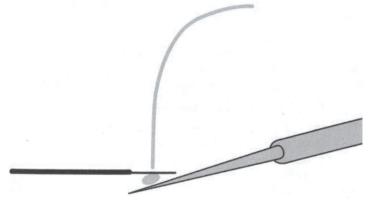

Figure 6.2 Tinning a wire.

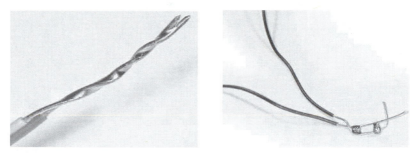

Figure 6.3 A happy solder joint (left) and a sad solder joint (right).

5. Twist the wires around one another like strands in rope. Again, apply a small blob to the iron and use the blob to conduct heat to the bundled wires. After a few seconds the tinned solder should re-melt and flow together; you may apply a little bit more solder to strengthen the joint, but only as much as can flow and distribute itself smoothly—like a wax-impregnated candle wick. Wait several seconds *without wiggling* for the joint to cool and harden (see figure 6.3).

    Blobs of solder on the wire or dull grey solder are signs of a "cold solder joint." Such a joint is neither electrically nor mechanically strong. Do it again.

    When tinning and soldering, be sure that you apply heat for the minimum amount of time needed to get the solder to flow, otherwise you may damage the components you are soldering (for example, melting the insulation off the wire).

6. Repeat this process until you get it right and feel comfortable with the "touch" of soldering—how much heat and solder to apply for how long, etc. It's a small step from here to cracking safes.

7. You can now move on to soldering wires to plugs and jacks. Tin wire and jack terminals as before, then solder together. You can bypass the tinning, if you wish, and solder the wire directly to the jack. If the terminal lugs on the jack have wire-sized holes, you can make your life easier by looping the end of the wire through the hole to secure it before soldering.

When soldering circuit boards (such as a simple amplifier kit recommended in chapter 1), use as fine a tip as possible. Keep it cleaned and tinned by frequent swipes across the sponge. Use solder sparingly to avoid blobs of excess solder bridging between separate pads on the circuit board.

Be advised that cold solder joints will come back to haunt you at the most inauspicious times (Amateur Night at the Apollo? *After* you get to Carnegie Hall? Grammy acceptance speech?), so it's worth getting soldering right before going on stage.

Chapter 7

HOW TO MAKE A CONTACT MIKE:
USING PIEZO DISKS TO PICK UP TINY SOUNDS

You will need:

- A battery-powered amplifier.
- A piezoelectric disk.
- About 8 feet of lightweight shielded cable.
- A plug to match the input jack on your amp, recorder, or mixer.
- Plastic insulating electrical tape.
- A can of Plasti-Dip or similar rubberized plastic paint (sold in hardware stores for dipping tool handles).
- Small spring clamps.
- Molex-style terminal block.
- Hand tools, soldering iron, and electrical tape.
- Sparklers, small blowtorch, guitar strings, metal scrap, Slinky, springs, and condoms.

The Piezoelectric Effect

Another common principle of reversible sound translation is the "piezoelectric effect," which depends on the electrical properties of *crystals*, rather than electromagnetism, as discussed in chapter 4: bang a crystal with a hammer and it will generate a pretty sizeable electrical signal (enough to light a flashlight bulb); conversely, if you send an electrical current into a crystal it will twitch.

Piezoelectric disks, made by bonding a thin layer of crystal to a thin, flexible sheet of brass, are everywhere today, inside almost everything that beeps: appliances, phones, toys, computers, etc. (see figure 7.1). Because they are manufactured in huge quantities they are incredibly cheap, and they happen to make even better contact microphones than they make speakers. Drum triggers and commercial contact mikes are often made from piezo disks and sold at absurdly marked-up prices.

Figure 7.1 Assorted piezo disks.

How to Make a Piezo Disk Contact Mike

1. Try to find a piezo disk that already has wires attached—soldering directly to the disc's surface is infuriatingly difficult. Better yet, get a few disks in case you break them. You can salvage them from all sorts of trashed electronic devices—from toys and alarm clocks to cell phones and computers—or buy them from Radio Shack or any number of Web-based electronic surplus outlets.

2. The disk may be encased in a kind of plastic lollipop. If so, *carefully* pry open the case and remove the disk. Try not impale yourself, but do not bend or scratch the disk, since this can result in the contact mike distorting. Prior work experience at the Oyster Bar or Clam Shack pays off here.

3. The disk may have a tiny circuit board attached. Snip off the connecting wires close to the circuit board, so that the wires attached to the disk are as long as possible. Remove the board.

4. Once removed, the disk should appear as a circle of gold- or silver-colored metal, with a smaller circle of whitish crystal within. Depending on the design, there will be two or three wires connected to the disk. One will always be connected to the *metal* portion, somewhere near the edge; this we will call the "ground" connection. One will connect to the *main* part of the inner crystal circle; this we will call the "hot" connection. In some cases there will be a narrow, tongue-like shape differentiated within the crystal, to which the third wire connects; this we will call the "curious but unnecessary" (CBU) connection.

5. Cut the connecting wires so that they protrude about 2 inches from the disk. Strip about 1/2 inch of insulation from the ends of the ground and hot wires; don't bother to strip the CBU wire. Tin the stripped ends. If there are no wires attached to the disk prepare it by tinning a small spot on the surface of the crystal and one on the

surrounding perimeter of the brass disk; solder fast and be very careful to apply only a minimum of heat, since the crystal surface is easily damaged.

6. Shielded cable consists of stranded wire inside insulation, surrounded by a layer of braided or twisted wire, which is in turn covered by another layer of insulation. A cross-section looks like tree rings or a target. Shielded wire is used to protect an audio signal from hum and other electromagnetic interference. Shielded cable comes with any number of internal conductor wires, but for audio purposes most cable has one or two internal conductors plus the shield. Unless otherwise specified, we only need cable with a single internal conductor plus shield; if your cable has two or more internal conductors (in addition to the shield) that's ok, but we'll only use one, so cut off the others.

Rule #9: Use shielded cable to make all audio connections longer than eight inches, unless they go between an amplifier and a speaker.

Cut a 5-foot section of shielded cable, the thinner and more flexible the better. Strip back 1 inch of the outside insulation. Unbraid the shielding and twist into a single thick strand. Now strip back 1/2 inch of the inner insulation, and twist the center conductor into a neat strand. Keep the two strands separate. Tin both strands, being careful not to melt back the insulation (see figure 7.2).

7. Twist together the hot wire from the center of the piezo disk and the inner wire from the shielded cable. Solder them together. Twist together the ground wire from the edge of the piezo disk and the shield from the shielded cable. Solder them together (see figure 7.3). Wrap both joints separately with a bit of electrical tape so that they cannot short out if they accidentally come in contact with each other. If soldering directly to the tinned disk do so quickly, as mentioned in step #4.

8. Strip the free end of the shielded cable as in step #5: 1 inch outer insulation, twist shield, 1/2 inch inner insulation, twist conductor, tin the wires. If you are connecting to your amplifier with clip leads, skip to step #10; otherwise proceed to the next step.

9. Unscrew the plug you are using to connect the contact mike to your amplifier/recorder/mixer. Slip the barrel back over the shielded wire toward the disk so that the

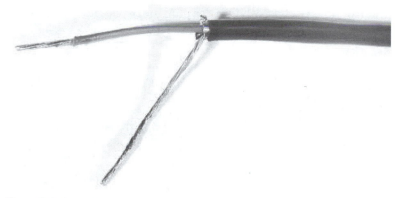

Figure 7.2 Shielded cable prepared for soldering.

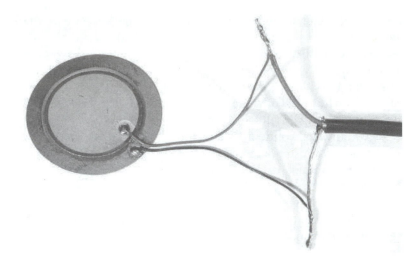

Figure 7.3 Piezo disk soldered to cable.

threaded portion faces the freshly tinned end. Unscrewing the barrel should reveal two solder tabs on the plug: the shorter one connects to the "tip" of the plug and the longer one connects to the "sleeve."

Solder the inner conductor of the shielded wire to the tip of the plug and the shield to the sleeve (see figure 7.4). Sometimes there are small holes in the connector tabs that you can hook your wire onto so that it is held in place before soldering. Otherwise you will have to tin the tabs and hold each wire against its respective tab while soldering—a job for three hands, a vise, or a fearless buddy with a steady hand. (If you are soldering to an XLR connector, such as those used on professional microphones, see chapter 10 for instructions on which wire to solder to which terminal.)

Now is as good a time as any to introduce the 10th Rule of Hacking, if it is not obvious already:

Rule #10: Every audio connection consists of two parts: the *signal* and a *ground* reference.

In the case of a contact mike the signal comes from the white part of the piezo disk, while the ground is the brassy bit; on the plug the tip carries the signal and the sleeve

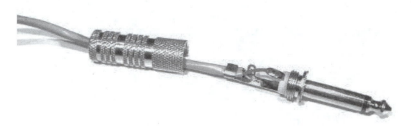

Figure 7.4 Cable soldered to plug.

is the ground. In future chapters I may get a bit sloppy and only refer to the signal when describing connections—always assume that a ground connection must accompany every signal.

10.   Plug into your amp and check that your new contact mike works—tapping the mike should make a solid thunking sound. If there is no sound, check the joints at both ends of the cable to make sure they are good and there are no shorts. If there is hum, you may have connected the hot and ground wires to the wrong conductor of the cable—de-solder and reverse them. If it works, screw the barrel down onto the plug and test again—sometimes squeezing the barrel down over a marginal solder joint will break or short it. A small piece of electrical tape can be used to isolate the connections if excess wire tends to short when the barrel is screwed down.

Whoops! Did you forget to slide the barrel onto the wire before you soldered? If so, de-solder the plug, go back to step #8, but don't feel too stupid—everybody makes this mistake. But remember:

Rule #11: Don't drink and solder.

11.   When you are sure you have an electrically functional contact mike, cover the ceramic side with a piece of electrical tape—you can trim it around the circumference with scissors or a knife, or you can wrap the edges over to the other side of the disk.

12.   Find a well-ventilated space. Open up and stir your can of Plasti-Dip. As per the instructions on the label, *slowly* dip the contact mike end of your cable into the goop until you have covered the wire past the electrical tape (see figure 7.5). *Slowly* withdraw it and hang it up (preferably outside) to dry. Go away and take a break—this stuff is stinky. You can dip a second layer after the first one dries thoroughly, which can take a few hours. More than three layers tend to muffle the sound, so don't overdo it without listening carefully after each new layer.

The tape and Plasti-Dip treatment serves several functions:

- It strengthens the connections between the wires and the piezo disk.
- It insulates the disk from electrical shorts, and prevents hum when you touch it.
- It waterproofs the contact mike, so you can use it to record underwater sounds, freeze it in ice-cubes, dangle it in a drink, etc.
- It deadens slightly the pronounced high-frequency resonance of the disk (similar to the effect of gaffing tape on the head of an unruly snare drum.)
- It looks really cool, and dipping is a treat after all that soldering.

Figure 7.5 Contact mike encased in Plasti-Dip.

The discovery of Plasti-Dip as the perfect contact mike sweater must be credited to the ingenious Robb Drinkwater of The School of the Art Institute of Chicago.

What to Try with Your Contact Mike

Contact mikes are great for greatly amplifying hidden sounds in everyday objects. The trick is making firm physical contact with the vibrating object.

Use double-stick tape or Blu-tak to attach the mike to the surface. Try: guitars, violins, drums, pots and pans, wrists and knees, foreheads, pinball machines. Use small spring clamps to hold things to the contact mike. Try: strips of metal, gaffing tape, rulers, popsicle sticks.

"Terminal strips" are used to make electrical connections in lamps and other appliances. They can be salvaged from discarded appliances or bought from any number of sources, including Radio Shack, DIY centers like Home Depot, and online electronic surplus retailers. Cut the terminal strip into small sections and clamp them onto the mike with a spring clamp. Insert thin objects into the terminal openings and hold them in place by tightening the screws (see figure 7.6). Try: Slinkies, springs, loose guitar strings, toothpicks, sate sticks, broom straws, porcupine quills, cactus needles.

This is an excellent way to replicate the old-fashioned phonograph cartridges used by John Cage in his visionary work of live electronic music, "Cartridge Music" (see "John Cage—The Father of Invention").

Many metals make unusual sounds as they heat and cool. Clamp a sparkler in the terminal block, light, and listen. Or clamp steel wire and heat with a torch (see track 7 on the CD).

Connect the contact mike to an amplifier and wire a raw speaker to the amplifier output jack. Place the speaker on its back, like a candy dish. Rest the contact mike inside the cone and turn up the gain. The contact mike should jump up and down as it feeds back with the speaker (a slightly higher-tech variation on the jumping speaker in chapter 5.)

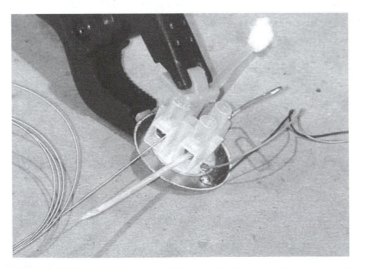

Figure 7.6 Terminal strip holding junk clamped to a contact mike.

John Cage—The Father of Invention

The influence of John Cage (1912–1992) on American avant-garde music cannot be overstated. Given the breadth of his impact as a composer and theoretician, his significance in the rise of hacker electronic culture is sometimes overlooked. Throughout his career Cage had a passionate curiosity for new sounds and compositional strategies. Lacking institutional support in the form of orchestral commissions and the like, Cage, the son of an inventor, chose to develop new instruments from everyday technological and commonplace objects. At the beginning of his career he literally made do with rubbish: his early percussion music, such as "First Construction in Metal" (1939), used brake drums and other scrap iron from junkyards. In the 1940s, Cage (together with Lou Harrison) inserted screws, washers, rubber erasers, and other pocket detritus into the strings of pianos to create the gamelan-like sounds of the "prepared piano." "Imaginary Landscape No. 1," composed in 1939 for piano, bowed cymbal, and record player, was the first documented piece of music to feature the DJ as a musical performer, while "Imaginary Landscape No. 4" (1951) was composed for a dozen ordinary radios.

In "Cartridge Music" (1960) performers substitute springs, twigs, pipe cleaners, and other thin objects for the needles in cheap record player pickups; the surprising richness of these enormously amplified "micro-sounds" rivaled the more labor—and capital—intensive synthetic sonorities coming out of the European electronic music studios, and opened the ears of a generation of sound artists to the splendor of the contact mike. "Hpschd" (1967–69), composed in collaboration with Lejaren Hiller, was one of the first works of computer music.

Cage's later music, such as "Études Australes" (for piano, 1975), or "Ryoanji" (for mixed ensemble, 1983–85), reverted to more traditional instrumental resources. (Cage once told me, "If I don't write for these virtuosos they'll have to play music by even worse composers.") But the ethos of hacking lived on in his continually surprising methodology and in his persistent invention of new performance techniques.

Once waterproofed with the electrical tape and Plasti-Dip, the contact mikes will also serve as affordable hydrophones and submersible mikes.

- Fill a plastic yogurt container with water, drop in the contact mike and pop it in the freezer. Listen as it freezes. Once frozen, remove the ice block from the container, float it in a bowl of hot water, and listen to it melt (see track 5 on the CD).
- Drop it in the water next time you go fishing and check if they're really laughing at you (see track 6 on the CD).
- Hold the mike in your mouth while you drink or chew, but please observe safe sex practices: put an extra layer of protection between you and electricity by encasing the contact mike in a condom or balloon, and

NEVER CONNECT THE DISK TO AN AC-POWERED AMPLIFIER OR RECORDER—ONLY TO BATTERY-POWERED EQUIPMENT.

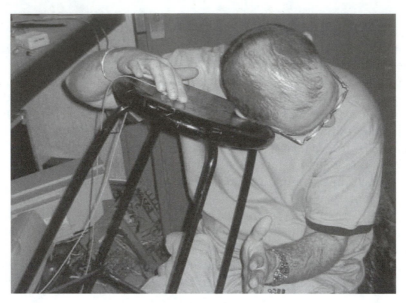

Figure 7.7 John Bowers enjoying his contact mike.

A few hours spent with a contact mike and a fistful of junk should convince you of the significance of the Second Law of the Avant-Garde (and the First Law of Pop):

Make it louder, a lot.

This is the credo of "Piezo Music" movement that sprang up in the aftermath of Cage's experimentation and the fortuitous invention of the economical piezo disk (see "Piezo Music" and figure 7.7).

Hi Fi

Ultrasonic transducers, such as those found in many motion-detecting alarm systems, contain small piezo disks (see figure 7.8). These disks usually have a slightly lower output

Figure 7.8 Some ultrasonic transducers.

Piezo Music

In the aftermath of Cage's "Cartridge Music" many sound artists sought affordable techniques for amplifying mechanical vibration and microscopic sounds. Since the early 1970s the proliferation of piezo disks in beeping appliances has effectively put contact mikes within reach of anyone with a soldering iron. Whether as pickups on bluegrass mandolins or as hydrophones for eavesdropping on whales, the disks have insinuated themselves into surprisingly diverse corners of our recorded soundscape, and have given rise to a genre of piezo music. Hugh Davies (1943–2004) (UK) and Richard Lerman (USA) were two of the earliest

Richard Lerman performing "Changing States 6."

innovators. Davies began inventing piezo-amplified instruments in the 1970s, the most poetic of which consists of a disk with short steel wires soldered around its rim. By plucking or blowing gently at these wires, he could elicit a wide range of surprisingly deep, marimba-like sounds, which he incorporated into composed and improvised work. Lerman (who has for many years maintained a wonderfully informative Web site with tips for working with piezo technology) uses similarly bewhiskered disks, but plays them with a small blowtorch: the whoosh of the gas creates an effect similar to that of bowing a cymbal, and while the wire heats and cools it snaps with gong-like solemnity (see figure above and track 7 on the CD). Collin Olan (USA) froze waterproofed contact mikes in a block of ice and recorded the cracks and whistles of escaping air bubbles as it thawed (see track 5 on the CD), while Peter Cusack (UK) used similar homemade hydrophones to record the breakup of ice on Siberia's Lake Baikal (see track 6 on the CD). Eric Leonardson (USA) performs regularly on his "Springboard": a plank of wood festooned with springs, wires, and other bits of scrap metal that, when heard through the piezo pickup, evoke the sound world of a Balinese Gamelan orchestra (see figure right).

"Springboard," Eric Leonardson.

level than the more common large brass ones (and are more expensive), but have a flatter frequency response. You will need to solder one connection to each side of the disk, since they have a different mechanical construction.

Interesting Historical Note

The term "piezoelectric" originates in the Greek word *piezen* meaning "to press." The discovery of the effect is credited to Jacques Curie and his brother Pierre. The latter, along with his wife, Marie Curie, is better known for his work with another rather energetic, if less user-friendly, phenomenon: radioactivity.

Chapter 8

TURN YOUR TINY WALL INTO A SPEAKER (OR HOW TO MAKE A PIEZO DRIVER): RESONATING OBJECTS WITH PIEZO DISKS, TRANSFORMERS, AND MOTORS

You will need:

- A battery-powered amplifier with output jack for external speaker.
- A second battery-powered amplifier, if possible.
- Your contact mike from the previous chapter.
- Another piezoelectric disk.
- Two plugs to match the amp's output connector.
- A female jack to match the plugs you are using.
- One small audio output coupling transformer (Radio Shack 273-1380 or equivalent).
- About 8 feet of lightweight shielded cable.
- A few feet of lightweight speaker cable or stranded hookup wire.
- Electrical tape.
- A can of Plasti-Dip.
- Small spring clamps or clothespins.
- A sound source, such as a CD player or radio, and cable to connect it to the amp input.
- Small DC motors (from pagers, cell phones, vibrators, etc.).
- Small speaker.
- Cork.
- Glue.

Piezo disks are used to make beeps because they do so very efficiently—they require very little current, and therefore are well suited to battery-operated devices. As loudspeakers they display a rather uneven, non-hi-fi response, but they can nonetheless be quite useful when coupled to other objects to make *speaker objects*.

To get the most vibration out of a piezo disk speaker it is necessary to feed it a very high voltage signal, albeit at a minuscule (and therefore harmless) current. A transformer is a kind of audio-lever that allows one to jack up the voltage of an electrical signal very easily. For this project we will wire up an *output transformer* backwards (see Rule #8) to step up the output voltage of a small amplifier from around 6 volts to over 200 volts. I learned this technique from Ralph Jones, a founding member of David Tudor's legendary ensemble, "Composers Inside Electronics" (see "Composing Inside Electronics," chapter 14).

The transformer will have a *primary* and *secondary* side. The primary will be designated as having an impedance of around 1000 ohms (1kOhm), and may have two or three wires. We will use the outer two wires—the center wire, if present, can be ignored. The *secondary* will usually have just two wires, and an impedance of 8 Ohms. In the case of the Radio Shack part, the outermost primary leads are blue and green and the secondaries are red and white.

1. Strip 1/2 inch of insulation off the ends of the primary and secondary wires and tin the ends.
2. Solder one of the *secondary* wires to the tip of a plug that mates with the output jack of your amplifier. Solder the other secondary wire to the sleeve of the plug. (If you are connecting to the amplifier via screw terminals or direct soldering, then omit the plug.) Polarity is irrelevant here—it does not matter which of the two secondary leads goes to the tip and which to the sleeve. If possible, slip the plug's barrel over the wires before you solder them up (as we did with the contact mike); there may not be sufficient wire length to allow this, in which case you can simply wrap some electrical tape around the connections later (after you have proven that the gizmo works, and being very careful not to squeeze the connections together to make a short).
3. Solder one of the *primary* wires to the tip connection of a female jack that mates with the plug you used on your contact mike (see chapter 7) Solder the other primary wire to the sleeve connection of the jack (see figure 8.1). Once again, polarity is irrelevant here—it does not matter which of the two primary leads goes to which connection.
4. Plug the plug-end of the transformer assembly into the external speaker jack of your amplifier or a boom box. You must use a connection designated for a *loudspeaker*, not a *headphone jack*, which cannot drive the very low 8-ohm load of the transformer.

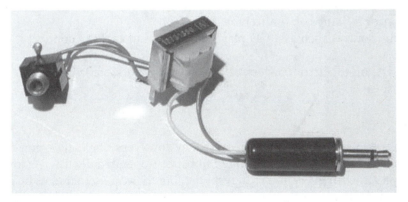

Figure 8.1 A transformer interface for driving a piezo disk.

If there is no proper external speaker jack you will have to de-solder the speaker leads from the speaker terminals and use clip leads to connect them directly to the *secondary* side of the transformer (instead of using a plug). Plug your contact mike (made in chapter 7) into the jack-end of the transformer assembly.

5. Plug a sound source into the amplifier input: a microphone, cassette recorder, CD player, radio, etc. Slowly raise the amp gain. The disk should start to radiate sound. If not, check your connections.

Use plastic spring clamps, clothespins, or tape to clamp the disk to different objects and resonate them with various sounds. Thin materials work better than thick ones: pie tins, etching plates, paper cups, tin cans, and balloons, rather than bricks, anchors, and baseball bats.

A quaint reverb unit can be made by sending signals into a spring or plate of metal using a piezo driver and picking them up with a piezo contact mike (you'll have to solder up a few more disks—go back to chapter 7). This is similar to the technique used in early plate reverb units common in recording studios before digital reverb, and also the principle behind David Tudor's famous "Rainforest" installation (see "David Tudor and *Rainforest*"), which used sculptural objects to transform sound material. You can patch the amp/driver/contact mike assembly into your mixer just as you would a reverb or effect processor: connect a send bus output to your driver-amplifier input, and bring the contact mike back to any console input to amplify and mix in the "reverb" with the dry signal.

Often flexing or dampening the object can affect the character of its filtering of the original sound—this is especially noticeable with the semi-rigid clear plastic packaging around toys, or clamshell cases from salad bars, but you should also try loose guitar strings, Slinkies, balloons, plastic bags, bubble wrap, vinyl records, drumheads, license plates, oil drums, buckets of water, bowls of Jell-O (see figure 8.2). Whether as a reverb substitute

Figure 8.2 A piezo driver and contact mike pickup being used to filter a sound through a sheet of plastic.

David Tudor and Rainforest

David Tudor (1926–1996) began his career as a leading pianist of the avant-garde. By the early 1950s he was serving as pianist for the Merce Cunningham Dance Company, and assisting in the realizations of both Cage's piano music and his electronic works. Tudor gradually abandoned the piano and emerged as the first virtuoso of electronic performance. Expanding on Cage's work with the "found" technology of radios and record players, Tudor embarked on the (at the time quite arduous) process of acquiring enough knowledge of circuit design and soldering to construct his own new instruments. He believed that new, object-specific, intrinsically *electronic*, musical material and forms would emerge as each instrument took shape: "I try to find out what's there—not to make it do what I want, but to release what's there. The object should teach you what it wants to hear." Although Tudor was not the first composer to make his own electronic instruments (he was inspired and assisted by pioneering composer/engineer Gordon Mumma), in no other composer's work is the ethos of music *implicit* in technology so fundamental and clear.

Beginning in 1968, Tudor composed a series of pieces under the title of "Rainforest," culminating in "Rainforest IV," developed in conjunction with a workshop in electronic performance that he gave in Chocurua, New Hampshire, in 1973 (see figure below). The principle underlying all the "Rainforest" works was similar: sounds are played through transducers affixed to solid objects; the objects filter, resonate, and otherwise transform the sounds; the processed sounds are directly radiated by the transduced objects, which serve as "sculptural speakers"; contact mikes on the objects pick up the vibrating surfaces of the objects, and these micro-sounds are mixed and heard through ordinary loudspeakers around the space. With an open-form score that encouraged experimentation in the design of sound generators and resonated objects, this work served as a creative catalyst for the workshop participants and, later, other young composers who were drawn to Tudor by word-of-mouth. They subsequently formed a loose collective ensemble called "Composers Inside Electronics." Over the next twenty-eight years, this group served as a laboratory for artist-designed circuitry and experimental electronic performance, presenting dozens of installations of "Rainforest IV" worldwide, as well as performances of works by individual members of the ensemble, which included over the years John D. S. Adams, Nicolas Collins, Paul De Marinis, John Driscoll, Phil Edelstein, Linda Fisher, D'Arcy Philip Gray, Ralph Jones, Martin Kalve, Ron Kuivila, and Matt Rogalsky.

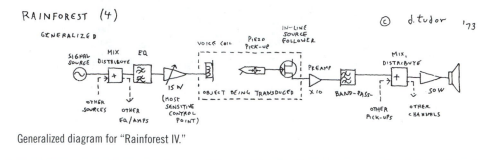

Generalized diagram for "Rainforest IV."

in a mixdown situation or as part of a live performance setup, this is a cheap, easy, fun route to unusual signal processing.

With all due respect to the First Law of the Avant-Garde, this transformer assembly does *not* do a very effective job of increasing the gain of a piezo disk when it is used as a contact mike—it is effectively limited to boosting the efficiency of a piezo *driver*. But don't take my word—try it for yourself.

You can create feedback by plugging a contact mike into the amp input and a piezo driver into the output, and attaching the two to the same object. Flexing or dampening the object can affect the feedback pitch, and turn a piece of garbage (such as the plastic packaging from toys) into a playable instrument—an electronic musical saw. You can configure several channels of amps, drivers, and contact mikes to send audio signals through a series of objects for multi-stage processing; using Y-cords you can branch off and mix after each resonator-object. Get together with your buddies, find a small garage, and form a piezo band. (See chapter 27 for more information on matrix processing.)

Whereas size does not greatly affect the loudness of a contact mike made from a piezo disk, it makes a big difference when you are making a driver. If you have a choice, use the largest possible disk and you get a bigger sound out of whatever you are driving. You will notice that this is not a "high fidelity" device: the sound is often limited to high frequencies, displays the peaked resonance inherent to a piezo disk, and can be quite distorted—larger disks have a wider frequency response, as well as being louder and less distorted than small ones. You can insert some equalization, in the form of an inexpensive "stomp box" graphic EQ, to process the signal driving the piezo disk and/or the contact mike picking up the vibrating object. Substituting a more powerful amplifier, such as a boom box with external speaker jacks, for the little 1/8 watt Radio Shack mini test amplifier, will also give you more volume before distortion. The benefits of equalizers and stronger amplifiers will be especially noticeable when you set up the matrices and feedback systems described above.

By the way, if you place your finger across an un-Dipped, bare piezo disk while it is being run as a driver, you may experience a mild, not entirely unpleasant electric shock. This demonstrates how high the voltage gets when jacked-up by the transformer. Electrical tape and Plasti-Dip will reduce distracting stimulation and protect the driver from damage. (Two considerably less-pleasant applications of transformer step-up technology are the Taser "nonlethal" stun gun and the "quaint" interviewing techniques popular at Abu Gharib and Guantanimo.)

Other Kinds of Drivers

In addition to piezo disks, small motors can be adapted as drivers. They are most effective for lower frequencies, and complement the rather tinny quality of the piezo—a sort of subwoofer-driver. Connect the two wires of any small DC motor (one that runs off batteries) directly to the output of your mini-amplifier (*not* through the output transformer). It should twitch in response to your sound source. Sometimes clamping the body of the motor directly to an object will be sufficient to transmit the vibration; sometimes you'll need to get clever with a cam on the motor shaft. Some motors work better than others (vibrators from pagers and cell phones tend to be good)—experiment. If you have a multimeter, you can use it to measure the resistance of the motor coil (touch the motor

Figure 8.3 A corked speaker.

terminals with meter's probes while setting it to the lowest range for measuring ohms (Ω)—you're looking for motors that measure between 4 and 12 ohms (see chapter 14 for advice on using a multimeter).

You can also make a pretty efficient driver by gluing a cork to the center of a small loudspeaker (see figure 8.3). Connect any sound source through an amplifier to the corked speaker and hold the speaker against a sheet of metal, drumhead, cymbal, etc. The cork should vibrate the material and process the original signal. You may want to pick up the vibrating surface with a contact mike. The end of cork can be treated to further affect the sound: a thumbtack brightens it (like a honky-tonk piano), while a piece of felt softens it, and wood is somewhere in between.

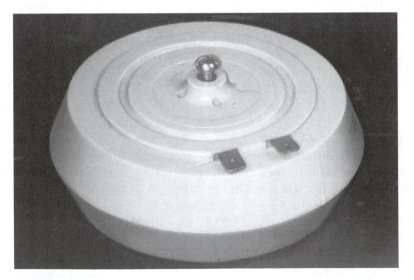

Figure 8.4 A Rolen-Star transducer.

Figure 8.5 A Bass Shaker.

A nice, simple spring reverb can be constructed by stretching a spring or Slinky between the center of a speaker cone (attach a small wire hook to the cone with epoxy) and a contact mike.

Finally, there are commercially available drivers. Richtech Enterprises still manufactures the "Rolen-Star" (see figure 8.4) wide-range driver originally used by Tudor for "Rainforest." Aurasound makes the "Bass Shaker," a low-frequency driver for use in car sound systems (you bolt them to the floor of your trunk and they turn the whole trunk into a big subwoofer) (see figure 8.5). These kinds of drivers do require 10–30 watts of power, however, and cannot be driven from a mini test amp or boom box. The "Soundbug" from FeOnic consists of a battery-powered amplifier and transducer package with a suction cup for affixing it to most smooth surfaces; it can be driven directly from the headphone output of a portable CD player, MP3 player, etc.

As "Drivers" (p. 44), shows, many artists have made creative use of the kind of "physical filtering" that can be accomplished by sending sounds through objects via all sorts of drivers.

Drivers

David Tudor's "Rainforest" is one of the most conspicuous compositions to use transducers to resonate materials, but other sound artists have employed similar technology to different musical ends. In "Music For Solo Performer" (1965) Alvin Lucier placed loudspeakers on the heads of drums and against cymbals, gongs, and other percussion instruments; the performer's amplified brainwaves were routed to the various speakers, and the low frequency (10–14 Hz) bursts played drum rolls on the percussion through the speaker cones. In later realizations Lucier attached solenoids to the outputs of some of the amplifiers, so they would tap against the bars of xylophones and gamelan instruments, and added corks to the speaker cones for similar effects. In Lucier's "The Queen of the South" (1972) sounds are played through transducers affixed to a sheet of plywood (or other large plate) onto which fine powder has been sprinkled; as the pitch, timbre, and loudness of the sounds are changed, the powder forms different patterns according to the vibrational modes of the plate.

Three stills from "The Queen of the South," Alvin Lucier, performed by the SAIC Sinfonietta

Berlin-based singer Ute Wassermann built her "Windy Gong" in 1995 (see figure below and track 8 on the CD). She sings into a mike, amplified through a small speaker with a cork attached to the center of the cone. The speaker is placed against the surface of a gong, which is in turn amplified with another microphone

"Windy Gong," Ute Wassermann

and contact mike. The vocal sounds are filtered and resonated by the gong, and the transformations can be manipulated by moving the speaker and microphone. In "Kupferscheibe" (1993–97) she extends long springs from speakers built into her clothing out to resonators encircling the performance area; her voice is processed by these spindly springs and heard, tin-can-telephone-style, through the megaphones.

For "Tisch" (1994–95) German artist Jens Brand installed speakers inside a circular plastic café table. The surface of the table is oiled, and eight empty wine glasses are placed on top. Very low frequency sound is played through the speakers. Although barely audible, the vibration from the speakers causes the glasses to move very slowly across the surface. When they make contact, they ring against one another. The piece ends when the last of the glasses tips over the edge and crashes onto the floor.

Nicolas Collins (USA) has been working with "backwards electric guitars" since 1981 (see figure below page and track 9 on the CD). In these instruments sounds are sent *into* guitar pickups or coils (scavenged from relays) whose fluctuating electromagnetic fields vibrate the strings of guitars and basses. The strings filter, resonate, and reverberate the original sounds (similar to the effect of shouting into a piano with the sustain pedal depressed), and are picked up, amplified, and further processed through distortion and other typical guitar effects. The filtering

Backwards electric guitar, Nicolas Collins

"Luftsdruckschwankungen" circuit from installation of "It's In The Air," Felix Hess, for the Stroomgeest exhibition at Groot Bentveld, Netherlands, 1996.

is "played" by fretting and dampening the strings, like a one-handed guitarist. This technique is an extension of the more familiar E-bow technology, which uses an electromagnetic pickup and driver in a feedback loop to resonate guitar strings.

Dutch sound artist Felix Hess has created beautiful large-scale installations with tiny circuits that drive piezo disks directly (see figure above). Pressed against small sheets of balsa wood by the weight of a stone, the piezos produce a cicada-like chirping of astonishing intensity.

Chapter 9

TAPE HEADS:
PLAYING CREDIT CARDS

You will need:

- An expendable tape recorder/player, or a loose tape head.
- Some magnetic media: cassettes, reel-to-reel tape, transit cards, credit cards, hard disks, etc.
- A battery powered mini-amplifier with considerable gain.
- An additional sound source, such as a CD or tape player.
- Optional: a surplus credit card reader.

Even in the age of CDs there's a lot of data sitting around in magnetic particles: music and phone messages on cassette tapes, personal data on your credit card, files on hard drives, virtual money on transit cards. Whereas a cassette tape player is still a pretty common device and we're all familiar with the sounds of cassettes, it's not often we get to *hear* the information on other magnetic storage media. But all it takes is a tape head and an amplifier.

A tape recorder translates audio signals into a fluctuating electromagnetic field through a tape head, the small metal Brancusi-esque object you can see inside a cassette player or answering machine (see figure 9.1). The tape head's undulating magnetism in turn aligns little tiny magnetic domains in the iron-like powder covering one surface of the recording tape, as if they were tiny compass needles. When the tape is played back the whole process reverses: the varying magnetic orientation retained by the mini-magnets on the tape now induces current flow inside the tape head which, when amplified, resembles pretty closely what went into the tape recorder earlier—another instance of the *reversibility* of electromagnetism discussed in chapter 4. It's not so different from translating sound vibrations into grooves cut into a record's surface, later followed by a needle whose wiggling is re-translated back into sound waves—only with tape it's magnetic fluctuations instead of shimmying grooves. Digital tape recordings, such as floppy disks or credit card stripes, are like cassette tape only simpler: the magnetic domains just flop back and forth between two states, 0 and 1, instead of tracing the nuanced contour of an analog waveform.

Figure 9.1 Tape heads.

Preparation

The easiest place to find a tape head is inside a broken or otherwise unwanted answering machine or cassette player. (If you have a functional boom box or other device that *records* as well as plays back tape, skip ahead to the "Recording" section below; if you have a working Walkman or other cassette playback-only device, skip to "Playback.") Many Web-based electronic surplus stores sell individual tape heads or credit card data readers at reasonable prices. The advantage of Aztecking a tape head (ripping it out of a still warm electronic body) is that audio wiring is attached, usually in the form of some shielded cable; in this case just cut the cable so as to leave as long a section as possible attached to the tape head. The answering machine will yield a simple mono tape head, while the Walkman will probably be stereo, but for the purposes of this experiment stereo is not very important, and you can get away with wiring up just one channel if you're feeling cheap or lazy.

The back-side of a stereo tape head will have four connections (as shown in the examples in figure 9.1); a mono head will have two. If the head has a cable attached, each pin will probably be attached to a separate wire in a multi-conductor shielded cable, and the shield will be affixed to the metal shell of the head. When wiring this cable from a *stereo* head to a *stereo* plug, solder "A" to the tip of your plug, "C" to the ring, and "B" and "D" and the shield to the sleeve; when wiring a *stereo* head to a *mono* plug, solder "A" and "C" to the tip of your plug and "B" and "D" and the shield to the sleeve; when wiring a *mono* head to a *mono* plug, connect "A" to the tip, "B" and shield to the sleeve (see figure 9.2).

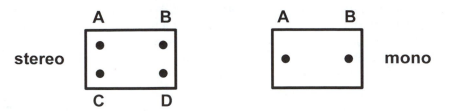

Figure 9.2 Wiring orientation for tape heads.

If the tape head arrives unwired, solder directly to connecting pins on the head, to the shield and to the tip of the jack, following the above routing instructions. Always use shielded cable to minimize hum, but bear in mind that tape heads are very hummy things by nature, and some noise is inevitable (in fact, you can substitute a tape head for a telephone tap coil to pick up electromagnetic fields, as described in chapter 3).

Playback

If your tape head is inside a functional tape player, remove it from the player *without* disconnecting the cable if possible. You will probably need to extend its wiring with a few feet of shielded cable—enough that you have room to move the head freely. Either cut the existing wires in half and splice in some additional cable, or de-solder the head's wiring at the circuit board (make careful note of which wire goes where!) and solder the extension cable between the board and the pigtails attached to the head.

If you are working with a loose tape head, plug it into a high gain amplifier, such as the Radio Shack mini test amplifier, a guitar amp, or the microphone input of a mixer. Press play on the cassette player or turn on the amplifier/mixer. Now rub the head over some recorded media: transit cards and credit cards, eviscerated cassette tapes, computer disks. If you're using cassette tape, it helps to stretch the audiotape across a sheet of cardboard, a tabletop, or some other flat surface and fasten it down with the sticky kind of tape at either end, or double-stick tape or spray adhesive on the back side. You will notice that one side (emulsion) will be MUCH louder than the other (backing). Digital data (credit cards, transit cards) tends to make a much louder sound than audiotape, and one that often sounds curiously like turntable scratching (see "Card Readers," below).

If you find it awkward to handle the tiny tape head you can lash it to the end of a popsicle stick or pencil with some electrical or gaffing tape, or solder it to a metal fingerpick (see figure 9.3).

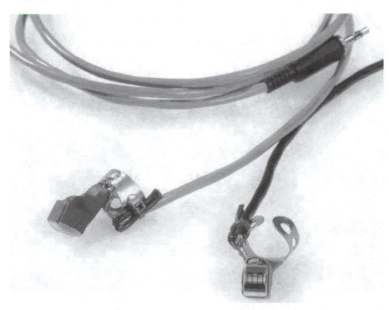

Figure 9.3 Tape heads mounted on fingerpicks, Nicolas Collins.

Tape

Although invented for straightforward recording and playback in the service of the Third Reich, and largely known today in its more benign role as a trustworthy musical amanuensis, magnetic tape has proven to be a wonderfully flexible performance medium in itself. Composers such Alvin Lucier ("I am sitting in a room," 1970), Steve Reich ("Come Out," 1966), Pauline Oliveros ("1 of 4," 1966) and Terry Riley ("Rainbow in Curved Air," 1969) have all made pieces derived from the properties of tape loops and tape delays. When the tape is taken off the reels it becomes surprisingly instrumental. In 1963 Nam June Paik, on the threshold of his transformation from composer to video artist, attached dozens of strips of prerecorded tape to the wall of a gallery in Wuppertal, Germany, and invited the visitors to play it back via handheld tape heads. According to legend, John Cage once did a similar thing in reverse. He fully covered a tabletop with blank tape, invited the public to scribble across it with tape heads attached to pencils through which electronic sound was playing; at the end of the evening the tape was wound onto a reel and played back for all to hear.

Laurie Anderson's "Tape Bow Violin" (built in 1977 in collaboration with Bob Bielecki—see "The Luthiers," chapter 29) substitutes a tape head for the bridge, and a strip of tape for the hair of the bow; the tape contains a recording that Anderson plays backwards and forwards as she draws the bow across the head (see figure below). "I began to work with audio palindromes, words that produced different words when reversed. Audio palindromes are not predictable like written palindromes ('god' is always 'dog' spelled backwards). With a lot of experimentation I produced songs for 'The Tape Bow Violin' that could be played forwards and backwards."

Years later, César Eugenio Dávila-Irizarry glued recordings of percussion instruments onto the body of the gourd typically used to make a *güiro* (a percussion instrument consisting of a gourd scribed with notches that are scraped rhythmically with a comb-like *raspa*); his new instrument is played with a hand-held

"Tape Bow Violin," Laurie Anderson.

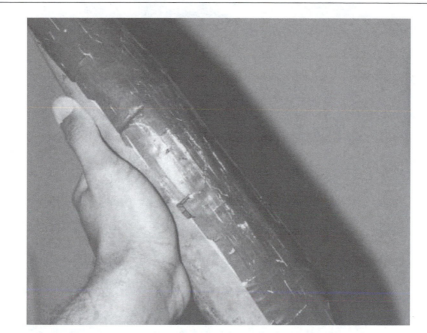

"Tape Güiro," César Eugenio Dávila-Irizarry.

tape head (see figure above). In the installation version of Mark Trayle's "¢apital *magneti¢*" (1999) visitors insert their credit cards into what appears to be an ordinary ATM; Trayle has programmed an internal computer to generate short musical compositions based on the data on each card, heard through speakers embedded in the ATM.

Recording

You can try *recording* with a hand-held tape head as well. Stretch cassette or reel-to-reel tape over a tabletop as above. If you are working with a loose tape head, plug a CD or cassette player into the input of a mini-amplifier; plug the tape head into its external speaker output. While playing the CD/cassette, move the tape head over the tape surface—keep the head in close contact with the tape. After a while stop recording and try playing back the tape—either by amplifying the head while moving it by hand across the surface, or reload the tape into a cassette or onto a reel and play it back on a tape recorder. Sometimes this works and sometimes it doesn't, so don't be too disappointed if you are unsuccessful.

You can get much better results if you start with a functional boom box or cassette recorder that you're willing to sacrifice on the altar of the weird. Disassemble the recorder to the point that you can carefully remove the record head from its mount in the cassette well. You will probably need to extend its wiring, as we described earlier in the "Playback" section. Mount some scrap cassette or reel-to-reel tape to a flat surface as we did above. Connect a signal to the boom box inputs, or tune in its radio. Insert a blank cassette in the well, or press that little prong with your pinkie, in order to enable the record function, and press the "record" and "play" keys to start recording. Move the head smoothly across

Figure 9.4 The "Scratchmaster" card reader (by Nicolas Collins, from the collection of Ted Collins).

the scrap tape. Press "stop," then "play," turn up the boom box volume, then retrace your movements over the tape—you should hear the original signal, altered by the inconsistencies in speed and smoothness between your two passes. You can speed up, slow down, and reverse your original sounds by changing the speed and direction of your playback motion. Or you can reload the tape into a cassette shell or onto a reel.

Card Readers

Surplus outlets often sell "card readers" from ATM machines, public telephones, etc. The reader consists of a tape head inside a housing that guides the card smoothly past it, along with circuitry needed to decode the digital data (see figure 9.4). Stealing credit card data is *advanced* hacking but for our immediate purposes you can discard the digital circuitry, wire the head up as shown in figure 9.2, plug into an amp, and end up with a very nice instrument for "scratching" cards.

Chapter 10

A SIMPLE AIR MIKE: CHEAP CONDENSER MIKE ELEMENTS MAKE GREAT MICROPHONES

You will need:

- An electret microphone element.
- 8 feet of lightweight shielded cable.
- Some plugs to match the jacks on your amp, recorder, or mixer.
- 9-volt battery and battery hook-up clip.
- An amplifier or mixer.
- Assorted resistors and capacitors.
- Packaging supplies as needed.
- Hand tools, soldering iron, and electrical tape.

We've saved the most normal form of microphone for last: after coils, backwards speakers, contact mikes, and tape heads we finally get around to your basic hear-my-song mike. From any number of sources (Radio Shack, Web retailers, electronic surplus outlets) one can buy, quite cheaply, high quality electret condenser microphone elements (see figure 10.1). You can also scrounge them from telephone answering machines and even some toys. These are the basic building blocks of recording microphones that can sell for several hundred dollars. All that stands between your $2.00 purchase and a pretty good mike is a handful of cheap components, a soldering iron, and some ingenuity.

If you have any choice when you go to buy an element, get a hold of some data sheets first and look for the highest signal-to-noise ratio and a flat, extended frequency response. If you have a choice between cardioid (directional) and omnidirectional pickup pattern bear in mind that the omnidirectional models usually have a smoother response curve—the quality of the sound tends to make up for its lack of directionality (many purists in the field of classical music recording use omnidirectional microphones exclusively).

Figure 10.2 shows the basic wiring. A 9-volt battery powers the mike through a resistor. A capacitor blocks this voltage from entering your amplifier or mixer. A switch turns the battery on and off—the microphone drains very little current, but the switch will help

Figure 10.1 Some electret condenser microphone elements.

your battery last for months. It's best to turn the mike on or off when it is *not* connected to your recorder or amp to avoid big thunks. Solder on whatever plug matches your recorder, amplifier, or mixer —I've included in figure 10.3 the rather odd connections needed if you use an XLR connector (used on the microphone inputs of most mixers and professional audio gear).

Electret microphone elements can usually be powered by a wide range of voltages. I've indicated a 9-volt battery in the figures, but two 1.5-volt batteries are usually sufficient—you can use AA, AAA, or even those tiny, absurdly overpriced button cells (see chapter 17 for advice on battery substitution). Sometimes a single 1.5-volt battery will suffice. If a data sheet is available from the manufacturer, it will tell you the safe voltage range; otherwise you'll have to experiment.

Occasionally one finds condenser microphone elements with three wires instead of two. This makes the job even easier. Instead of combining signal and battery power on a single wire, one wire will be designated as the signal, and will connect directly to the tip of the plug or pin 2 of the xlr; another will be labeled "power" and will connect to the "+" of the battery; the third (invariably the shield) connects to both the connector ground and the battery's "–" terminal (see figure 10.4).

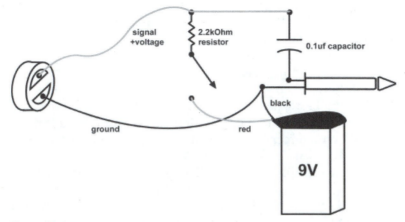

Figure 10.2 Basic electret microphone wiring.

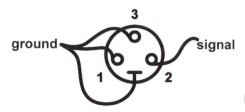

Figure 10.3 Wiring an XLR microphone connector.

The mechanical packaging is trickier than the electronic wiring. The tiny electret element can be glued into a plastic drinking straw or encased in heat-shrink tubing, and the cable run down to a small box containing the battery, resistor, capacitor, switch and jack. Or you can drill a hole in a small box, insert a plastic grommet into which the mike fits, build-in the remaining components, and run a cable out of the box to a plug. The issue of packaging is not merely aesthetic: the shape and mass of the material can affect the frequency response and directionality of the microphone. You may want to "ear-test" various options. The challenges of the mechanical design process may increase your tolerance of Neumann's mark-up, but it's worth it.

Two of these tiny mikes attached to a pair of headphones make a great binaural recording set-up (but look out for feedback if you monitor through the headphones while recording). Mount one at the focus of a parabolic reflector (a satellite dish or kid's snow-saucer) for a hyper-directional mike for wildlife sound recording. These mikes are cheap enough to embed recklessly in musical instruments—they're great inside accordions and melodicas, and in mutes for trumpets and trombones.

Even the least expensive of electret microphone elements has a surprisingly extended bass response—often extending down to 20Hz or lower. They are very susceptible to wind noise and breath pops; you'll want a windscreen of some kind (scrap foam rubber will do) and may need to roll off the bass to avoid overloading your recorder input under certain circumstances. But their low frequency response also makes them excellent for picking up subsonic pressure waves, such as those produced by opening and closing doors, wind gusts and some barometric changes—roll off everything *above* 30Hz and the remainder is weather.

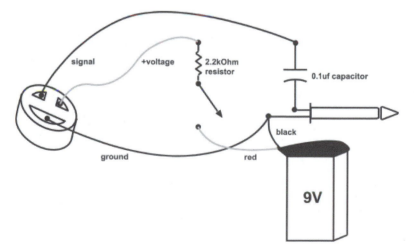

Figure 10.4 Wiring a 3-wire electret microphone.

PART III
TOUCHING

Chapter 11

LAYING OF HANDS I (ST. VITUS' DANCE): TRANSFORMING A PORTABLE RADIO INTO A SYNTHESIZER BY MAKING YOUR SKIN PART OF THE CIRCUIT

You will need:

- A battery-powered AM radio.
- Batteries for the radio.
- Small screwdrivers, flat and/or Phillips, as required to disassemble the radio.
- Plastic electrical tape and some stranded hook-up wire may be needed.
- Optional: cigar box, double-stick foam tape.

How to Choose a Radio

It should be cheap enough that you won't be too angry if it never works again. The AM band is more important than the FM, but it doesn't matter if the radio picks up both. It should have *analog* tuning (i.e., a dial) rather than digital presets or scan buttons. Older radios are usually better than newer ones. Larger radios are easier to work with than tiny ones, and often produce a wider range of sounds. Small boom boxes are great, and you can use the tape head for other experiments (see chapter 9). It's better if it has a built-in speaker, not just a headphone jack, but a headphone jack *in addition to* a speaker can be useful. And most importantly: **IT MUST BE BATTERY POWERED!** Beware: an alarm clock radio with a built-in "backup battery" is *not* suitable, since it requires AC power to function as a radio.

Laying of Hands

Install the batteries and confirm that the radio works *prior* to disassembly; if not functional, return it to the store. If it works, remove the batteries.

Remove screws holding radio together. Put them somewhere safe (like a cup, *not* loose on top of the workbench), taking care to make a note of location if they are of different sizes. Some screws may be hidden beneath stickers or under the batteries. Gently separate the halves of the radio. If plastic wedge-fasteners are used you may need to twist a thin flat screwdriver or clam shucker along the seams. Don't force it—check for hidden screws if it resists. Avoid tearing wires. Once open, make note of any wires connecting the two halves of the radio or the circuitry to the speaker, battery, antenna, etc., in case they get torn later (see the Fourth Rule of Hacking).

Locate and remove the screws holding the circuit board to the radio housing. Carefully remove the circuit board from the chassis. Sometimes adhesive may be used as well as screws. Knobs and switches may intrude into slots in the case and require bending the plastic to release the board. Circuit boards, especially cheap ones, can be very brittle, so don't bend it!

The side of the board with most of the little bumpy colorful things (resistors, capacitors, chips, etc.) is called the "component side"; the side that consists mostly of little wiggly lines (usually silver or copper colored, sometimes under a translucent green wash) is the "solder side." Turn the board so that the solder side is accessible. Replace the batteries; depending on the construction of the case you may have to hold the batteries in place using plastic electrical tape, or extend the battery leads with extra wire. If it has a telescoping antenna this may need to be disconnected in order to expose the circuit board—you probably won't need to reconnect it. Remove the volume and tuning knobs if they are large enough to cover over parts of the circuit board, leaving short nubbins by which you should still be able to adjust settings.

Turn on the radio and tune it to a "dead spot" between stations or at the end of the dial. Lick your fingertips, like a safecracker in a film noir. Touch the circuit board lightly in different places with your fingers until you find a location that affects the radio's sound (see figure 11.1). Search for touch points that cause the radio to start to whistle, squeal, or "motorboat." Tune the radio across the band, and continue to experiment with finger placement. Try several fingers at once. The moisture on your fingertips increases conductivity, and makes your touch more sensitive, but I suggest you do not lick the circuit board directly. And, observing Seventh Rule of Hacking, avoid shorting points on the circuit board with screwdriver tips, bare wire, or full immersion in drool.

Don't worry if you don't get new sounds immediately—it's a bit like trying to make your first sound on a trumpet or flute, or learning to ride a bike. Sometimes you have to work a while before you find a sweet spot, but then you'll lock in and form a tight feedback relationship with the instrument, and the sounds should pour forth (see track 10 on the CD). It can take up to an hour to make your first squeal. If you can't get anything after an hour, try another day or another radio.

What's happening?

As Ol' Sparky has demonstrated on far too many occasions, flesh is an excellent conductor of electricity. By bridging different locations on the board with your fingers you are effectively—if haphazardly—adding free-range resistors and capacitors to the existing circuit. Your body literally becomes part of the circuit. Varying the pressure (or dampness) of your finger changes the values of these components. Depending on the location and pressure, you may end up merely re-tuning the radio, or affecting its loudness, but you may change the radio into very different kind of circuit, like an oscillator. This happens when the output of a gain stage (such as an amplifier) flows back through your skin into an input—voilá, feedback, the musician's friend!

Figure 11.1 Laying of hands.

A radio contains several of the same basic modules as a classic analog music synthesizer: oscillators, amplifiers, filters, frequency shifters, ring modulators. Your skin re-tunes these modules, patches them together, and adds feedback paths. Moving your fingers and changing the volume, tuning, and band selections reconfigure this synthesizer to make different sounds—a whistling oscillator, modulated white noise, a signal processor chopping fragments of radio broadcasts, etc.

You may not know exactly what you are doing, but you should soon acquire a sense of touch: what points work best, how does pressing harder affect the sound, etc. This is a very direct, interactive sense of control similar to that which a "real" instrumentalist, such as a violinist, uses to articulate and intonate notes. This principle of direct contact with circuitry is relatively rare among commercial electronic instruments, but has often been exploited by experimentalists (and is the soul of the infamous Cracklebox).

Later we will modify circuits by replacing your flesh with specific "knowable" components—the effect may be more predictable and stable, but the sense of touch will be diminished. In the future if things start to sound *too* controlled, remember you can always add your body to the circuit. And if your eviscerated radio becomes too predictable, try a friend's or open another—different radios respond differently.

The Cracklebox

Legend has it that the inspiration for the Cracklebox springs from the out-of-body experience of an adolescent Michel Waisvisz after he attempted to play his father's shortwave receiver by laying his hands on its 240 volt-powered circuit board. He recovered, the radio was nailed against the wall of their house in Delft to prevent further mishap, and Waisvisz's vision of an electronic instrument that could be played by intuitive touch was eventually safely realized in the late-1960s in collaboration with the engineer Geert Hamelberg. After building a number of different keyboard-sized instruments, in 1975 Waisvisz worked with engineers at STEIM, a music research foundation in Amsterdam, to design the very portable and affordable Cracklebox. Four thousand Crackleboxes were sold, and the original instrument has recently been reissued and can be bought online. Touch circuits had been employed in the expressive keyboard controllers of the maverick synthesizer designers Donald Buchla in 1965 and Serge Tcherepnin in the early 1970s, but the Cracklebox was the first mass-produced electronic musical instrument that incorporated the player's skin as the primary variable component in a sound-generating circuit.

The Cracklebox

Older-style radios sometimes have tuning coils whose colorful slotted tops are just asking for the twist of a screwdriver. Doing so may diminish or disable the radio's ability to pick up stations, but can add whooshy noise and rhythmic motorboating sounds to your instrument's palette.

When you are through experimenting you may want to reassemble the radio—this is the safest way to carry it around, and to insure its future functionality as a radio. But if you are so enamored of your electronic Ouija board that you cannot bear to seal it up again, welcome to the most hardware part of hacking: finding a box. Cigar boxes work great: using double-stick tape, you can stick down the circuit board (solder side up), speaker, and related parts. Close the lid to transport, open it to play. Don't do this with metal boxes, as they may short out the circuit, but wood or plastic are fine.

A tickled radio often swoops over a very wide frequency range, but if the built-in speaker is small you might never hear the bass end. Try placing a telephone pickup or a guitar pickup on the speaker and plug it into an amplifier of some sort—a mini-amp, or a guitar amp, or a mixer and speakers. The coil will pick up lower frequencies than a small speaker will actually reproduce. Alternatively, drop an amplified contact mike onto the speaker: listen as it bounces around, adding a percussive edge to the radio's squeals—like the bottle caps around the calabash of an mbira.

If your radio has a headphone jack you can listen to it over headphones, or connect it to a *battery-powered* amplifier—if this amp has a larger speaker than the radio it should give you a louder, fuller range signal. Do *NOT* connect from the headphone jack into any amplifier, mixer or recorder that connects to AC (Mains) power at the wall.

EXTREMELY IMPORTANT NOTE: DON'T EVEN *THINK* ABOUT "LAYING HANDS" ON ANYTHING THAT PLUGS INTO THE WALL!! AND NEVER PLUG YOUR RADIO'S HEADPHONE JACK INTO AN AC-POWERED MIXER OR AMPLIFIER UNLESS YOUR ARE 101% CERTAIN THAT THERE IS NO POSSIBLITY OF A GROUND FAULT (I.E., NEVER)!

An Alternative

The primary electronic function needed to transform the radio into an oscillator is *amplification*. Although the radio's filtering, frequency shifting, and chopped noise add considerable character, you can get similar results by laying damp fingers upon a simple battery-powered amplifier circuit, such as those described in chapter 1.

Chapter 12

TICKLE THE CLOCK (LAYING OF HANDS II): FINDING THE CLOCK CIRCUIT IN TOYS

You will need:

- An electronic toy.
- Small screwdrivers.
- A Sharpie-style fine-tip permanent marker.
- Optional: two test leads with alligator clips and a resistor in the range of 1kOhm–4kOhm.

Hacking is a lot like hot-rodding your car: you don't need to be able to build a car from scratch to swap in a 4-barrel carburetor, but it helps to know what a carburetor looks like before you get too creative with the wrench. We'll use a simple but useful hack as a step toward identifying basic electronic components, and introduce some electronic axioms along the way.

How to Choose a Toy

As with the radio, select a toy that is expendable, not too tiny, and has a built-in speaker. A toy that makes sound is preferable to a mute one, and sampled sounds (like voices, animal sounds, or instruments) are more rewarding than simple beeps. The more buttons and switches the better, generally speaking. Keyboards are a gamble: some cheap Yamahas hack magnificently (the PSS-140 is especially satisfying), while others have curiously limited potential for interesting modification. Cheaper is usually better—the more expensive toys (and almost all that put out video) often use crystal clocks, which are more difficult to hack. And, of course: **THE TOY MUST BE BATTERY POWERED!**

Clocks

The majority of electronic toys manufactured since the late-1980s are essentially simple computers dedicated to running one program. In most, a crude clock circuit determines the pitch of the sounds and the speed of its blinking lights, graphics and/or program

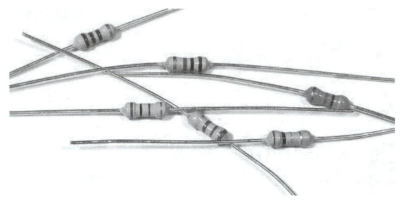

Figure 12.1 Some resistors.

sequence. (This is true for many older analog toy circuits as well.) If you can locate the clock circuit and substitute one component, you can transform a monotonous bauble into an economical source of surprisingly malleable sound material.

What's Under the Hood?

Open up the toy, carefully noting wire connections in case one breaks. Study the circuit board and try to identify the following types of components:

- Resistors: little cylinders encircled by colorful 1960s retro stripes (see figure 12.1).
- Capacitors, in two basic forms (see figure 12.2):
  Small discs of dull earth tones, or colorful squares;
  Cylinders, upright or on their side, fatter than resistors, with one stripe at most.
- Transistors: three wire legs supporting a small black plastic blob or metal can (see figure 12.3).

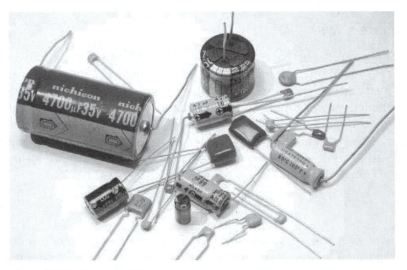

Figure 12.2 Some capacitors.

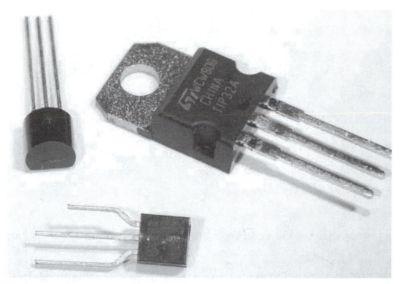

Figure 12.3 Some transistors.

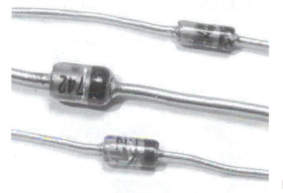

Figure 12.4 Some diodes.

- Diodes: cylinders, smaller and less colorful than resistors, usually marked with one stripe, glass, or plastic (see figure 12.4).
- Integrated Circuits (ICs): usually black or grey, sometimes like rectangular bugs with legs on one, two or four sides; sometimes a malignant looking black circular blob oozing up from the circuit board (see figure 12.5).

Figure 12.5 Some Integrated Circuits.

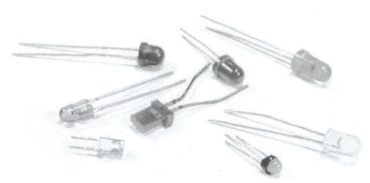

Figure 12.6 Some LEDs.

- LEDs (Light Emitting Diodes): colorful sources of light (see figure 12.6).
- Other things you'll learn about later.

More and more toys are being made these days with "surface mount devices" (SMDs)—insanely tiny, rectangular versions of the above building blocks (see figure 12.7). Until you gain some hands-on experience with them you can despair of distinguishing the various different types of components, and decoding and hacking these toys will be a doubly foggy experience.

We're looking for *resistors*, especially those lying near an IC, flanked by a disc or square capacitor.

Laying of Hands, Again

As with the radio hack we did earlier, your fingers are usually the most direct form of circuit manipulation and testing. Get the circuit making sound. Position it so that you can touch the solder-side of the circuit board, if possible while looking at the component

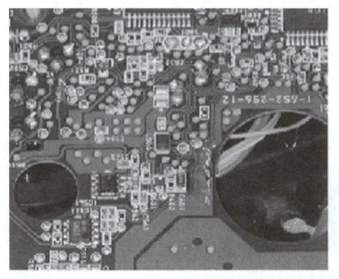

Figure 12.7 Circuit board with surface mount components.

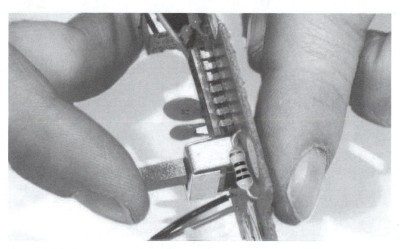

Figure 12.8 Finding the clock resistor (finger on right).

side. Lick one fingertip and place it across various connections; in particular try to connect across points at either end of a resistor, so that your finger parallels the resistor's connection (see figure 12.8). When your finger bridges a resistor that is part of the clock circuit you should hear the pitch slide up a bit, or the tempo speed up. If the circuit has lots of connections, and you are having trouble finding the spot, concentrate on those resistors lying close by small capacitors, usually near the biggest IC on the board. If the circuit is too small for your fingers, clip a test lead to each end of a resistor in the range of 1–4kOhm, and touch the free ends of the leads to the ends of various resistors on the circuit board until you hear the pitch go up.

When you think you've found a hot spot, mark it on the circuit board with a Sharpie.

If the circuit incorporates the above-mentioned SMDs, most of the components *and* connections will be on the same side of the board, and it may be difficult to distinguish the capacitors from resistors. Go after the blips with *two* shiny solder blobs at either end, rather than three or more, and you're more likely to hit one of the timing components. Good luck—it can be very frustrating, and at a certain point you may want to give up, go out, and find yourself another (older) toy with bigger, more recognizable components.

If you have no success finding the spot, the toy may use a crystal for the clock timing, rather than a simple circuit with a resistor and capacitor. You'd best put it aside and try another. On the other hand, sometimes you'll get lucky and won't even need to lay a finger on the circuit board to find the clock resistor: some toys, such as the "Microjammer" guitars, include a pitch control knob or slider.

What's Happening?

Electric current flows through wire like water through a fat pipe. Resistors are like skinny pipes, or the rust-laden risers of NYC loft buildings: the higher the resistance (measured in chantworthy Ohms), the less current flows. Capacitors also resist the flow of electric current, but resist it more at some frequencies than others, in a manner that defies liquid analogies. Capacitance is measured in soukable Farads, usually in small enough amounts to be called "microfarads" or "picofarads." (Yes, the vocabulary of hardware is much cuter than that of software.)

When a resistor and a capacitor are combined in the feedback loop of an amplifier, they resonate at a frequency that can be adjusted by changing the value of either of the two components; with enough gain the circuit starts to oscillate, just like a mike and speaker feeding back. Make the resistor or capacitor *smaller* and the frequency goes up; make either *larger* and the frequency goes down. When the frequency gets too high to hear, it enters the range of a useful clock rate for a computer or a digital toy (or a way to summon your dog).

When you place one resistor in parallel with another you *lower* the net resistance (think of it as adding an additional pipe for the current to flow through.) Your skin is a resistor (as we demonstrated in the previous chapter)—when you press your finger across the circuit board contacts you effectively decrease the size of the resistor on the other side of the board. More current flows and the pitch goes up.

Chapter 13

HACK THE CLOCK (LEARN A NEW ALPHABET): CHANGING THE CLOCK SPEED FOR COOL NEW NOISES

You will need:

- The electronic toy from the previous experiment.
- Some hookup wire.
- Test leads with alligator clips.
- A few resistors of different values.
- A potentiometer, 1megOhm or greater in value.
- Soldering iron, solder, and hand tools.

Wet fingers are fine for making the clock go faster. But we all know that the Third Law of the Avant-Garde states:

Slow it down, a lot.

To slow it down we need to make the resistance *larger* instead of smaller. Which means removing the clock resistor (once you are sure which one it is) and replacing it with a larger one—instead of bridging it with your finger (as we did in the last chapter) which can only make the pitch go up.

1. Locate the clock resistor you identified in the previous experiment. Wedge a small flat-bladed screwdriver under the resistor. Melt the solder on the underside of the circuit board at one end of the resistor, and lever the screwdriver to lift that end free from the solder connection (see figure 13.1). Now grip the resistor with a pair of pliers and pull it free of the board as you melt the other solder joint. Put it somewhere safe and don't lose it! If the circuit already has a pitch-control potentiometer ("pot"), de-solder and remove it entirely.

2. Strip and tin the ends of two pieces of hookup wire (approximately 3–6 inches long). Press the end of one into one of the holes left after removing the resistor from the component side of the circuit board. Melt the solder on the solder side of the board as you press the end of the wire through the hole. Touch up the solder joint with a bit of fresh solder to make sure it is solid. Repeat with the second wire into the other hole. Your circuit board should now have two colorful whiskers sprouting from among the other, vertically challenged components (see figure 13.2). If you removed a pot from the board, there may be more than two holes; solder a wire to each of them.

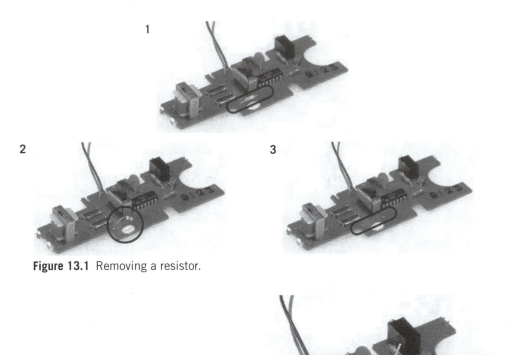

Figure 13.1 Removing a resistor.

Figure 13.2 Resistor whiskers.

The copper traces on printed circuit boards can be very delicate, and the twisting of the wires as you go through the following experiments can tear the trace, sometimes irreparably. It is a good idea to provide some kind of "strain relief" for them. The easiest method is to bend them gently so they lie flat against the board, and then tape them down with electrical tape to prevent them from moving at the point they pass through the board (see figure 13.3).

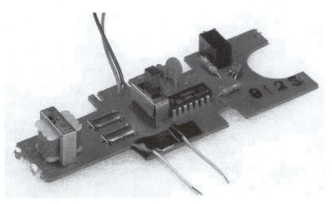

Figure 13.3 Whisker strain relief.

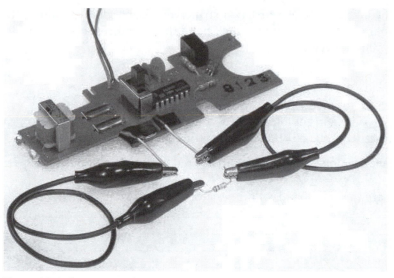

Figure 13.4 A remote resistor.

3. Attach a clip lead to the free end of each of the wires. Clip the resistor you removed between the other ends of the clip leads, effectively re-inserting it to the circuit (see figure 13.4). If you didn't damage anything in de-soldering, the circuit should behave as it did before the operation. If it doesn't, you may need to "restart" the toy by removing and reinstalling the batteries (see Rule #12, below).

4. Those colorful stripes around the resistor indicate its value. Look at the decoder chart in figure 13.5 below:

Resistor Color Codes

Color	Value	Multiplier
black	0	1
brown	1	10
red	2	100
orange	3	1,000
yellow	4	10,000
green	5	100,000
blue	6	1,000,000
violet	7	10,000,000
gray	8	100,000,000
white	9	1,000,000,000

Color	Tolerance (for end band only)
no color	+/– 20 percent
silver	+/– 10 percent
gold	+/– 5 percent

Figure 13.5 Resistor color codes.

Study your resistor. The first two stripes represent number values, the third is a multiplier, and a final gold or silver band the tolerance. So if the bands go: brown, black, yellow, silver:

Brown = 1
Black = 0
Yellow = multiply by 10,000
silver= +/–10 percent tolerance
So we get: 10 x 10,000=100,00 Ohms (or 100kOhms) +/–10 percent

Another example: orange (3) orange (3) red (x 100) gold = 3300 +/– 5 percent. Get it?

5.   What are the color bands of the resistor you removed?

_____
_____
_____
_____

What is its value? _____

6.   Go to your resistor assortment and find a resistor at least twice as big, and one about 1/2 the value. Clip the larger one into the circuit and the pitch should go down. Replace it with the smaller one and the pitch should go up. If either one does not work it may be so extreme a value that the circuit shuts down, so replace it with one whose value is somewhere between the original resistor and the non-functional one. In the event of such a crash, observe the 12th Rule of Hacking:

Rule #12: After a hacked circuit crashes you may need to disconnect and reconnect the batteries before it will run again.

(Count to five before replacing them.)

7.   Substituting resistors should give you a good idea of what values produce what kind of sound, but you will probably want to vary the pitch/speed more fluidly. A potentiometer is a continuously variable resistor. In order to extend the pitch downward you need a pot whose maximum value is *greater* than the resistor you removed. Since most clock circuits use rather large resistors (100kOhm or larger) you will probably need a pot whose maximum value is 1megOhm (1,000,000 Ohms) or greater.

Pots have three terminals, which are labeled A, B, and C in figure 13.6. The resistance between the outer two (A and C) is fixed at the designated value of the pot, which is the

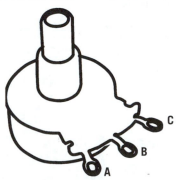

Figure 13.6 The three terminals of a potentiometer.

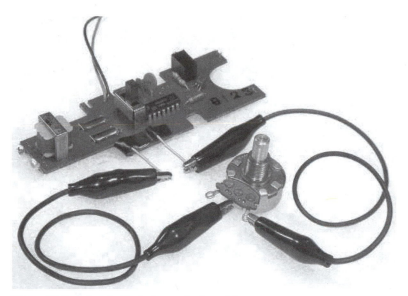

Figure 13.7 Pot substitute for a clock resistor.

pot's absolute maximum resistance (i.e., 1megOhm). As you rotate the shaft of the pot clockwise the resistance between the center terminal B and the outer terminal A goes *up* from 0 Ohms to the maximum value, while the resistance between B and the other outer terminal C goes *down* from the maximum to 0—like a seesaw. Reversing the pot's rotation tips the seesaw back the other way.

Remove the resistor from the clip leads attached to the whiskers on your circuit board. Clip the free end of one of the leads to the center terminal (B) of your pot, and clip the other to the end terminal C (see figure 13.7). Rotate the pot and listen. The circuit will probably crash if you raise the pitch past a certain point and you'll have to restart it (see Rule #12, above). But as long as you stay below that point in the pot's rotation you should be able to coax a pretty wide range of sounds out of your circuit. If the toy appears to shut down when the clock is at its slowest, but restarts on its own when the pitch is raised again, the problem may be simply that the sound is going too low to be heard on the built-in speaker; try putting a telephone pickup on the speaker and amplify it through a bigger speaker (as suggested for the radio in chapter 11).

If there is no appreciable change in pitch or tempo you may have picked the wrong resistor as the clock timing component. Solder it back into the board and use your finger to search again for the hot spot.

If you removed a pitch-varying pot from the circuit (instead of a fixed resistor) you will have to experiment with connecting the terminals of your new pot to various combinations of leads from the circuit board before you find the correct hookup. Substituting a pot of larger value than the built-in one should give you a wider range of pitch/speed variation. Note: one could also change the clock frequency by varying the *capacitor* in the clock circuit, rather than the resistor, but it is difficult to make a capacitor continuously variable over a wide range, and therefore this is generally a less practical approach to the problem of "playing" the clock.

Chapter 14

OHM'S LAW FOR DUMMIES: HOW TO UNDERSTAND RESISTORS

You will need:

- The electronic toy from the previous experiment, or a new one.
- Some hookup wire.
- Test leads with alligator clips.
- An assortment of resistors.
- A potentiometer (1 MegOhm or greater in value).
- A multimeter.
- Soldering iron, solder, and hand tools.

Now it's time for a smidgen of theory—sorry.

Measuring Resistance

A multimeter is a device for measuring various electronic properties, such as testing the voltage of a battery to see if it's dead or alive, or checking the value of a resistor. Meters come with analog readouts (a wiggling needle) or digital displays—simple digital meters are cheap these days and generally more useful. Most meters have a multi-position rotary switch for selecting different measurement modes (DC voltage, AC voltage, current, resistance, etc.) and the range of values measured and displayed.

Grab a meter, turn it on, and select the Ohm setting (Ω). Measure some resistors to confirm your prediction of value from the color code, and to acquaint yourself with this new tool. Most meters have a few ranges for resistance—experiment and see how changing the range affects the readout. You will notice that a handful of "identical" resistors" (i.e., all marked orange-orange-yellow for 330kOhm) will probably measure slightly different values—an indication of the 5 percent or 10 percent tolerance mentioned in the previous chapter. Measure between the different tabs of a pot (you may need to use clip leads between the meter's probes and the terminals of the pot unless you have three hands) as you turn the shaft, and observe the seesaw change in resistance. Try measuring the resistance of your skin—you'll need to use the highest setting in the Ohm range. Notice that the resistance decreases the harder you press the probes into your skin (ouch!), the closer together you place them, or the wetter your fingers are.

Series and Parallel (Ohm's Law)

You may recall that a finger pressed on a circuit puts your flesh in *parallel* to the existing components, *lowering* the net resistance, *increasing* the speed of the clock and raising the pitch of the toy. In order to lower the pitch you had to remove the on-board resistor and substitute a pot of larger value. This demonstrates an aspect of Ohm's Law so essential to hacking that we will appropriate it:

Rule #13 (Ohm's Law for Dummies): The net value of two resistors connected in parallel is a little bit less than the smaller of the two resistors; the net value of two resistors connected in series is the sum of the two resistors.

To make a clock *slower* than it already is you must add a pot in *series* with the resistor on the board: de-solder one end of the resistor and connect the pot between this loose end of the resistor and the hole out of which it came (see figure 14.1). Because the toy will never run faster than its "stock" speed, this configuration minimizes the risk of freeze and crash.

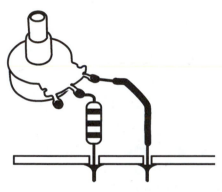

Figure 14.1 Potentiometer and resistor in series.

To make the clock only go *faster* you connect the pot in *parallel* (essentially substituting it for your finger in the test we did in chapter 12): leave the resistor in place on the board, and solder wires from the two tabs of the pot to the two ends of the resistor (see figure 14.2).

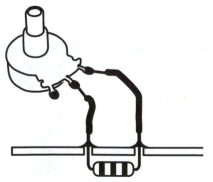

Figure 14.2 Potentiometer and resistor in parallel.

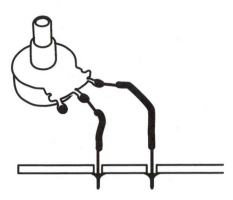

Figure 14.3 Potentiometer alone.

To make the clock go slower *and* faster you remove the resistor entirely and connect a pot of *larger* value than the removed resistor in its place (see figure 14.3).

Finally, if you want the toy to go slower and faster but never crash, put the original resistor in series with the pot with clip leads, then substitute progressively smaller resistors for your original value until you find one that lets the circuit run at the maximum speed before crashing, with the pot in the fully clockwise (i.e., 0 Ohm) position.

If all this doesn't make sense in the abstract, check it out. Use the meter to measure some series and parallel combinations of fixed resistors. Then try some of these modifications to a toy clock circuit until you feel comfortable with The Law.

Theory class is over. Take a moment to read about some of the first artists to puzzle over Ohm's law as they struggled to make their own electronic instruments (see "Composing Inside Electronics"), then get back to work.

Composing Inside Electronics

The 1970s were a pivotal time in the evolution of the technology and culture of electronic music. Synthesizers were still impractically expensive for young musicians, but Integrated Circuits—the guts of those costly machines—were getting cheaper in inverse proportion to their sophistication. New chips contained 90 percent of a functional circuit designed by someone who really knew what he was doing; the remaining 10 percent could be filled in by someone relatively clueless. The trick was finding the right chips: in the days before the World Wide Web, information was much more segregated, with precious few leaks. When data did trickle down from the engineers to amateurs, through magazines with titles like *Popular Electronics* or *Wireless World*, it was often passed from hand to hand like samizdat literature.

A musical community formed around this exchange of information. It included the "Composers Inside Electronics" who worked with Tudor (see "David Tudor and *Rainforest*," chapter 8,) students of David Behrman (see track 11 on the CD) and Robert Ashley at Mills College in Oakland, California (including Kenneth Atchley, Ben Azarm, John Bischoff, Chris Brown, Laetitia de Compiegne Sonami, Scot Gresham-Lancaster, Frankie Mann, Tim Perkis, Brian Reinbolt, and Mark Trayle), students of Alvin Lucier at Wesleyan University in Middletown, Connecticut (Nicolas Collins and Ron Kuivila), of Serge Tcherepnin at California

"Pygmy Gamelan" (1973), electronic circuit composition, Paul De Marinis.

Institute of The Arts in Valencia, California (Rich Gold), and other musicians and artists scattered throughout the United States and (more thinly) Europe. Some participants were mere muddlers, who built beautiful, oddball circuits seemingly out of pure ignorance and good luck. Others became astonishingly talented, if idiosyncratic, designers. The prolific Paul De Marinis included bits of vegetables as electrical components so his circuits would undergo a natural aging process ("CKT," 1974), incorporated sensors that responded to a person's electronic field ("Pygmy Gamelan," 1973; see figure above), and built automatic music composing circuits that anticipated later trends in computer music ("Great Masters of Melody," 1975)—one of which could be played by a bird ("Parrot Pleaser," 1974.)

The European electronic music scene of the time was much more stratified—there was a well-established state-funded tradition of collaboration between composers and professional engineers, and homemade music circuitry never caught on there to the degree that it did in the United States (I have never seen a photograph of Stockhausen holding a soldering iron). There were notable exceptions, however. Andy Guhl and Norbert Möslang (Switzerland; see top, next page) formed "Voice Crack" in 1972, and over the next thirty years honed their skills at "cracking" everyday electronics and became virtuoso performers with their new instruments, including circuits for extracting sound from blinking lights (see track 19 on the CD), radio-controlled cars, radio interference, and obsolete Dictaphones. Christian Terstegge (Germany) has been making elegant sound installations and performances with homemade circuitry since the early 1980s. In his 1986 work, "Ohrenbrennen" ("Ear-burn"; see figure bottom, next page and track 12 on the CD) four oscillators are controlled by photocells inside small altar-like boxes containing candles; the pitches of the oscillators rise in imperfect unison, punctuated by swoops that trace the sputtering of the candles as they burn down.

Toward the end of the 1970s the first affordable microcomputers came on the market. Cajoled by the visionary Jim Horton (USA), a handful of musicians

Circuitry by Norbert Möslang.

invested in the Kim-1—a single A4-sized circuit board that resembled an autoharp with a calculator glued on. Programming this thing in machine language (and storing the program as fax-like tones on a finicky cassette tape recorder) was an arduous, counterintuitive, headache-inducing process, but coding offered one great advantage over building circuits: it was easier to correct a mistake by re-programming than by re-soldering. Over the next ten years Apple, Commodore, Atari, Radio Shack, and others introduced increasingly sophisticated machines (and eventually disk drives) which gradually reduced the angst-factor of programming, and homemade circuits faded into anachronism, until the anti-computer backlash of "Circuit Bending," as proselytized by Reed Ghazala (see chapter 15), brought "chipetry" back into fashion.

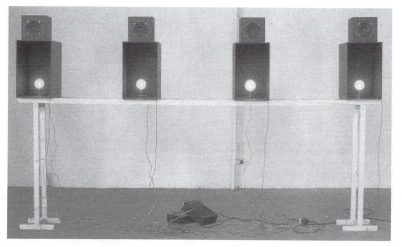

"Ohrenbrennen" (Ear-burn), Christian Terstegge.

Chapter 15

BEYOND THE POT:
PHOTORESISTORS, PRESSURE PADS, AND OTHER WAYS
TO CONTROL AND PLAY YOUR TOY

You will need:

- Electronic toys and radios from the previous experiments.
- Some hookup wire.
- Test leads with alligator clips.
- An assortment of resistors and pots.
- A few different photoresistors.
- A flashlight.
- A soda straw.
- Some loose change.
- Anti-static foam from packaging Integrated Circuits.
- A small sheet of corroded conductive metal, such as iron, copper, or aluminum.
- A lead from a mechanical pencil.
- Some paper and a soft pencil.
- Some fruit and or/vegetables.
- A telephone pickup coil.
- A multimeter.
- Soldering iron, solder, and hand tools.

You've opened a toy, tickled the clock, replaced its timing resistor with a potentiometer, and learned a bit of theory about swapping resistors—what's next in the way of toy hacks?

Photoresistors

A photoresistor (or photocell, as it is sometimes called) changes its value in response to light level: the resistance gets *smaller* when it is exposed to a bright light, and gets *larger* in the dark (see figure 15.1). The lowest resistance in bright light is anywhere from 100 to 2000 Ohms, depending on the kind of photoresistor; the "dark resistance" is very large,

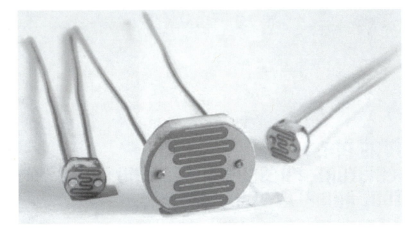

Figure 15.1 Some photoresistors.

typically around 10 megOhms. Because this is higher than most pots, and because most clock circuits use pretty large resistors, photoresistors are a convenient variable resistor for slowing down toys a lot.

Photoresistors are pretty cheap. Sometimes they come with data on the range of resistance, sometimes not. In addition to different "light" (minimum) and "dark" (maximum) resistances, different photoresistors will respond at different speeds to changes in light level—some are more sluggish than others. All these factors affect how they perform in a musical circuit. You can test them with a multimeter, but ultimately your ear is the best guide to picking the best photoresistor for your circuit. Don't be disappointed if it takes a while to find the perfect one.

Select a photoresistor. It is a small disk with two wire leads; one side of the disk has a fine network of thin lines, the other is blank. The side with lines is more sensitive to light than the other. Remove the pot from the clock circuit of your toy and, using clip leads, attach the two leads of the photoresistor where the pot tabs were connected, or solder it directly in to the holes left when you removed the resistor (see figure 15.2). Listen to how

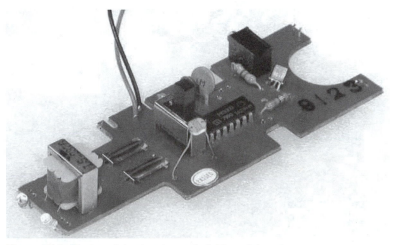

Figure 15.2 Photoresistor in place of clock resistor.

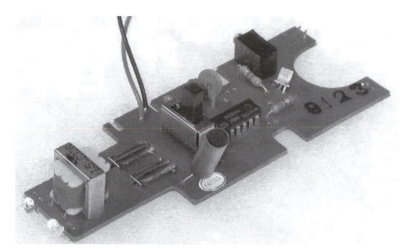

Figure 15.3 A shy photoresistor.

the circuit behaves when you pass your hand over the photoresistor or shine a flashlight on it. If you have more than one type of photoresistor listen to how different ones affect the circuit .

You can put the photoresistor at one end of an opaque tube (such as a drinking straw painted black) to make it very directional in its light sensitivity: it will only respond to light aimed directly down the tube (see figure 15.3). This is the core technology of certain carnival shooting galleries, where each "gun" fires a light towards similarly blinkered targets.

You can place the photoresistor in your mouth and make a very expressive controller that responds to changes in both the light level as you open and close your mouth, and and in the conductivity of your saliva-laden tongue (a suggestively naughty extension of the licked-finger-on-circuit-board effect).

> **ONCE AGAIN: DON'T EVER *THINK* OF TRYING THIS WITH ANY CIRCUIT THAT IS EVEN BATTING ITS EYELASHES AT A WALL OUTLET!**

Try placing a fan between a light source (such as flashlight) and the photoresistor, or reflecting light off a record turntable (put some delicately crumpled aluminum foil on the turntable instead of a record)—you should hear a vibrato effect or other wobbly modulation, which changes as you vary the speed of the fan or turntable.

If the toy has blinking lights or LEDs you can tape the photoresistor against one of the lights and the toy will *self-modulate* itself to produce interesting patterns. Two toys with blinking lights and photoresistor-controlled clocks can modulate each other—curiously erotic electronics! The more toys, the greater your chances of creating artificial life.

A photoresistor can be a good compromise between the fluid, if somewhat unpredictable (and occasionally dangerous), effect of the finger on the circuit board and the more controllable but less expressive potentiometer. You can use it as a very responsive *performance* interface to interpret hand shadows or flashlight movement, or as an installation sensor, reacting to ambient light and the shadows cast by visitors. We'll look at more photoresistor applications in chapters 18 and 22.

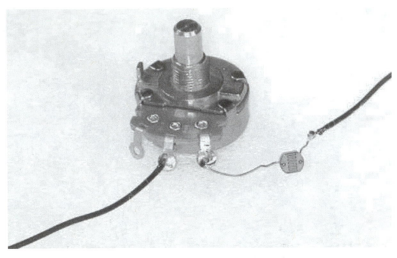

Figure 15.4 A potentiometer and photoresistor in series.

Although the zigzagged side is more sensitive to light than the backing, most photo-resistors are made of translucent material, so that light striking the back will affect its resistance as well. It is important to cover the back if you want the greatest range. Besides burying the photoresistor in an opaque straw, you can seal off the back with black paint or electrical tape.

If you want to both the gestural quality of the photoresistor and the controllability of the pot, you can combine the two: if you wire a pot in *series* with a photoresistors (see figure 15.4), the pot will determine the *maximum* frequency of the clock in full light, and darkness will cause the speed to go *down* from that maximum. If you wire the pot in *parallel* with the photoresistor (see figure 15.5), the pot will set the *minimum* frequency of the clock in full darkness, from which the speed will go *up* as light increases.

In total darkness, the photoresistor has a very large resistance—as high as 20mOhm—much higher than any commonly available pot. Photoresistors can be strung together in series to drive a clock down into the glacially slow range.

Figure 15.5 A potentiometer and photoresistor in parallel.

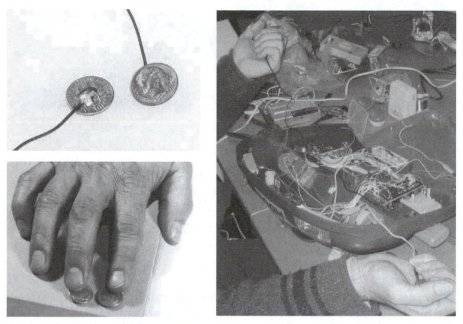

Figure 15.6 Coin electrodes and their performance.

Electrodes

Let's not forget the heady spontaneity of our youthful experiments with flesh-controlled circuitry back in chapter 11. If you want to use your fingers to connect points on the board that are widely separated, or you just want a more formal playing surface, dimes or other silver-plated coins make excellent electrodes. Strip 1/4 inch of insulation off both ends of a few 5 inches pieces of wire. Solder one end of each wire to one of the "sensitive points" you've found on the circuit board, and solder the other end to a dime or other silver-plated coin (copper tarnishes too quickly to use in an urban or coastal environment—think of the Statue of Liberty). Arrange the dimes in a pattern that lets you bridge them easily with your fingers, but avoid direct shorts (see figure 15.6). By the way, I suspect it is illegal to solder U.S. currency, so you might refrain from playing this one in the presence of the Secretary of the Treasury.

A nice way to combine the control certainty of a potentiometer with the gestural expression of finger-on-circuitry is to parallel the pot and a pair of electrodes, as we did with the photoresistor in figure 15.5. When you solder your hook-up wires to the lugs of the pot leave an extra 1 inch of bare wire sticking up through the solder hole. When you go to mount the pot in the box that will hold the circuit (see chapter 17), drill small holes to line up with the wire ends and two more about 1/2 inch away. Dress the bare wires up through the panel at the pot and then down again, so that they form two parallel strips (see figure 15.7). You will have convenient electrode contacts immediately adjacent to the knob so you can slip your finger back and forth between precision adjustment and touchy-feely playing.

Figure 15.7 A potentiometer with electrodes in parallel.

Cheap Pressure Sensors

The squashy black "antistatic foam" in which Integrated Circuits are sometimes packaged has interesting electrical properties. Put a piece between two coin electrodes and measure the resistance as you squeeze them together—it gets lower as you apply more pressure (see figure 15.8). This homemade pressure sensor can be used in place of a pot or photoresistor to make a pressure-sensitive controller for performance or installation (under chair legs to measure weight, for example). (Antistatic foam can also be bought in sheets from various online retailers, if you can't find any high tech garbage pail from which to scrounge.)

Vegetables and fruit also have resistive value. This value changes as they dry out or are squished. You can try substituting small slices of produce for the antistatic foam in the above experiment, or poke bare wire directly into carrots or apples. As some of you may remember from childhood science experiments, it is also possible to make a battery out of fruit or vegetable, but this lesson will wait until another day.

Arty

A pencil lead from a mechanical pencil makes an excellent, if delicate resistor (see figure 15.9). Attach two clip leads to the clock resistor contact points in your toy. Clip one wire to one end of the pencil lead, and scrape the jaws of the other along the lead. Resistance is proportional to the distance separating the contact points, so the pitch of the toy should go down as you move the clip further from the end.

Figure 15.8 Pressure sensor.

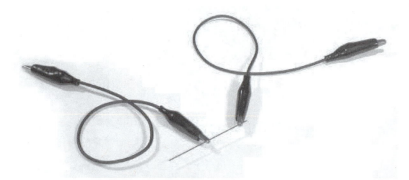

Figure 15.9 A pencil lead resistor.

And the use of graphite as a resistor is not limited to pencil leads. Draw two blots near the edge of a piece of paper, and clamp the jaw of a clip lead to the paper at each blot; clip the other ends of the leads to the clock resistor contact points in your toy (see figure 15.10). Draw a line between the two blots and get the toy running—as you widen the pencil line linking the blots, or draw additional lines, the pitch should go up. Why? The wider the graphite path between the clips the lower the resistance (think fat pipes versus skinny pipes.)

Almost a Short Circuit

Sometimes a toy can be induced to make curious sounds if you make new connections between various locations on the circuit board. Take a resistor of about 1000 Ohms (1kOhms). While listening to the toy, press one end of the resistor to a solder point on the solder side of the board; then touch the other end to various other points—if the circuit

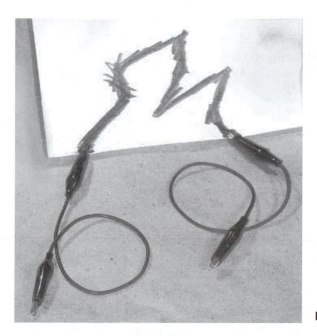

Figure 15.10 Drawing a resistor.

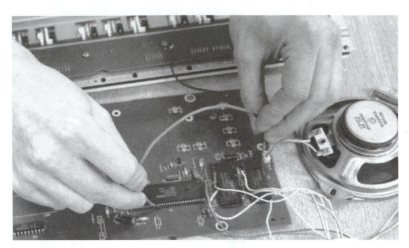

Figure 15.11 Phil Archer bridging the circuit board.

board is large you may need to use a clip lead to reach all over (see figure 15.11 and track 13 on the CD). You may (or may not) get some interesting sounding circuit malfunctions. Disconnect *immediately* any connection that seems to cause heat, smoke, or flame.

Try different value resistors, goings as low as 100 Ohms, but avoid shorting out the board with straight wire unless it's the only thing that works (see the 7th Rule of Hacking). If you find that the best sounds happen with the smallest value resistor, you can try a straight wire, but do so gingerly and be prepared to remove the wire as soon as you feel or smell trouble. You can also try using pots or capacitors instead of resistors. You can go back to your radio and experiment with using resistors to jump between the hot spots you bridged with your damp finger.

Once you find a useful connection you can solder the resistor permanently into place, or add a switch to connect and disconnect it as a performable change (see next chapter for switch information).

This technique is a the heart of Reed Ghazala's wonderful "Circuit Bending" philosophy of hardware hacking (see "Circuit Bending"), and is a very powerful and creative tool for extracting unusual sounds from almost any found circuit.

Rusty

A corroded metal plate and a nail can serve as a quasi-random variable resistor, as we demonstrated in chapter 5. Choose any two points on the circuit board that produce a change when they are connected to one another—this could be the clock resistor solder pads, or any of the hot spots we've just described bridging with resistors. Solder a short wire to each point, long enough to be grasped in the jaws of a clip lead. Clip the other end of one of the leads to a nail and the other lead to a sheet of rough or corroded metal (copper flashing, rusty baking sheet, file, etc.). Lightly scrape the nail across the metal and listen to the circuit twitter—the corrosion and intermittent hop, skip, and jump of the nail over the rough micro topography yields an ever fluctuating resistance that can be steered (if not exactly controlled) by adjusting the pressure and speed of movement.

Circuit Bending

Traditionally, making functional electronic objects has necessitated a fair grasp of theory and a pretty clear idea of what you wanted to make *before* you picked up your soldering iron. David Tudor, Gordon Mumma, Composers Inside Electronics, and other musical designers of the 1970s chipped away at these assumptions. Being self-taught, they had only piecemeal knowledge of electronic theory and were less concerned about doing things "properly" than about making something that sounded cool. Immersed in a musical ethos that valued chance, they were highly receptive to accidental discoveries—in the pursuit of the "score within the circuit," they relished wandering down side paths, rather than race-walking toward a predetermined goal.

More recently Reed Ghazala pushed serendipity back to the fore of electronic practice with his fervent advocacy of what he dubbed "Circuit Bending." Like Waisvisz (see "The Cracklebox," chapter 11), as an adolescent in the late 1960s Ghazala encountered the sounds of accidental circuit interaction: an open amplifier left in his desk drawer shorted against some metal and began whistling. After some experimentation, Ghazala added switches so he could control the shorting, and Circuit Bending was born. He developed a series of techniques for modifying found circuitry—especially electronic toys, whose sonic sophistication grew in direct response to the boom of semiconductor technology in the 1980s—without the benefit of the manufacturer's schematics, or any engineering knowledge whatsoever. In 1992 he began publishing instructive articles in *Experimental Musical Instruments* (an influential journal for instrument builders) and acquired a cult following. In 1997 he launched his Web site and today a cursory Web search will reveal news groups, festivals, and workshops for Circuit Bending all over the world.

Circuit Bending is freestyle sound design with a postmodern twang—the perfect escape for artists bored by the powerful, but often stultifyingly rational, software tools that increasingly dominate music production, but still hooked on the digitally inspired cut-and-paste aesthetic of scavenging, sampling, and reworking found materials. With its defiantly antitheoretical stance and emphasis on modifying cheap consumer technology, bending has a natural egalitarian appeal (as well as some odd orthodoxies: looking at my instruments as I was setting up a demonstration at the "Bent 2004" Festival at The Tank Gallery in New York City, an audience member inquired, "Are they bent or hacked?" When I looked baffled he elaborated: "'Bent' means you have *no* idea what you are doing when you open up the circuit; 'hacked' means you have *some* idea"). But Bending's try-anything extreme experimentalism can produce wonderful results never anticipated by the original designers of the device being bent.

Phil Archer (UK) and John Bowers (UK) are representative of the emerging generation of hackers, who effortlessly combine bending with Tudor-era contact mike technology and sophisticated computer programming. Archer did the "classic" bend to his Yamaha PSS-380 keyboard: exposing the circuit-board, placing the inverted instrument on the performer's lap, and making arbitrary connections between components on the board with a stripped piece of wire (see figure 15.11

"CD Player Slide Guitar," Phil Archer.

and track 13 on the CD). "These connections," he writes, "induce tones, bursts of noise and corrupted 'auto-accompaniment' sequences from the device which are unpredictable in their details but generally 'steerable' overall with practice. The precision and control afforded by the standard keyboard interface is eschewed in favour of direct contact with the circuit, and the performer is continually forced to rethink and re-evaluate their relationship with the instrument in light of the sonic results." Most of his other instruments have a Frankenstein quality: a midget Hawaiian guitar whose single string is played by the sled mechanism from a CD player (see figure above); a set of small percussion instruments whacked and scraped by motors from a dot matrix printer; a music box mechanism activating "Bent" electronic keyboards.

John Bowers—in an ongoing struggle against his training as a computer scientist—"reinvented" what he has dubbed the "Victorian Synthesizer" (see chapter 5 and track 4 on the CD): it produces sounds with speakers animated directly by batteries, bereft of intervening electronic circuitry. Corroded metal, mercury-filled tilt-switches, and a handful of screws and washers complete instruments that could indeed have been built in the nineteenth century. His other "Infra-Instruments" combine similar electro-mechanical technology (mixing bowls filled with motors, magnets, contact mikes and guitar pickups (see figure top, next page); microphones embedded in a plank of wood; strings, stones, and guitar pickups strewn across a table with computers and rock effect boxes).

Notable younger Benders include Knut Aufermann (Germany/UK), Xentos "Fray" Bentos (UK), Joker Nies (Germany), David Novack (USA), and Sarah Washington (UK). Britain's particularly vibrant bending scene (including an "all bending ensemble," P. Sing Cho—see track 14 on CD) has roots in the prevalence of toys as affordable, alternative noisemakers among improvisers in the 1970s—most

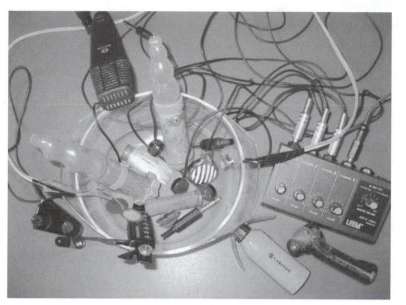

"Mixing Bowl," John Bowers.

significantly Steve Beresford. As Sarah Washington says, echoing Tudor from four decades ago, "I am an improvising musician…the choice of sounds is down to the circuit—whatever it comes up with is fine by me" (see figure below).

"Mao Tai," Sarah Washington.

Motor-Mouth

Noise, flashing lights, and frenetic activity—the essential attributes of any disaster are also the core components of any successful toy. After messing around with the sounds and lights, don't forget the motors that make tickled Elmo twitch and Billy Bass flap his tail. Some pretty sophisticate computer code goes into this electromagnetic choreography, and you can eavesdrop on it by placing a telephone tap coil on a motor and connecting the coil to your amplifier. There is often a beautiful rhythmic interplay between the toy's original sounds, blinking lights and movements, and a thorough hack can bring all this futurist polyphony to the ear. And don't forget to try another coil on the toy's speaker to make the basic sounds louder and wider range (as we did with the radio in chapter 11).

Interconnecting Toys

Once you've opened and hacked a few toys don't be afraid to experiment with interconnecting them. First connect a clip lead between the grounds ("–" end of the batteries) of both toys. Then use the clip-lead-and-resistor technique we described above to make random connections between any point on one toy and any on the other. Use a jumper between the clocks and you may get the toys to cross modulate each other; if you connect clock points between two circuits and remove the resistor from one, you can sometimes drive both in sync from a single clock.

Remember that you can also link circuits through blinking lights and photoresistors, as described earlier in this chapter.

Lest you get too distracted by the gizmo-factor of all these add-ons, don't forget the humble laying of hands. On larger circuit boards with multiple components (such as musical keyboards) a few damp fingers brushed against the circuit board can raise delightful havoc with the normal behavior of the toy—the Yamaha PS-140 is especially susceptible to fleshly corruption (see figure 15.12).

Figure 15.12 Mike Challis playing his hacked Yamaha PS-140.

Figure 15.13 "Sled Dog," hand-scratchable hacked CD player by Nicolas Collins.

Beyond Toys

Most of the techniques described in this chapter can be used to extend the radio you opened up in chapter 11 as well: electrodes can be used to pull the radio's ticklish spots to the outside of a box, and make it easier to bridge multiple points with your fingers; pots, photoresistors, pressure pads, resistors, and rusty nails can be used to link these points as well. Toys and radios are cheap and plentiful, and thus an obvious flashpoint for hacking insurgency, but the same methods can be applied to almost any electronic circuit: CD players (see figure 15.13), old cell phones, rock effect pedals ("stomp boxes"), cassette players, answering machines—you'll never know until you try them. You can buy hundreds of different kinds of electronic kits—from strobe lights to electronic wind chimes—from online retailers (see Appendix A) and experiment with these kinds of modifications as you build them—hacking goes faster if you don't have to disassemble first. After savoring bespoke electronics you'll never accept off-the-rack again.

Chapter 16

SWITCHES:
HOW TO UNDERSTAND DIFFERENT SWITCHES,
AND EVEN MAKE YOUR OWN

You will need:

- The electronic toy from the previous experiments.
- Some hookup wire.
- A Single-Pole Double-Throw switch (SPDT), momentary or toggle.
- A plank of wood, some short nails, and a large ball bearing.
- Soldering iron, solder, and hand tools.

This is possibly the most boring chapter in the book. Skip over it if you wish, but don't tear it out, because it may prove useful later.

Switches are useful for turning power on and off to a circuit to save battery life, for turning on and off specific sounds or functions, and for resetting a circuit if it freezes up. They are often described in catalogs, on Web sites or in packaging by arcane abbreviations. Here are the main distinguishing features.

Mechanical Style

A switch can be *momentary* pushbutton, like a door bell, that changes state (turns something on) when you press it, and returns to its default state (off) when you release it; or it can be a push-on/push-off switch that alternates but holds its state. It can be a *toggle* switch with a handle, like a traditional light switch, that stays where you put it until you switch it back. There is also the *rotary* switch, like the cycle selector on a clothes washer, with which you select between several positions, rather than just on and off. *Slide* switches, like the rotary switch, can select between two or more positions (see figure 16.1). There are a few other oddball switches we'll discuss if they become relevant.

Figure 16.1 Assorted switches.

Number of Throws

A switch is also described by the number of mutually exclusive connections it makes when moved or "thrown." A simple pushbutton that turns something on in one position, but does nothing in the other, is called a "Single Throw" (ST) switch (see figure 16.2a). If the switch alternates between two possible connections, it is a "Double Throw" (DT) switch (see figure 16.2b)—this could be a pushbutton, a toggle, or a slide switch. Rotary switches that can make several different connections are classified by the number of connections, i.e., a five-position switch would be abbreviated as "5T" (see figure 16.2c).

Number of Poles

Sometimes a single handle or button can switch two or more separate circuits simultaneously (think of the huge double-bladed switches in *Frankenstein*, thrown by one ominous handle). Most pushbutton and toggle switches are either "Single Pole" (SP; see figure 16.3a), meaning that they switch only one circuit, or "Double Pole" (DP; see figure 16.3b), which switches two circuits. The dotted line on the schematic representation indicates that the two sections switch in tandem.

Terminal Designations

In a Double Throw switch the solder terminal that is normally *off*, or unconnected, is designated "Normally Open" (NO). The one that is normally *on*, or closed, is the "Normally

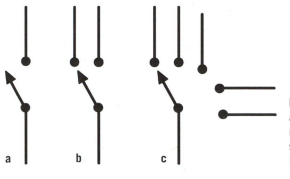

a   b   c

Figure 16.2 a. Schematic representation of a Single Throw (ST) switch. b. Schematic representation of a Double Throw (DT) switch. c. Schematic representation of a Five Throw (5T) switch.

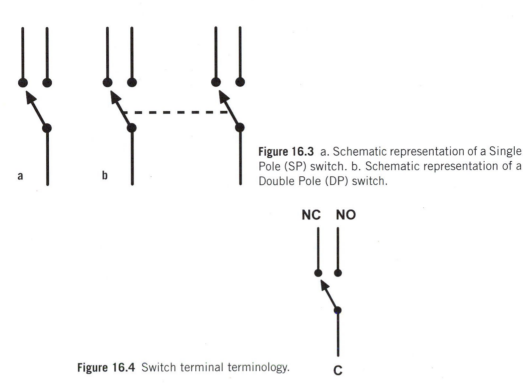

Figure 16.3 a. Schematic representation of a Single Pole (SP) switch. b. Schematic representation of a Double Pole (DP) switch.

Figure 16.4 Switch terminal terminology.

Closed" (NC). The terminal that is connected, by the movement of the button or toggle, to the NO or NC terminals is the "Common" (C; see figure 16.4).

Reset Switch

You may have noticed that your toy occasionally freezes up, usually when the clock is run too high or too low, or you short out some part of the circuit. As per the 12th Rule of Hacking, momentarily removing the batteries will usually fix the problem. But this gets tiresome. We can add a reset switch that lets you press a button or throw a toggle to disconnect the batteries temporarily, without the bother of actually removing them. You'll need a SPDT (Single Pole Double Throw) or DPDT (Double Pole Double Throw) switch. It can be a *momentary* switch, if the toy already has a built-in power on/off switch; if you want to use the reset switch as a power switch as well, then get a toggle switch instead.

Cut one of the wires connecting the batteries to the circuit board. Solder one end of the cut wire to the switch's Common terminal (C); solder the other end to the Normally Closed (NC) terminal. If the battery wire is very short you may want to extend one or both sections with some additional hookup wire. If the switch has more than three connectors, or they are unmarked, you should use a multimeter to figure out the switch logic.

With a momentary switch, the switch is normally *closed*, so the battery voltage flows into the C terminal and out through the NC terminal to the circuit; when you press the switch the C flips its connection to the NO terminal, breaking the connection to the NC terminal and disconnecting the batteries from your circuit. Next time your circuit crashes, return the clock speed pot to a middle setting, restore any other weird connections to their "safe" states, press the switch for a moment, and (hopefully) the circuit will "re-boot" when you release it—easier than removing the batteries, especially in front of a restless crowd at CBGBs or The Royal Albert Hall.

Figure 16.5 A homemade tilt switch.

If you use a toggle switch the circuit will stay in the off state when switched, so it will function as a power on/off switch as well.

Toggle or momentary switches can also be used to switch on and off the resistive jumpers you made in the chapter 15, or to switch between a fixed clock and a variable one.

Homemade Switches

Switches are useful, often essential, things. Unfortunately, they can also be the most expensive part of a hack: resistors, capacitors, wire, and many other electronic components you use in hacking typically cost fractions of a penny, but a switch can set you back $1.00–$3.00. However, with a little mechanical ingenuity you can fabricate your own switches out of paperclips, springs, brass fasteners, and other scraps of metal—classic prison technology, like making a shiv from a bedspring.

You can construct a nice multi-position tilt switch by hammering a ring of brads into a piece of wood, and soldering a wire between each nail and a point on the circuit board that needs switching (see figure 16.5). You can use this switch to select different circuit hot-points to connect to an output jack (see above) or jumper the almost-shorts you found in chapter 15. Variations on this design can be made with loops of wire, strips of copper, or even blobs of mercury (once a common switch element, now banished behind the sign of a skull and crossbones—see figure 16.6).

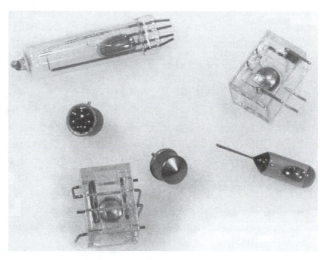

Figure 16.6 Some commercial tilt switches.

Chapter 17

JACK, BATT, AND PACK:
FINISHING TOUCHES:
POWERING AND PACKAGING YOUR HACKED TOY

You will need:

- The electronic toy or radio from the previous experiments.
- A battery-powered mini-amplifier.
- Some hookup wire.
- One or more jacks for external audio connection.
- Some 1kOhm resistors.
- A battery holder (if appropriate—see text).
- A box of some kind to house your circuit.
- Soldering iron, solder, and hand tools.

It's almost time to "close" your first hack, as they say in the O.R., but let's look at a few final modifications before Frank rises from the slab.

Jacks

Beyond retuning the clock and finding some musically-viable almost-shorts, the most significant change you can make to a toy is replacing the little speaker with a big one, thereby confirming the Second Law of the Avant-Garde (introduced in chapter 7). A telephone tap coil resting on the little speaker is one approach, as discussed already. But if your circuit is *never* going to be played by saliva-drenched fingers it's safe to try a wired connection directly to an amplifier.

By adding a jack to connect the circuit to an external amp and decent-size loudspeaker you not only make the sound much louder, which lets you hear more detail, but you will also hear low frequency components that aren't audible through the tiny, parent friendly speakers inside most toys. It's easy to do:

1. Find the wires leading from the circuit board to the speaker.
2. De-solder them from the speaker terminals or cut them as close to the speaker as possible.

3.   Solder these two wires to a female jack of your choice; usually it doesn't matter which wire goes to which terminal, but you must always have one wire going to the shield/sleeve connector and one to the hot/tip connector.

4.   Plug it into a decent sound system and listen. Start at a low volume setting, since the output of a toy can be surprisingly loud. If there's lots of hum, reverse the hot and ground connection at the jack. If there's no sound at all, check your soldering. You may find that the raw sound is too much—too noisy or abrasive, too much extreme high or low—but that's where the equalization on a mixer, amp or "stomp box" can help you carve the sound you want out of the toy's raw material.

Let me repeat:

DO *NOT* ATTEMPT THIS MODIFICATION ON A CIRCUIT THAT WILL BE MAKING INTIMATE ELECTRICAL CONTACT WITH YOUR BODY (SUCH AS THE WET-FINGERS RADIO).

As long as you're adding one jack, why don't you see if there are any other interesting signals running around the circuit board yet unheard?

1.   Solder a wire from the shield/ground connection on a jack to the place on the circuit board where the "−" terminal of the battery connects, or to the shield/ground terminal on the main output jack, if you've added one already.

2.   Solder another wire to the hot tip of the jack and strip and tin the other end.

3.   Solder a 1kOhm resistor to the tinned end of the wire.

4.   Plug a cord between the jack and a battery powered amplifier.

5.   Turn the volume up just a little bit. Poke the free end of the resistor around the circuit board and listen to the different sounds (see figure 17.1). Adjust the volume as needed. Sometimes you can find very odd noises that seem completely unrelated to the basic sound of the toy. Hold on to the body of the resistor, rather than the bare wire, to minimize hum.

Figure 17.1 Phil Archer hunting for interesting sounds.

6. When you find a place you like, solder down the free end of the resistor. Wrap the bare wire and resistor lead in electrical tape to prevent shorts (you can shorten the resistor leads prior to soldering to minimize the amount of bare wire running around your circuit, itching for a short circuit.

7. If you wish, add another jack and repeat the process, discovering and decanting hidden sounds. Or add a multi-position switch (like a rotary switch) to select among different circuit points to connect to a single jack.

If you get sound when one or the other of your two jacks are connected to the same amplifier/mixer, but not with *both*, you have probably unintentionally crossed your grounds. De-solder one of the two incompatible jacks from its wires (the speaker jack, if used, is the first choice) and swap the "hot" and "ground" connections.

You may have noticed that most audio devices with built-in speakers and jacks for headphones switch off the speaker automatically when the headphone plug is inserted. This is accomplished with what is known as a "cut-out jack," which can be purchases at any retailer carrying electronic connectors. The jack's terminals will be designated "tip" or "hot," "sleeve" or "ground," and "normally closed" (NC)—like the switches we discussed in the previous chapter. You wire it as shown in figure 17.2.

Solder a wire between the jack's shield/ground and the circuit ground, in parallel to the speaker's ground connection (do not disconnect the speaker ground.) De-solder the wire from the speaker's hot terminal and solder it instead to the jack's tip/hot. Solder a new wire from the speaker's hot terminal to the NC terminal on the jack.

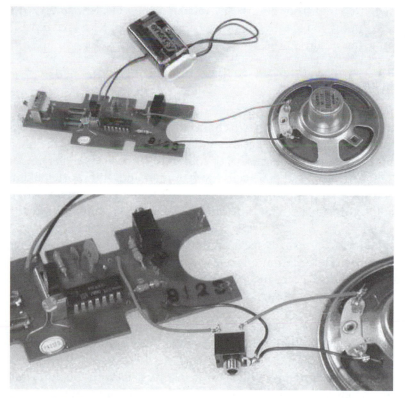

Figure 17.2 Wiring a cut-out jack.

Turn on the circuit. You should hear the sound through the built-in speaker as usual. Now plug a cord from the cut-out jack to your amplifier—the speaker should shut off while the signal passes to your amp through the patch cord. If not, check your wiring logic and soldering joints—it's easy to make a mistake.

> VERY IMPORTANT: BE VERY CAREFUL CONNECTING A HACKED CIRCUIT TO A MIXER OR AMPLIFIER THAT GETS ITS POWER FROM THE WALL. IT'S BEST TO TEST FOR ANY POSSIBLE ELECTROCUTION HAZARD BY GINGERLY TAPPING THE CIRCUIT BOARD, JACKS, AND POTS WITH A DRY FINGER AND FEELING FOR ANY BUZZ OR TINGLE. ALTERNATIVELY, LET A SQUIRREL RUN ACROSS THE BOARD.

And always remember the 14th Rule of Hacking:

Rule #14: Kick me off if I stick (Zummo's rule).

Always have a buddy nearby when there is a risk of electrocution, and chant this mantra before you power up.

An excellent insurance against electrocution is to insert what is known as an "audio isolation transformer" or a DI box between your circuit and the AC-powered world (these can be purchased from almost any retailer selling electric guitars, microphones, keyboards, etc.) but if you are unsure of your power grid, JUST STAY AWAY FROM IT! Use a telephone tap on the speaker instead, if you must get loud.

Battery Substitution

Almost all toys use batteries that put out either 9 volts or 1.5 volts. Most 9-volt batteries basically look the same: bricks with two connectors that resemble android navels. 1.5-volt batteries come in all sorts of packages: cylindrical ones, like D cells (the biggest kind, in the flashlights that Southern sheriffs beat people with), C cells (smaller), AA cells ("pen-light" flashlight batteries), and AAA cells (even thinner and a bit shorter, like some metric mismatch of an AA battery), and button cells (the watch and camera batteries that are infernally small, come in a zillion different sizes and shapes, and are way too expensive and hard to find).

Nine-volt batteries are usually used singly, but 1.5 volt are often combined to add up voltage to power a circuit—commonly one will find them in sets of two, three, or four. The larger (and heavier) the battery the more *current* it provides, which means it lasts longer and can power a larger circuit, so:

Rule #15: You can always substitute a *larger* 1.5-volt battery for a smaller one, just make sure you use the same number of batteries, in the same configuration.

This means you can replace those little button battery cells with the same number of AA cells and run the circuit much longer and much cheaper, and afterwards you can find replacement batteries anywhere. All you need to do is:

1. Disconnect the existing battery holder, noting which wire connects to the "+" end of the battery stack, and which connects to the "–" end.
2. Get a battery holder for larger batteries of your choice.
3. Connect it to the circuit, observing the proper polarity.

Some low-current 6-volt circuits (i.e., using four AA, AAA, or button cell batteries) will run on a 9-volt battery, and might even react to the additional juice with extra perkiness, but others will succumb to cardiac arrest. Unfortunately there's really no way to know until you try it, so proceed with caution (and a duplicate circuit, if at all possible) and stop if you smell smoke or feel a component on the circuit board getting hot.

As you accumulate circuits you will be tempted to minimize your energy costs by using a single battery (or set of batteries) to run several devices. This, unfortunately, is *not* a good idea: sharing often induces noise, weird interference, and interaction, especially if you try to connect more than one of the circuits to the same amplifier.

Rule #16: It's always safer to use separate batteries for separate circuits.

How big a battery to upgrade to has as much to do with fitting them inside the device as any electrical consideration, which brings us to our next topic.

Packaging

As your first hack nears completion you'll want to think about how to package it. You have a few basic style choices:

Stealth: Keep the original packaging, with added knobs, switches, and jacks, as needed (see figure 17.3).
Camp: Go for other recycled housing, such as a cigar box, a BandAid tin, or a human skull (see figure 17.4). David Tudor favored plastic soap boxes. Since the rise of the DVD, plastic VHS boxes fill the dumpsters outside rental shops, and they make perfect homes for circuit boards.

Figure 17.3 Stealth packaging: bent keyboard by Alex Inglizian.

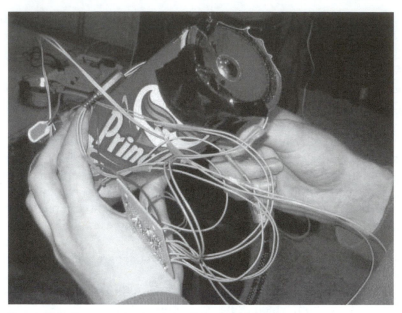

Figure 17.4 Camp packaging: circuit by André Bosman.

Sandwich: Two slabs of acrylic plastic or thin wood with a circuit board in between (see figure 17.5).

Traditional: One of those plastic or metal boxes from Radio Shack or elsewhere that make your product look "professional" (or boringly geeky, depending on your perspective; see figure 17.6).

Figure 17.5 Sandwich packaging: David Behrman's "Kim 1" microcomputer.

Figure 17.6 Traditional packaging: small amplifier by Nicolas Collins.

The decision is partly topological (how do I fit in the all new jacks, pots, and switches?), partly practical (what's the easiest material to drill?), but largely aesthetic (what looks coolest?). Remember that a bare circuit board will short out if placed in a metal box unless it is isolated from the metal with standoffs of some kind, or you cover the metal or circuit board with electrical tape or a sheet of cardboard.

Cigar boxes are great because they can usually be had for free, and you can open them easily to change batteries or touch the circuit. If the clock speed is controlled by photoresistors inside the box, the pitch will glide up and down as you open and close the box, like a cubist trombone. Unfortunately, the wood of a cigar box is sometimes a little too thick for some jacks and pots to mount easily—you may need to countersink the mounting holes in order to secure any nuts that screw down; alternatively, you can pass shielded cable through holes in the wood and solder plugs or jacks directly to the ends.

Now that your first hack is resting comfortably in a beautiful box, the time has come to show it off. Pick up the phone and book that gig!

PART IV

BUILDING

Chapter 18

THE WORLD'S SIMPLEST OSCILLATOR: SIX OSCILLATORS ON A TWENTY-CENT CHIP, GUARANTEED TO WORK

You will need:

- A plastic prototyping board ("breadboard").
- 1 CMOS Hex Schmitt Trigger Integrated Circuit (74C14, CD4584 or CD40106).
- Assorted resistors, capacitors, pots, and photoresistors.
- Some small signal diodes, such as 1N914.
- Some solid hookup wire.
- A plug to match your amp.
- A 9-volt battery and connector.
- A battery powered mini-amplifier.
- Hand tools.

In the contrarian spirit of hacking, the first circuit we build from scratch is based on the *misuse* of an Integrated Circuit (IC) never intended for making sound. The "Hex Schmitt Trigger" is a CMOS digital logic building block consisting of six identical "inverters." An inverter takes a logical input, 1 or 0, and puts out its opposite (so 1 becomes 0, 0 becomes 1). This particular version of the inverter is useful to us because it runs for a long time on a 9-volt battery, it is very cheap, and it contains a circuit element known as a "Schmitt Trigger" whose fine points you don't need to understand at this point but, trust me, transforms the chip from a simple digital no-man (as opposed to a yes-man) into a versatile sound generator.

The Hex Schmitt Trigger may be labeled with the numbers 4584, 40106, or 74C14. There may be prefixes, suffixes, or additional number strings that you can ignore, but chips with a different "innerfix" may not work: if labeled 74HC14 or 74AC14 they will not run on a 9-volt battery, and so are less suitable for this project. If you purchase them sight-unseen (i.e., online), make sure all your Integrated Circuits have a "dual in-line" (DIP) specification, not "surface mount devices" (SMD), as the latter are infernally small and difficult for prototyping.

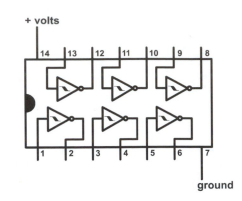

+ volts

ground

Figure 18.1 74C14 pinout.

Internal configuration and connections are shown in figure 18.1.

We will build our circuit on a "solderless prototyping board," commonly referred to as a breadboard. On it you can assemble and rearrange circuit designs quickly, without damaging components. It consists of a plastic block with lots of little holes, beneath which are strips of wire arranged in a matrix (see figure 18.2). These strips, called "buses," run in one or two long horizontal strips along the top and bottom edges of the block, and in numerous shorter vertical strips that extend above and below a central groove.

There are some variation on the designs show here: some breadboards are longer, have only one horizontal bus and the top and bottom, instead of two, or consist of multiple modules on a metal plate, but they all depend on the same underlying bus and matrix system.

The holes are the right diameter for the leads of most electronic components (resistors, capacitors, integrated circuits, etc.) and hookup wire. Circuits are built up by inserting components into the holes on the board and connecting them by linking rows and columns of the matrix with short strips of wire.

Your First Beep

Place the breadboard on the table so the trough-like central groove runs horizontally, from left to right. Strip, twist, and tin 1/2 inch from the ends of each lead of a 9 volt-battery hookup clip. Insert the end of the red wire in one end of a horizontal bus on the upper edge of the breadboard and the black wire in a horizontal bus along the lower edge. Anything

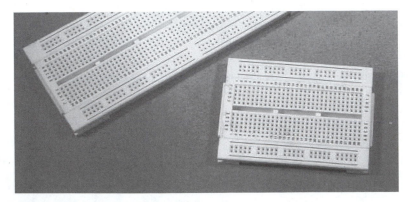

Figure 18.2 Some solderless breadboards.

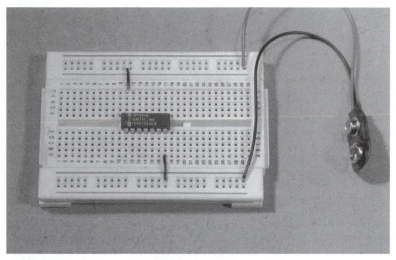

Figure 18.3 74C14 in place, with power connections.

inserted in the upper bus will now be connected to +9 volts, while anything inserted into the lower one will be connected to ground (0 volts).

Press a Hex Schmitt Trigger IC into the breadboard, taking care not to bend over any pins. Be sure that the notch and/or small dot is at the left side, as shown in figure 18.3. Use a jumper to connect pin 14 to the +9 volt bus and pin 7 to the ground (0 volt) bus. If there are two horizontal buses at the top and bottom be careful to link to the active one.

If the breadboard is longer than the one shown, the upper and lower horizontal buses may be "broken" in the middle, rather than extending the full length of the board. If so, you will notice a slightly larger gap in the pattern of 5-holes, gap, 5-holes, etc. You can surmount this difficulty by jumping the gap with a small piece of wire, as shown in figure 18.4.

Connect a 0.1 uf capacitor between pin 1 and the ground bus. You do so by pushing one lead of the capacitor into a hole in the vertical bus into which pin 1 has been inserted, and the other end in to a hole in the horizontal ground bus—you can use any holes in

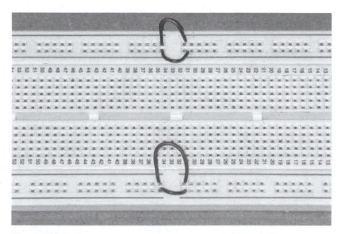

Figure 18.4 Using jumpers to join split power buses.

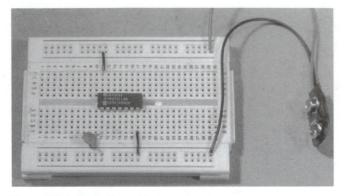

Figure 18.5 Capacitor added.

these buses, but with components with closely-spaced leads (such as capacitors) it's easier to use holes that are close together (see figure 18.5).

Connect a resistor of about 100kOhm between pin 1 and pin 2—you can bend it like a croquet wicket (see figure 18.6).

Connect the tip/hot of a jack or plug to the pin 2 bus, and the sleeve of the jack to any point along the ground bus. You can solder some light-gauge solid insulated wire to the jack, and strip and insert the ends into the busses, or you can connect clip leads from the plug's terminals to short pieces of bare wire inserted in the appropriate buses (see figure 18.7).

Snap the battery into its hookup clip. Connect the jack/plug to your amplifier, turn it on and listen (watch the volume—this circuit is *loud*!) You should hear a strident, steady pitch—a square wave. If not, check your connections: it's very easy to be off by one hole to the left or right when you insert component leads and jumper wires; if there are double power buses at the top and bottom of the board make sure you've connected the chip and other components to the buses you are using (and bridge the gap if the buses are split, as shown in figure 18.4). If the chip is HOT disconnect the battery immediately and start checking your connections.

If the circuit still doesn't seem to make any sound, make sure the component values are correct—too small a capacitor or resistor will cause the circuit to oscillate at a frequency too high for you to hear (you might notice the dog complaining, though); very large values

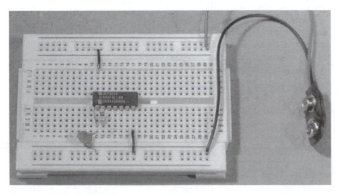

Figure 18.6 Resistor added.

Figure 18.7 Jack added.

produce sub-audio frequencies, the slow tick-tock of a metronome. Check that none of the chip's pins have been folded, yogi-like, *under* the chip instead of into a hole. Make sure you didn't put the chip in the board backwards, or didn't invert the battery leads. If the circuit oscillates, but erratically, and is sensitive to placing fingers on chip pins and component leads, then you may have forgotten to connect the + and – power to the chip, or connected them to the wrong pins, or left one leg of the capacitor or resistor uncon-nected (this chip will sometimes work even without power hooked up). When in doubt, triple-check all connections.

Your First Schematic

This is as good a time as any to start getting familiar with *schematic* representation, which conveys a circuit design independently of the physical arrangement of its components on a breadboard (see figure 18.8).

The big triangle represents one Inverter—any of the six in the 74C14 package; the flat left side is the input, which could be pin 1, 3, 5, etc., while the pointed right side is the output (2, 4, 6, etc.) The zigzag line is the resistor, between input and output. The two vaguely parallel lines (one straight, one curved) symbolize the capacitor, connected between the Inverter's input and the ground bus. Ground is represented by the weird runic arrangement of three lines. The signal output appears as a single line with an arrow head at the end. This is the signal that would go to the tip of a plug; the ground half of the connection is implied, rather than drawn in (see Rule 10). Likewise the power connections to the chip (+ 9 volts to pin 14, ground/– 9 volts to pin 7) are implicit.

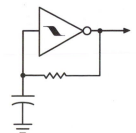

Figure 18.8 Schematic representation of our oscillator.

Figure 18.9 Potentiometer-controlled oscillator: schematic and photo.

The translation from this symbolic schematic to the mess of wires and components on the board may not seem obvious at first, but once you get more familiar with the language of electronics you'll see that the schematic is a useful way to represent the way a circuit *functions*, rather than just the way it goes together.

Variations

You are justified in taking great satisfaction in producing your first electronic tone, but after a while you may wish for a change of pitch. Try substituting different resistors and capacitors and listen to the effect. Take a pot or photoresistor and use it instead of a fixed value resistor—the wiggly resistor symbol in the schematic above can be taken to mean any form of resistor, including variable ones such as pots or photoresistors. We can specify that the resistor is a potentiometer if we use the symbol shown in figure 18.9—"A" and "C" are the ears of the pot, while "B" is the nose (as shown in figure 13.6 in chapter 13.) A photoresistor is shown in figure 18.10. A photoresistor turns this simple oscillator circuit into a wonderful, Theremin-style instrument controlled by light and shadow (see figure 18.11 and track 12 on the CD).

The capacitor determines the *range* through which the variable resistor will sweep the pitch. Too small a capacitor (less that 0.001uf) and the circuit will make sounds that only dogs and bats can hear. Larger values (greater than 5.0uf) lower the pitch range to that of rhythm—you'll hear the oscillation as a tick-tock instead of a buzz. Capacitors 1uf or larger are often *electrolytic*, and take the form of a little plastic cylinder. Electrolytic capacitors have polarity, like a battery: one leg will be labeled "+" or "–" When using electrolytic capacitors, be sure to observe the correct polarity and hook the "–" side to the ground bus

Figure 18.10 Photoresistor-controlled oscillator: schematic and photo.

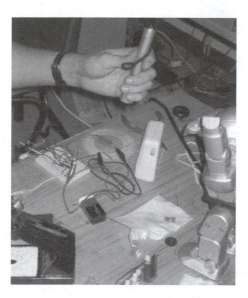

Figure 18.11 Playing a photoresistor-controlled oscillator with a flashlight.

(in a schematic the "–" side of the capacitor is indicated by the curved line). The circuit will work if the capacitor is connected backwards, but it may not be as stable. Electrolytic capacitors usually have their value printed quite clearly. The smaller, flat capacitors often employ an arcane code of "most significant digit + multiplying factor" (like resistor color code)—the easiest way to familiarize yourself with this argot is to buy a few capacitors of known value and look for correspondences between the numbers printed on the capacitor and its actual value. Or you can download a capacitor identification table from the Web.

When you use a pot you will notice that at one extreme of the rotation the pitch will go too high to be heard. It will drain much more current at this ultrasonic pitch, and shorten battery life. Therefore, you may want to put a modest resistor (try around 10kOhm) in series with one leg of the pot (see figure 18.12) to set a maximum pitch that is within the range of hearing (as we demonstrated in chapter 14 to limit the upper frequency of a toy clock.).

Similarly, if you wire a pot in series with a photoresistor, you can use the pot to set the upper pitch limit of a light-control instrument, combining the accuracy of the pot and expressiveness of the photoresistor (as we did with the toy clock in chapter 15). You can also use bare wires (with or without coins soldered to the ends) to make a "laying of hands" oscillator, as with our radio and toy experiments, or the STEIM "Cracklebox." Substitute

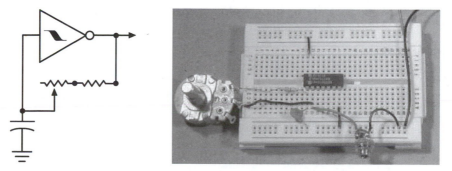

Figure 18.12 Potentiometer with resistor for fixed upper frequency limit.

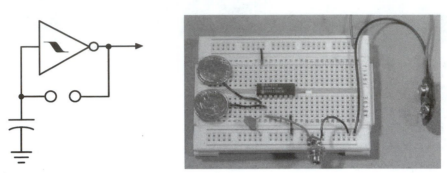

Figure 18.13 An electrode-controlled oscillator.

the electrodes for the resistor or pot by connecting one to the inverter's input and one to its output (see figure 18.13); if you connect the electrodes in parallel to a pot (as shown in figure 15.7 in chapter 15) you can use both elements to control the pitch. Experiment with the various types of variable resistors discussed in chapter 15, including the pressure sensor, rusty plate, and graphite tricks. Many of these alternate resistors (especially the pencil lead and drawing-on-paper) are often more effective or obvious with oscillators than with toy clocks.

Why? (If You Care)

This circuit oscillates because of the principle of argumentation. Each Inverter stage, represented by the small triangle in the schematic, puts out the opposite of whatever signal appears at the input: if a binary "1," represented by 9 volts, is applied to the input, then a "0" (0 volts) is sent to the output. That 0 flows through the resistor back to the input. When the 0 appears at the input the output goes to 1, which flows back to the input and the whole process begins again, causing the circuit to flip back and forth between two states, generating a square wave. The speed of the flip-flopping (the pitch we hear) depends on the values of the resistor and capacitor—just like in our earlier clock experiments, the smaller the values the higher the pitch. It's like the Monty Python argument sketch, or a dispute in a bar: I disagree with everything you say, so our output keeps flipping between yes and no according to how fast each of us can reply. The resistor and capacitor act like booze—the more you add the slower the argument goes, ergo the lower the pitch.

Having brushed you off earlier, I will now confide that the Schmitt Trigger part of the Inverter prevents indecisiveness in the argument: the inverter snaps completely from one state to the other, from 0 to 1 and back, and never vacillates in between.

Polyphony

As you might be able to intuit from the schematic or any dormant knowledge of Greek, the *Hex* Inverter has six identical sections. You can make an additional oscillator with any of these sections, just duplicate the connections we made for our first oscillator with another set of components, attached to another set of pins: capacitor between any input and ground; resistor, pot, or photoresistor between that input and its appropriate output; connect the output via a jack to the amplifier.

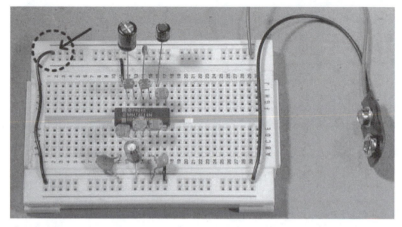

Figure 18.14 Parallel ground and + voltage buses.

Remember when working on the "top" side of the chip (pins 8–14) that the capacitor must go between the chip and *ground*, not to the + supply that mirrors the ground bus on the upper side of the board. If there are two parallel horizontal buses at the top and bottom of the board, you can connect a wire jumper between the lower ground bus and the upper bus that is not +9 volts; the second upper bus is now an additional ground bus, to which you can connect the capacitor on the upper half of the chip (see figure 18.14). Be careful to connect to the new ground bus, not the 9-volt bus, and don't accidentally link the ground and power buses together with a wire, or you will have a flat, hot battery on your hands. Alternatively, you can push the grounded legs of the capacitors into a vertical bus to either side of the chip, and jumper that vertical bus to the lower ground bus, creating a secondary, ground "mini-bus" (see figure 18.15).

Also remember that every oscillator output signal needs a ground connection to its output jack, as well as a signal from the output pin.

You can use different size capacitors for each oscillator, so each of the six covers a different range, from low BPM to ultrasonic pitches, or you can add a switch to select different

Figure 18.15 Satellite mini ground bus.

Figure 18.16 Joysticks.

capacitors for each oscillator. A joystick is an expressive device for controlling pairs of oscillators (see figure 18.16). You can salvage one from an unneeded game controller (perhaps the one you will eviscerate in chapter 29). A proper analog joystick consists of two potentiometers controlled by the *X–Y* movement of a shaft. If you de-solder the joystick from its original circuit you will notice the familiar three terminals on each of the small pots; connect two terminals of each pot to one oscillator. You may need to try various connections before you arrive at the most satisfying interaction between the two oscillators, but when you get there you'll be rewarded by square waves careening off each other like radio-controlled mosquitoes.

To mix more than one oscillator to a single jack, connect each output to the jack through a resistor of about 10kOhm (see figure 18.17)—anything from 3kOhm to 1mOhm will work, but use the same value for every oscillator if you want then all the same loudness (otherwise those that pass thru the smaller resistors will be louder than those mixing though the larger ones (see chapter 27 for more information about "proper" mixing). Don't jumper the oscillator outputs together with plain hookup wire, which will probably cause them to stop running.

You can add a tilt switch (see chapter 16) to select different oscillator outputs as you tip and wobble the circuit, instead of mixing them all together all the time.

The resistors form a simple linear mixer, through which one can hear each oscillator distinctly. If you mix the outputs together using a component called a "diode" instead, you'll

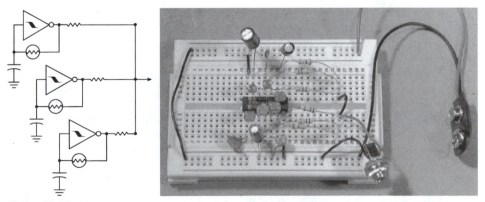

Figure 18.17 Six oscillators mixed through resistors (only three shown on schematic).

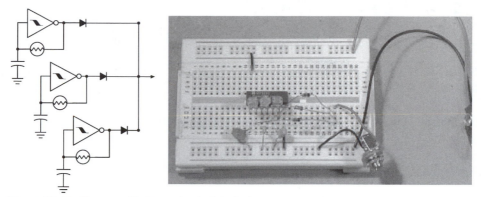

Figure 18.18 Three oscillators mixed with diodes.

Figure 18.19 Diode orientation.

notice that the individual oscillators interact and distort in an archetypically "electronic music" way—they produce a "ring modulation"-type sound, in which sum and difference frequencies are exaggerated and the individual source pitches obscured (see figures 18.18 and 18.19). If some of the oscillators are running at low frequencies (in the metronome range) while others are in the audio range, the low ones may appear to gate the high ones on and off (see chapter 20 for more advice on cross-modulating oscillators).

If you sum more than three oscillators together with diodes you might notice that the signal gets oddly noisy; if you don't like this artifact you might mix three to one jack and three to another for a nice stereo sound field, or mix up the orientation of the diodes. Sometimes this diode-mixing works connected to some kinds of amps and mixer and not to others. If a multi-diode mixer does not work with your amplifier, try connecting an additional 10kOhm resistor between the output point (where all the diodes tie together) and ground.

Diodes are odd little devices that only allow signals to pass in one direction. Current flows toward the end indicated by the single stripe that appears at one end of the component. The orientation of the diode doesn't really affect the sound as long as *all* of them face the same direction—all the stripes at the chip side or all at the jack side; you can mix up the orientations, but the sound will change. Why they make such a cool sounding mixer for oscillators is a somewhat complicated story, and pretty irrelevant to appreciating their sonic contribution, so I won't try to explain it. This brings us neatly to Rule #17:

Rule #17: If it sounds good and doesn't smoke, don't worry if you don't understand it.

Six square-wave oscillators make a wonderful din. With six photoresistors or electrode pairs, control is somewhat unpredictable but nonetheless intuitive and playable. There's a glorious tradition of music made with masses of homemade oscillators, from David Behrman (see track 11 on the CD) through Voice Crack and beyond. Try it.

Caveat

There is a corollary of sorts to Rule #17 that is worth bearing in mind:

Rule #18: Start simple and confirm that the circuit still works after every addition you make.

Don't assume after you get one oscillator buzzing that you can smote the remaining five in one blow. When you find yourself gazing down at a rat's nest of wires that makes neither sound nor sense, strip your board back to one oscillator and start over, one voice at a time, listening as you go.

Chapter 19

FROM BREADBOARD TO CIRCUIT BOARD:
HOW TO SOLDER UP YOUR FIRST HOMEMADE CIRCUIT

You will need:

- Your bread-boarded circuit from the previous chapter.
- A full duplicate set of parts used in the circuit.
- A prototyping circuit board.
- 14-pin IC socket.
- Solid and stranded hookup wire.
- Hand tools and soldering iron.

The breadboard is great for trying out circuit designs—mistakes are easily undone—but not very stable if you want to take your music on the road. At some point you may wish to solidify the circuit. This means soldering the components down onto a generic "Printed Circuit Board" intended for prototyping and developing new designs (as opposed to the board inside a toy, radio, or mixer, configured for one particular circuit). These boards come in various styles, with patterns of individual copper pads that can be linked together with components and bits of wire any way you wish (see figure 19.1). Some designs, such as Radio Shack part #276-170, mimic a typical breadboard almost exactly, and make it much easier to transfer your circuit from breadboard to soldered board (see figure 19.2).

If the board you've chosen is larger than needed for your one-chip circuit, you may want to cut it down before you start soldering on parts—scribe along the dotted line with a sharp knife, then snap the board over the edge of a table. Alternatively, you can build your first circuit at one end, and add designs as you develop them. Once you've got your circuit board ready, start by placing a 14-pin IC socket on the side of the board that does not have the copper paths and pads (this is the component side—the other side is the solder side). Push the pins gently through the holes, insuring that, if there is a matrix of rows and columns like on the breadboard, the socket is similarly positioned, with a rows fanning out from each pin, not shorting them all together. Make sure all the pins go though fully, and none are bent over on top of the board. Solder the socket pins carefully: avoid letting blobs of solder short together adjacent pins or copper traces (see figure 19.3). The IC is inserted into this socket after you have finished all your soldering.

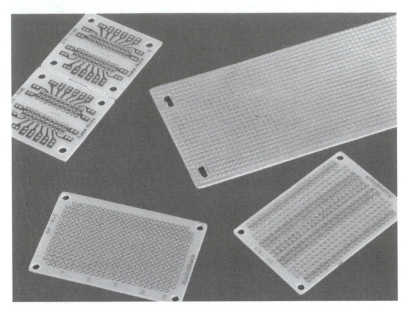

Figure 19.1 Assorted printed circuit boards, showing solder side.

This protects the chip from damage by the heat of the iron and makes it easier to replace the chip if it blows out.

Now solder an identical set of resistors, capacitors, and other components onto the board, following their placement on your breadboard. Use thin, insulated solid wire to make interconnections on the board—strip insulation off the ends, as you did to make the jumpers for the breadboard; link points by running the wire along the component side of the board, passing it through holes where appropriate, and solder to the pads (see figure 19.4). Make sure the uninsulated ends of wire do not short against each other or adjacent

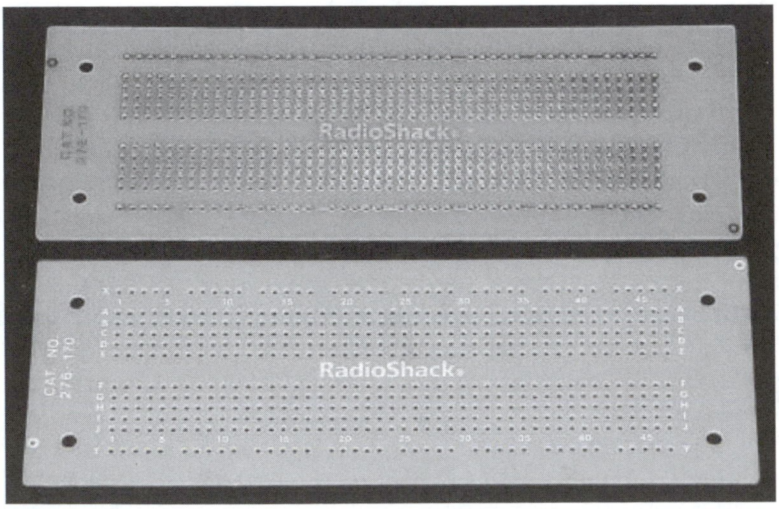

Figure 19.2 Printed circuit board mimicking breadboard, showing solder-side (top) and component-side (bottom).

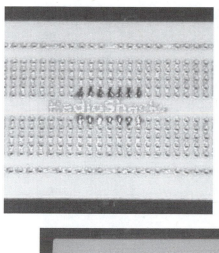

Figure 19.3 Socket soldered to PC board, solder-side view.

Figure 19.4 Completed circuit.

solder pads. Use stranded, rather than solid, wire for the pots, jacks and photocells, so the wire can flex easily without breaking when you mount the circuit in a case. Don't forget that every jack needs signal connection and a ground wire (Rule #10).

If you use an exact clone of a breadboard (such as the Radio Shack board), it will have ground and +9-volt buses you can wire to just like on the breadboard. If you are working with another design, you may have to create your own satellite mini-buses (as we did on the breadboard in the previous chapter) or another kind of "virtual bus" by linking the ground ends of all the capacitors and the chip ground together with wire.

If you want to add an on/off switch, solder the black wire of a 9-volt battery clip directly to the ground bus on the circuit board. Solder the "NO" terminal of a toggle switch to the +9-volt line (red wire) so you can turn the circuit on and off without having to remove the battery, then solder a wire from the "C" terminal of the switch to the board.

Rule # 19: Always leave your original breadboard design intact and functional until you can prove that the soldered-up version works.

This makes it much easier to debug any mistakes, by comparing the working version on the breadboard with the miscreant on the circuit board (see figure 19.5).

Put the chip in the socket after all soldering is finished, and check to make sure its orientation is correct (i.e., pin 14 goes to +9 volts, pin 7 to ground, not vice versa). Check that you did not make unintentional "solder bridges" between traces when soldering. (After transferring your first design to a circuit board you will see how important it is to have a good soldering iron with a very fine tip). Compare your connections against the

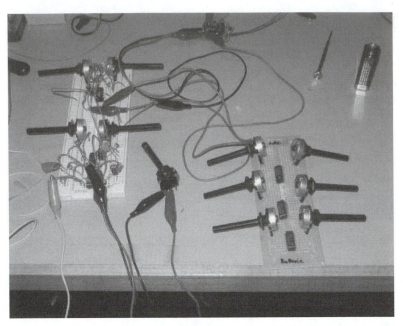

Figure 19.5 Breadboarded and soldered circuits, side by side.

breadboard one more time before connecting the battery and turning on the circuit. If the battery or chip gets hot when the circuit is on, shut it off immediately and check again for mistakes.

If your soldered circuit doesn't seem to work, compare the placement of every part and wire between the breadboarded version and the soldered one—look sharp, since it's easy to miss a connection by one hole. Check for wires you pressed though the board but somehow forgot to solder, as well as blobby grey cold solder joints. Make sure there are signal and ground connections for the audio output, and that both battery leads go to the right places.

If the circuit makes sound, but is much quieter than the breadboarded version, or just acts weirder than it should, check to make sure you remembered to hook up the battery's "+" and "−" connections to pins 14 and 7 of the chip—sometimes the circuit *almost* works without a direct power hookup, by sucking voltage through other connections you have made (spooky!). Another tip for keeping this (and any other) circuit running cleanly is to solder a 0.1uf capacitor between the "+" pin (14) and the "−" pin (7), keeping it as close to the pins as possible (not at the other end of the board and linked by wires). This "decoupling" capacitor helps filter noise that can spread through power supply connections.

A circuit board that mirrors your breadboard exactly makes the transfer process much easier. If you can't obtain such a board you must make adaptations carefully, checking your connections as you go. Once you have transferred a few designs, and get comfortable with the "topology of circuitry," you can choose various sizes and patterns of circuit board that give you the freedom to rearrange your designs between prototype and final version, or shrink them down to fit in tiny boxes. Larger boards can always be cut into smaller sections for simple one-chip circuits, such as our first oscillator.

Figure 19.6 A boxed photoresistor-controlled Hex Oscillator.

When your circuits start to get complicated you may find that regular hookup wire is too thick and messy on the board. To lighten up, and move from spaghetti to capellini, buy yourself a roll of what is called "wire wrapping wire." At 30 gauge, it's real thin, stays in place when snaked around the board, and comes in nice, bright, child-friendly colors.

Once you've confirmed that everything works you can move on to finding a box and drilling a mess of holes (see chapter 17 and figure 19.6). That's the fun part.

Chapter 20

MORE OSCILLATORS: OSCILLATORS THAT MODULATE EACH OTHER

You will need:

- A breadboard.
- One CMOS Quad NAND Gate Schmitt Trigger Integrated Circuit (CD4093).
- Assorted resistors, capacitors, pots, and photoresistors.
- Some solid hookup wire.
- A jack to match your amp.
- A 9-volt battery and connector.
- An amplifier.
- Hand tools.

The 74C14 offers you a fast, cheap, easy route to oscillators whose pitch can be easily swept over a wide range. With another chip from the same CMOS family we can implement some more advanced control functions commonly associated with classic analog synthesis.

Gated Oscillator

The Schmitt Trigger circuit element that turns each Inverter in the 74C14 into a potential oscillator is also found in other CMOS digital circuits. Most useful is the CD4093 Quad NAND Gate (see figure 20.1)

This chip contains four identical NAND gates. There are two gates on each side of the chip, but unlike the spawning salmon of the 74C14, they are arranged in mirror symmetry, like rutting elks: the outputs of each gate face each other, rather than the same direction. Note that this chip has the same power connections as the 74C14 Hex Inverter chip we used in the previous two chapters: + voltage to pin 14, ground to pin 7. All of which brings us to an important new Rule:

Rule #20: All chips may look alike on the outside without being the same on the inside—read the fine print!

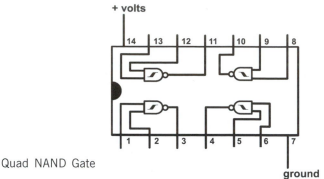

Figure 20.1 CD4093 Quad NAND Gate pinout.

A NAND gate is a variant of the basic binary function of an AND gate, which for two inputs generates the following outputs:

Input A	Input B	Output
0	0	0
1	0	0
0	1	0
1	1	1

You see that the output only goes "true"/1 when both inputs are true/1—democracy in action: we go to the zoo because it's the place both kids agree would be fun.

A NAND (NOT+AND) gate adds an inverter stage after the AND logic to flip the output like this:

Input A	Input B	Output
0	0	1
1	0	1
0	1	1
1	1	0

Democracy is replaced by contrarian despotism: dad avoids turning off the highway to visit Mammoth Caves specifically because both kids have been whining to see it for one hundred miles.

The added inverter stage introduces the principle of knee-jerk denial (discussed in chapter 18) that transforms this logic circuit into a "gateable oscillator."

Hook up the circuit shown in figure 20.2. Note that the basic design is similar to our earlier oscillator: a capacitor between an input and ground; a feedback resistor from the output back to the input. But where each stage in the Hex Inverter package had just one input, each NAND gate has *two* inputs. Because of the combinatorial logic of the NAND gate, the second input of the gate can be used as a control input to turn the oscillator on and off: the output of the circuit will only change state (i.e., oscillate) when the control input is held "high" (+9 volts). If you connect the second input of the gate to ground (0) the circuit stops oscillating and the output remains in a "1" state (see figure 20.3).

Try both configurations. Remember to hook up power to the chip as you did with the 74C14 (+9 volts to pin 14, ground/– to pin 7). Plug a bit of wire into the breadboard near

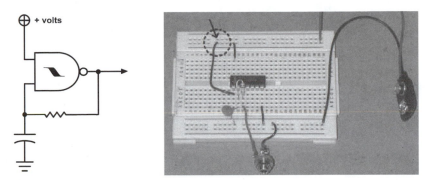

Figure 20.2 Basic NAND Gate oscillator, enabled.

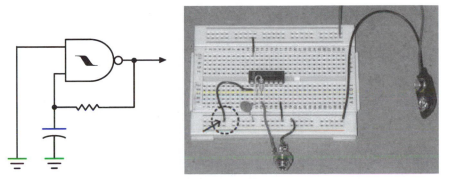

Figure 20.3 Basic NAND Gate oscillator, disabled.

the gate input (pin 1 in figure 20.2 and figure 20.3) and alternate connecting the other end to the + and ground buses. The two inputs to each gate are identical—it doesn't matter which you use for the "control input" (the one with the wire moved between + and ground) and which for the "feedback input" (the one with the capacitor and feedback resistor), as long as you don't mix up the two and connect the capacitor and to one and the feedback resistor to the other, for example. And you can use any of the four NAND gates on the chip—they function identically—the photos show just one of four possible hookups.

Total Control

The oscillator oscillates when the control input is connected to +9 volt; it turns off when the control input is connected to ground. Big deal, you say, we can do this by simply connecting and disconnecting the battery. But, because the oscillator's output consists of a square wave swinging between "true"/+9v and "false"/ground, we can also use the output of one oscillator to switch another oscillator on and off. Breadboard the circuit shown in figure 20.4. Use a large capacitor (4–10uf) and 1 megOhm pot for Oscillator 1 (shown here using pins 1, 2, and 3), and a 0.1uf capacitor and pot or photoresistor (as here) for Oscillator 2 (using pins 4, 5, and 6).

The control input on Oscillator 1 is tied directly to +9 volts, so it runs all the time, as we demonstrated earlier in figure 20.2). But the control input of Oscillator 2 is connected to the *output* of Oscillator 1, which gates Oscillator 2 on and off as it swings between ground and 9 volts. If the Oscillator 1 (the control oscillator) has a large capacitor and runs

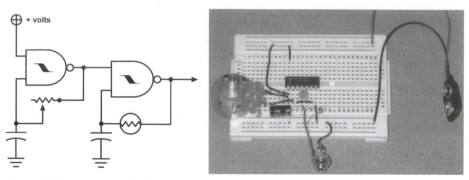

Figure 20.4 A gated oscillator.

slowly (like a metronome), you can hear Oscillator 2 (the modulated oscillator) switch on and off at a regular tempo. As we tune Oscillator 1 higher and higher, the obvious on/off function transforms into a kind of frequency modulation that is heard as a change in the tone color rather than tempo.

Very cool flangey noises occur when the control oscillator and the modulated oscillator are both in the audio range and are very close in frequency—try using .1uf capacitors and identical photoresistors for both stages. Now substitute 10uf capacitors and 1 megOhm pots for both stages: careful tuning of the pots results in interesting polyrhythms.

You can cascade three or four oscillators (see figure 20.5) to create tone clusters or rhythmic patterns, depending on capacitor sizes. As you can see, you'll have to configure parallel or satellite ground buses for the top-side gates as we did for the multi-voice oscillators in chapter 18 (see figure 18.14 and 18.15).

Experiment with different value capacitors and pots for the different stages. You can use photoresistors, electrodes, or any of the other alternative resistors discussed in chapter 15, for the resistors/pots in these circuits.

Note that even though a control input might be connected to +9 volts we still need to connect +9 volts to pin 14 and ground (– voltage) to pin 7. The connections to the supply voltages have two distinct functions in our circuit: through pins 14 and 7 they provide *power* to the chip, needed to run its internal operations—this is the "gas." But + and – voltage also have *logical* value, and are evaluated as part of the (admittedly simple) mathematical calculations that the circuit performs in order to oscillate. As with our previous circuit with the 74C14, sometimes this chip will make sound *without* proper power connections, but it will be "coasting," and probably will not perform reliably (or go up hills)—which brings us to Rule #21:

Rule #21: All chips expect "+" and "–" power connections to their designated power supply pins, even if these voltages are *also* connected to other pins for other reasons, withhold them at your own risk (or entertainment).

By the way, I've chosen the CMOS family of integrated circuits (of which the 74C14 and the CD4093 are members) for our experiments because they consume very little current and can run on a wide range of voltages, which makes them ideal for battery operation. They are also rather difficult to blow up.

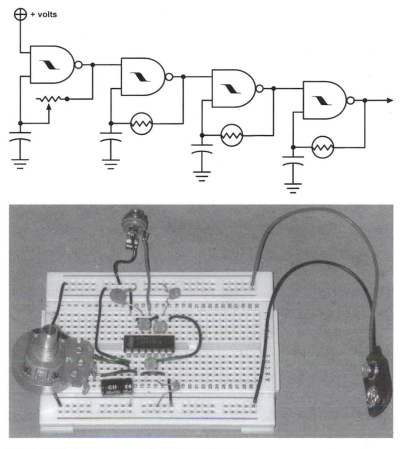

Figure 20.5 Four cascaded gated oscillators.

Chapter 21

EVEN MORE OSCILLATORS:
DIVIDERS, FEEDBACK LOOPS, AND INSTABILITY;
USING OSCILLATORS AS CLOCKS FOR TOYS

You will need:

- A breadboard.
- One CMOS Hex Schmitt Trigger Integrated Circuit (74C14) or CMOS Quad NAND Gate Schmitt Trigger Integrated Circuit (CD4093).
- One CMOS Binary Counter/Divider (CD4040).
- Assorted resistors, capacitors, pots, and photoresistors.
- Some solid hookup wire.
- A jack to match your amp.
- A 9-volt battery and connector.
- A piezo disk.
- An amplifier.
- A hacked toy.
- Hand tools.

Dividers

The musical applications of digital logic circuits go well beyond simple oscillators. Once you accept that an audio square wave can be regarded as a simple alternation between two binary numbers (0 and 1), the logical and arithmetic functions on which all digital calculations are based can be seen as potential sound transformations. For example, a chip that performs division, such as the CD4040 12-Stage Binary Divider, can be used to generate several harmonically related pitches from a single master oscillator (see figure 21.1).

Breadboard the circuit shown in figure 21.2. Note that the 4040 has 16 pins, but the power connections have a similar diagonal arrangement to the 14-pin chips we've used so far: ground connects to pin 8, +9 volts to pin 16. You also need to connect ground to pin 11, designated "rst" (for reset), or the chip will not run. A master oscillator, built from one section of a 74C14 or 4093, is connected to pin 10, the clock input of the divider chip

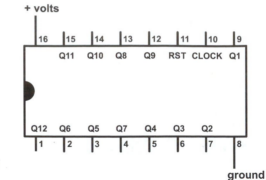

Figure 21.1 CD4040 12-Stage Binary Divider pinout.

(4040). Don't forget to hook up +9 volts and ground to the 74C14/4093 as well. The 4040 has 12 cascaded stages, each of which divides the frequency by 2; outputs are provided for the clock signal divided by 2, 4, 8, 16, etc, all the way to 4096.

Connect the shield of your audio jack to the ground bus, and attach a 4 inch piece of solid hookup wire to the hot connection. Connect this hot lead first to the output of the clock oscillator (master output) by inserting it into the vertical bus at pin 10 on the 4040, and tune the clock to a high frequency audio pitch. Now listen to Output Q1 (clock frequency/2) by pressing a wire into the bus at pin 9, and note that it sounds an octave lower. Output Q2 sounds an octave below that (clock/4), Output Q3 an octave below that (clock/8), etc.

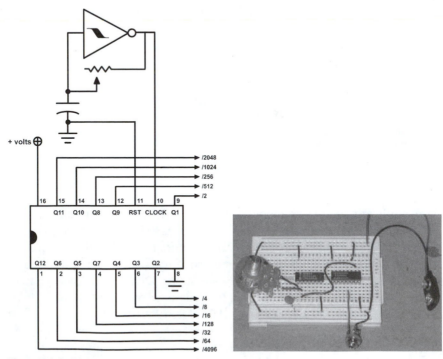

Figure 21.2 Divided oscillator.

You can use switches to select amongst these different subharmonics. The switches can be anything: momentary pushbuttons, toggle switches, our homemade tilt switch from chapter 16, or just some wire jumpers on the breadboard. Because of the thick texture and low frequencies of this circuit, you may want to listen to it over a larger loudspeaker than that of the tiny test-amplifier. If you want to *mix* multiple outputs to build up a rich wave-form, make sure you send each output through a resistor before tying together (as we did with the multiple oscillators in chapter 18, figure 18.17). Because of the simple harmonic relationship of the octaves you will note that the differences in mixes are subtle: a slight shift in overtone balance, rather than an impression of distinct voices being added.

If you slow the master oscillator down to the rate of a tempo, rather than a pitch, the various outputs become subdivisions of the beat—good for setting up nested rhythmic patterns.

Random Acts of Kindness

Disconnect the oscillator circuit from the clock input (pin 10) and connect a short piece of solid wire sticking up into the air from the breadboard. Sometimes your body carries enough of an electrical charge that if you touch the end of the wire the noise of your flesh will often trigger the divider—listen to the different divisor outputs as you experiment with brushing and squeezing the wire. Sometimes it helps to connect a large resistor (100kOhm–1mOhm) between the clock input pin (pin 10) and either ground or +9 volts to stabilize the circuit when you are not touching it. An excellent ghost detector, by the way.

Some Applications for Oscillators

The oscillator circuits we've made have a number of applications beyond just plugging into an amplifier and droning away.

Clocks for Toys

Sometimes you can use the output of a high frequency oscillator as a substitute for the clock circuit in a toy. Breadboard an oscillator (using the 74C14 or 4093 design) that runs too high to hear—use a capacitor between 100 pf and .01 uf and a pot to adjust the speed. Connect the ground of the toy (– battery point) to the ground on your oscillator (– battery bus). Disconnect the timing resistor of the toy (as we did in chapter 13) and solder a jumper to each of the pads at either end of the resistor. Plug the free end of one of the wires into the output point of the oscillator. Does the toy run? You may need to disconnect and reconnect the batteries, and adjust the oscillator speed with the pot. If it doesn't work, try the lead from the *other* resistor pad; you might have to connect the unused resistor pad to ground. If neither configuration works try another toy or give up. But if it does work you can proceed with applying all of our oscillator variations (gated, divided, etc.) to modifying the toy's performance.

Power Struggles with Crickets

As I alluded earlier, this family of Integrated Circuits consumes only tiny amounts of power, which makes them well suited to battery power. Power consumption is directly proportional to the frequency of the oscillator. To wax technical for a moment, the chip only uses power when it changes state from low to high or back again; the lower the frequency, the less power consumed in a given period of time—a metronome built with this chip can run for a year or more on one battery. A high-pitch audio squealer will go through batteries faster—disconnecting the battery when you leave the breadboard for the day is a good idea in any case.

Although the output signal is very hot (swinging 9 volts peak-to-peak, compared to .7 volts of a typical CD player output), it carries very little current. This means you have to plug the circuit into a power amplifier in order to drive a speaker—if you wire the oscillator output directly to an ordinary speaker you will probably hear nothing. But these CMOS chips can drive a piezo disk directly: connect the oscillator's output to the hot wire of a disk (center) and connect the circuit's ground bus to the metal of disk's ground (don't use the chapter 8 transformer in this configuration). Low frequency pulses yield a pleasing clicking sound, while audio pitches buzz like insects and frogs on a sultry summer evening. If it's too quiet for your taste, clamp the piezo disk to a cookie sheet, or place it on a wooden matchbox with a stone on top, or glue it to the wing of a balsa glider. Dutch sound artist Felix Hess has made beautiful large-scale installations with multiple small circuits pinging piezo disks (see "Drivers," chapter 8). If you leave the piezo disk inside the plastic lollipop packaging this resonator will also increase the loudness of the chirping.

Volume Control

Because these oscillator circuits put out such a hot signal, they may overload the input to your amplifier or mixer, causing distortion (not always a bad thing—see chapter 23) or limiting the useful range of your faders. If you want to drop the level down to a volume that matches your other line-level equipment (like a CD player), try adding the circuit shown in figure 21.3 to the output of each oscillator, or, if you are mixing multiple signals, after the summing resistors.

Alternatively, if you want fade the volume up and down, rather than just drop it down to normal line level, you can add a volume control pot at the output of the oscillator, as

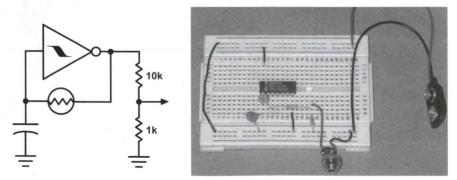

Figure 21.3 A volume dropping circuit.

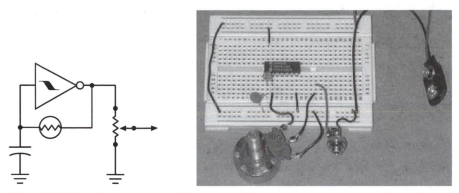

Figure 21.4 Continuous output volume control.

shown in figure 21.4. Any pot whose value is 10kOhm or greater will do. If you can find a pot designated as having an "audio taper" it will make the fade sound smoother (see chapter 27 for a discussion of pot characteristics, and information on making simple mixers).

More Randomness

Once you get the hang of these basic oscillator circuits and the way they are *supposed* to work, don't be afraid to experiment with alternate configurations, even if you have no idea what you're doing (see Rule 16). It is almost impossible to destroy the chip by making "wrong" connections between its various pins; at worst, certain configurations will be mute. Try random connections and component substitutions. Create multiple feedback paths by linking the outputs of some oscillators to the inputs of others—you can do this with plain wire, resistors, capacitors, pots, photoresistors, etc. Add multiple electrode touch contacts to set up feedback paths through your skin. You may need to add pull-up resistors to the inputs of the circuits to start them oscillating: connect a resistor in the 100kOhm–1mOhm range between the input pin and +9 volts of the various stages of your circuit. Arranged in matrices, sometimes the oscillators produce unstable, complicated patterns of pitch and rhythm not displeasing to the ear (or brain). When you hear something good, stop and make very careful notes of what is wired to what, because you may never find it again. And no one will ever be able to explain why it sounds the way it does.

Chapter 22

ON/OFF (MORE FUN WITH PHOTORESISTORS): GATING, DUCKING, TREMOLO, AND PANNING

You will need:

- Two sound sources to turn on and off, such as radios, cassette players, or CD players with output jacks.
- Some photoresistors.
- A flashlight.
- A basic oscillator circuit on a breadboard from one of the previous chapters.
- Some LEDs (Light Emitting Diodes).
- Some heat shrink tubing (optional).
- Assorted resistors, capacitors.
- Some solid hookup wire.
- Some plugs and jacks.
- Clip leads and Y-cords.
- A 9-volt battery and connector.
- Two amplifiers.
- Hand tools.
- Plastic electrical tape.

As we have seen in our earlier experiments with toy clocks and simple oscillators, the photoresistor changes resistance in response to changes in light level. This change is resistance in turn affects the speed of a clock or pitch of an oscillator. A photoresistor can also be used as a kind of gate or volume control to pass, block, or fade any audio source (such as the output of a CD player, a hacked toy, or a microphone).

Flashlights

In a clean, well-lighted place, clip together the simple circuit shown in figure 22.1.

Connect the "hot" or tip of any audio signal (such as the output of a portable cassette or CD player) to one lead of the photoresistor and connect the other lead of the photoresistor to the "hot" of your amplifier input. Connect the shield/ground of the audio source

Figure 22.1 A basic photoresistor gate circuit.

to the shield/ground of the amplifier input—remember Rule 10 (every audio connection needs signal and ground) but note that, for the sake of clarity, the ground lines between connectors have been omitted in the schematics. Turn on the amp, play the cassette/CD, and confirm that audio passes through.

Now take the whole rat's nest into a dark place, like a closet, or turn off your lights and draw the blinds. The sound should get quieter. Turn on the flashlight and pass the beam across the photoresistor—the sound should get louder when the cell is lit, quieter when the cell is dark. This super simple circuit won't shut off the sound completely, but you should hear a significant volume difference between light and dark. The back-side of a photoresistor is usually translucent, so total darkness and quieter level can only be achieved if you fully enclose the cell—in your hand for example, or you can cover the back with black electrical tape. Make sure you don't let the leads short out or the signal will pass through unattenuated all the time (you should spread them apart before applying the tape).

You can increase the dynamic range of this circuit (the difference in loudness between "on" and "off") by adding a resistor of about 10kOhm between the *output* side of the photoresistor and ground, as shown in figure 22.2. Without getting into unnecessary technical detail, the resistor "clamps" the output to ground when the circuit is off, thereby minimizing bleed-through of the input signal, and increasing the depth of the muting when the circuit is "off".

This circuit is an absurdly simple but nonetheless very effective light-controlled audio gate. You can use it with any audio signal. It is a "passive" signal processor, which means that it needs no batteries (although the flashlight does). The only requirement is darkness, which makes it well-suited for stage use, camping trips, or persons with difficulty paying the electrical bill.

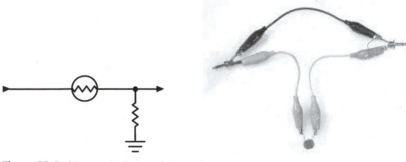

Figure 22.2 Clamped photoresistor gate.

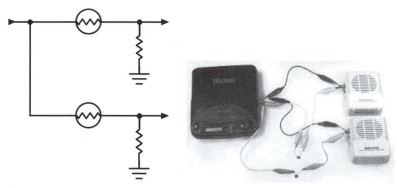

Figure 22.3 Light-controlled panner.

Ping Pong, Pong Ping

By adding a second photoresistor and some more connectors we can expand our gate into a light-controlled "panner" or "mixer." Hook up the configuration shown in figure 22.3.

Connect an audio signal (such as the output of a CD player) through two clip leads to two photoresistors. Clip the other leg of one photoresistor to the hot/tip of a plug connected to one amplifier, and connect the other leg of the second photoresistor to the hot/tip of a plug connected to a second amplifier. Link together the grounds on all three connectors with two more clip leads. Seek the cover of darkness, play your source material, turn on the amplifiers, and pass the flashlight beam back and forth across the two photoresistors: the sound should pan between the two speakers, following the movement of the light across the two cells.

Now rewire the circuit slightly, as shown in figure 22.4. This time connect one audio source (i.e., a CD) through a clip lead to one leg of a photoresistor. Connect a different source (i.e., a cassette player or second CD player) through a second clip lead to one leg of the second photoresistor. Connect the second legs of both photoresistors through clip leads to the input of one amplifier, and link all the grounds together as before. Carry the whole mess into darkness. Now when you pass a flashlight across the two photoresistors you should be able to cross-fade and mix between the two sources, like cutting between turntables.

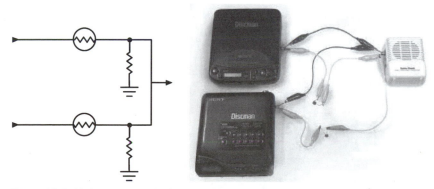

Figure 22.4 Light-controlled mixer.

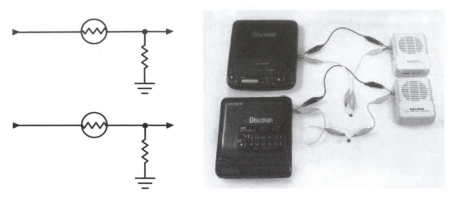

Figure 22.5 Patchable optical panner/mixer.

You can solder up this circuit with two input jacks and two output jacks as shown in figure 22.5, so it can be used as either a panner, a mixer or a two-channel gate. To make a panner, use a Y-cord to connect a single audio source to both input jacks, and patch the outputs to two amplifiers. For a mixer, connect a different source to each input, and use a Y-cord to mix the outputs of both photoresistors to a single amplifier input. For a two-channel gate hook two sources to two amplifiers with no interconnections, as shown in the photograph.

This basic panner/mixer circuit can be expanded with more photoresistors, inputs and/or outputs to make four-channel panners, multi-channel mixers, etc.

Flashlight controlled circuits like these gates, panners, and mixers (and our earlier photoresistor-controlled oscillators) occupy a distinguished place in the early history of live electronic music: similar circuits can be heard in the work of David Tudor, Lowell Cross and other early hacker-composers.

Blinkies

An LED is a small and cheap source of light that can be controlled electronically. The LED has one shorter leg, and if you look closely you will notice that one side of the lower rim of the LED is slightly flattened—the short leg and flat side indicate the "—" connection of the LED, the other leg is the "+" connection (see figure 22.6).

Breadboard the circuit shown in figure 22.7. It should light up. Swap the polarity of the LED and observe that it only lights in one orientation. Substitute different values for the resistor and note the change in brightness: the smaller the resistor, the brighter the light,

Figure 22.6 LED orientation.

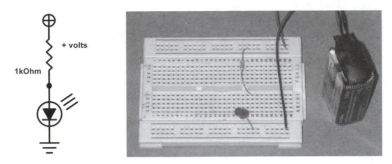

Figure 22.7 Lighting an LED.

but only to a point, after which the LED will burn out. Don't use a straight wire—1kOhm is a good value to start with if you are using a 9-volt battery.

Rule #22: Always use a resistor when powering an LED, otherwise the circuit and/or LED might blow out.

Breadboard the circuit shown in figure 22.8. This is the simple oscillator from chapter 18 (you could also use the 4093-based design in chapter 20, with the gating input pulled up to + 9 volts so it runs constantly), but now we are connecting the oscillator's output to an LED instead of to an amplifier. The circuit blinks the light instead of clicking the speaker. We want it to blink at an observable rate, so we use a reasonably large capacitor (4–10uf) and pot (1 megOhm) to keep the oscillator in the metronome range. If it doesn't blink you're probably using too small a resistor, or have omitted some connection. Vary the speed and watch the effect. Fun enough just to look at, but wait—it gets better!

Now take the LED and hold it against the photoresistor as shown in figure 22.9. Spread the leads of the photoresistor and LED apart so they do not touch each other, then wrap the photoresistor and LED in electrical tape so that they are sealed from outside light. Be very careful not to let any of the wires touch each other or the circuit will not work—you can wrap each of the four wires separately if this helps. Replace the LED in the figure 22.7 circuit with this bundle, add an input and output jack for the photoresistor as in figure 22.2, and it should look like figure 22.10.

Now run some audio through the photoresistor while you vary the speed of the oscillator (remember to link the audio input and output grounds with a clip lead, but you

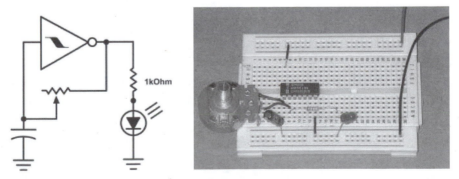

Figure 22.8 Blinking an LED with an oscillator.

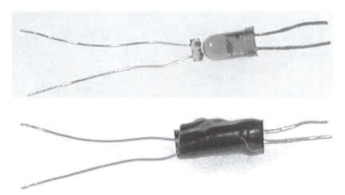

Figure 22.9 LED and photoresistor kissing (top) and bundled in electrical tape (bottom).

needn't clip this ground to the breadboard ground). You should hear the cassette/CD get chopped on and off as the LED blinks. You can add the 10K clamping resistor to increase the on/off isolation, as shown in the schematic in figure 22.10 (but omitted from the photo for clarity).

As you speed up the oscillator into the audio range the on/off rhythm is replaced by a kind of a distorted, buzzing, sound. Experiment with different size capacitors until you find a good range of speeds. If you want to *see* what's happening as well as hear it you can add a second LED in parallel as an indicator light (and we all love blinking lights, useful or not,) as shown in figure 22.11.

We can extend this basic oscillator/LED/photoresistor design to create an automated version of our flashlight-controlled panner/mixer. The circuit shown in figure 22.12 uses one stage of the Hex Schmitt Trigger to make an low-frequency oscillator; a second stage simply inverts the clock signal from the first, so the two blinking lights are always out of phase—remember that an inverter always outputs the opposite state of the input signal: you will note that one LED is always off when the other is on. When wiring a stage of the 74C14 as a simple inverter you need no capacitor to ground or feedback resistor, as you have in the oscillator circuit.

Use a Y-cord or clip leads to connect a CD player to both circuit inputs and connect each circuit output to a separate amplifier; adjusting the oscillator frequency changes the

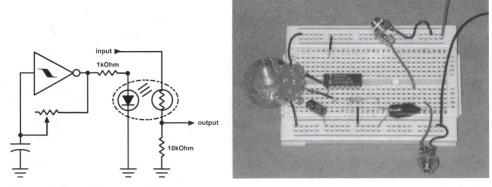

Figure 22.10 A blinking-LED-controlled gate.

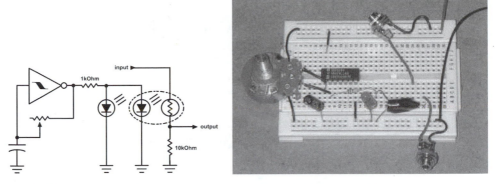

Figure 22.11 A blinking-LED-controlled gate with second indicator LED.

panning speed—Psycho-Pan-Scan! Hook up two different audio sources to the two circuit inputs, mix both circuit outputs to one amplifier input (Y-cords or clip leads), and adjust the oscillator to cut between the two signals —Super Crab!

Remember to link all the input and output jack grounds together, but (as with the basic gate circuit) you do not need to connect the oscillator's ground bus to the ground of the input and output jacks (in fact these circuits are cleaner if the audio ground and oscillator ground are *not* connected to one another).

The basic concept of the blinking LED chopping audio can be extended from simple oscillators to more complicated control circuits. You can connect the various outputs of the Divider circuit shown in chapter 21 to multiple LED/photoresistor gates to chop multiple sound sources in rhythmic patterns—Hacking Dub! Or drive the LED with the output of the cascaded gated oscillators we made in chapter 20—crazy rhythms! Just don't forget to include a resistor between each divider output and its LED.

As with the flashlight-in-the-closet experiment, these circuits do not produce a total mute when off—some of your audio signal will continue to bleed through even when the LED is off. The amount of bleed will depend largely on the specific photoresistor used and how effective it is shielded from outside light. The photoresistor should have as large a difference as possible between "on" and "off" resistance, but is best picked by ear, by sub-

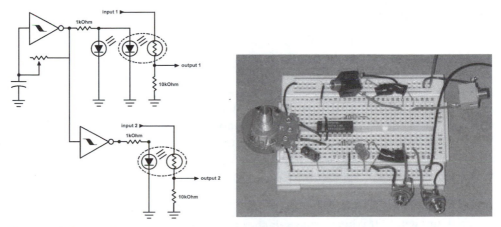

Figure 22.12 A blinking-LED-controlled panner/mixer.

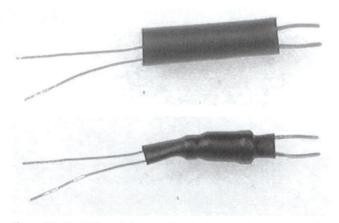

Figure 22.13 LED and photoresistor in heat shrink tubing, before shrinking (top) and after shrinking (bottom).

stituting different choices into the circuit. Moreover, the slight leakage of the "off" audio will be masked by other sounds in your mix unless this circuit is being used all by itself.

If the masses of electrical tape offend your sensibilities, you can put the photoresistor and LED inside an opaque soda straw, or the plastic sleeve of a mini plug or guitar plug—you may want to put some BluTak or opaque silicon sealant into the ends of the tubes to prevent light leakage—once again, be careful to avoid shorting the leads against one another. Heat shrink tubing is another tidy solution to light isolation (see figure 22.13). Slide narrow pieces around the legs of the LED and photoresistor to insulate them from shorting against one another, if you wish. Slide a wider piece over the LED and cell, nuzzle the two components tightly together, and apply heat from a hair-dryer to shrink the tubing tight around them. Voilá! A microelectronic "Bruit Secret."

This type of optical gating is much prized by audiophiles for its sonic purity. The complete separation of the audio ground from the oscillator's ground contributes to the high quality of the sound. Only a few small, if confusing, additions stand between these simple circuits and some very expensive studio noise gates, compressors and limiters.

Other Uses for Photoresistors

As you should grasp by now, the photoresistor is a resistor like any other, but for its Nosferatu-like response to light (it shrinks from it). You can substitute a photoresistor for most resistors and pots, and then modulate that resistance with a light—either performed (flashlights, shadows, etc.) or automated as we have in this chapter (with blinking LEDs). If you already have a toy or oscillator whose pitch is controlled by a photoresistor, press a blinking LED against the cell and hear what happens (similar to the toy cross-modulations we tried at the end of chapter 15). Modulating the pitch of a photoresistor-controlled audio oscillator with an LED blinking at a genre-appropriate beats-per-minute yields a pleasingly Disco-tinged "syn-drum" swoop; a pot in series with the photocell makes it possible to adjust the general pitch range.

Sometimes, if its "on" resistance is low enough, a photoresistor can be substituted for a low-current switch. If your toy has switches to trigger sounds or enable functions, try

Figure 22.14 Photoresistor as substitute for switch in a toy.

paralleling one of those switches with a photoresistor: connect the two photoresistor legs to the points on the toy's circuit board that are joined when the switch is closed (see figure 22.14).

Shine a flashlight at the photoresistor, or link it to an LED driven by a slow oscillator. The function associated with the switch should be triggered when the flashlight hits the photoresistor or when the LED is on—if so, you've got a simple solution to automating some of the toy's functions; if not, try another switch or another toy. Don't use the photoresistor as a substitute for the on/off switch of a circuit or between the circuit and its speaker, since it can't pass enough current.

Chapter 23

AMPLIFICATION AND DISTORTION: A SIMPLE CIRCUIT THAT GOES FROM CLEAN PREAMP TO TOTAL DISTORTION

You will need:

- Something to amplify: an electric guitar works best; a contact mike, telephone pickup or CD player will do.
- One of your oscillator circuits
- A breadboard.
- A CD4049 CMOS Hex Inverter.
- Assorted resistors, capacitors, and pots.
- Some solid hookup wire.
- Assorted jacks and plugs.
- A 9-volt battery and connector.
- An amplifier.
- Hand tools.

In addition to turning sounds on and off, there are many occasions when we want to make something LOUDER (see the Second Law of the Avant-Garde). Loudness comes in different flavors, and a little experimenting with the CD4049 Hex Inverter demonstrates several of them. This is yet another example of a digital logic chip being "misused" for analog purposes. Its internal configuration and pinout are shown in figure 23.1. Note that the 4049 is a rare exception to the general rule of corner pins for power hookup in CMOS chips (as in the 74C14 Hex Schmitt Trigger, the 4093 NAND Gate, and the 4040 Divider circuit we used in previous chapters). If you are at all dyslexic, now is the time to hold onto your hat with both hands: although the ground connects to pin 8 as expected, + volts connects to pin 1. The NC by pins 13 and 16 indicates "no connection." Note also that the 4049 inverters face the opposite direction than those in the 74C14. IMPORTANT: do not substitute the 74C14 Hex Schmitt Trigger for the 4049 in the examples in this chapter—the 74C14 *is* an inverter, but has a different internal circuit design that won't work properly in these configurations (if I may wax technical, the 4049 omits the Schmitt Trigger circuit essential to making our oscillators snappy, but incompatible with the designs in this chapter).

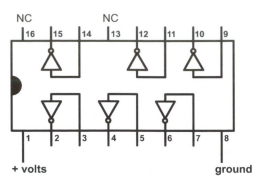

Figure 23.1 CD4049 Hex Inverter pinout.

Preamplifier

Hook up the circuit shown in figure 23.2. This is a general purpose preamplifier circuit, useful for increasing the signal of low-level sound sources (such as microphones, contact mikes, guitar pickups and coils) to the line level signal strength typical of CD players, cassette decks, computers, etc. After preamplification these signals can be intermixed with line-level sources using simple, passive mixers (see chapter 27). A preamplifier is not the same as a power amplifier—this circuit will not power a loudspeaker effectively—for that you need another kind of design, shown in chapter 28.

This preamp circuit has five basic components:

1. The CMOS Inverter stage. As with our oscillator circuits, the six sections of the 4049 chip are interchangeable.
2. The input resistor, RI, generally around 10kOhms.
3. The feedback resistor, RF, generally larger than RI (see below).
4. The input capacitor, CI, generally around 0.1uf.
5. The output capacitor, CO, generally around 10uf.

Your guitar (or other sound source) connects to the jack at the *right* hand side of the breadboard as shown, while the output emerges from the *left* jack—a needed Semitic twist on the right-to-left orthodoxy we've been observing in our circuits so far.

The gain—how much the circuit amplifies the incoming signal—is determined by the ratio of RF/RI. So, if RF = 100kOhms and R1 = 10kOhms, the gain is 10, which means that any signal you plug into the circuit comes out 10 times louder. If RF = 10mOhms and RI = 10kOhms the gain is 1,000, which makes it much MUCH louder. By substitut-

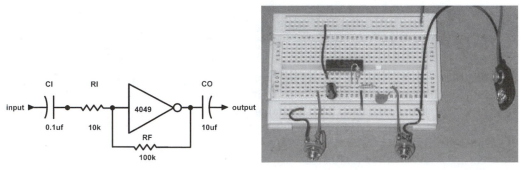

Figure 23.2 A basic preamplifier.

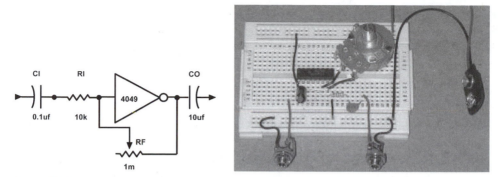

Figure 23.3 Preamplifier with variable gain.

ing a large pot (i.e., 1 megOhm) for the fixed resistors we can vary the gain of the circuit, as shown in figure 23.3. For a typical preamp (as you might use for a contact mike or coil) you may wish to wire up a 10k resistor in series with a 1 megOhm pot: this lets you adjust the amplification smoothly from unity gain (signal out = signal in) to a gain of 100 (output = 100 x input).

The input and output capacitors (CI and CO) block the DC voltage present in the circuit from the reaching whatever you're plugging into. Don't think about them too much if they bother you, just put them in. They are necessary for the stability of the circuit, and usually don't affect the sound much—which brings us to our next topic.

Tone Control

You may notice some noise or high frequency oscillation at very high gain. You can minimize these unwanted artifacts by putting a *very* small feedback capacitor (CF) in parallel to the feedback resistor as shown in figure 23.4. Try values in the range of 10–100 pf (picofarad)—the "small" 0.1uf capacitors we have been using in our oscillators are *way* too big.

Beyond getting rid of the noise or unwanted oscillation, this "feedback capacitor" sets the upper limit of the frequency response of the circuit. By substituting slightly larger capacitors you can transform our preamp into a simple "Low Pass Filter" tone control—one that blocks all frequencies above a certain pitch, while letting those that are lower pass through.

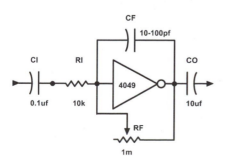

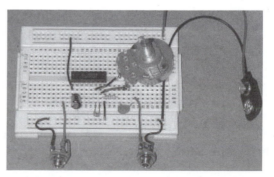

Figure 23.4 Adding a feedback capacitor.

Connect a CD player to the circuit and adjust it for low gain, so as not to distort the listening amplifier. Try different value feedback capacitors: 10pf, 100pf, .001uf, .01uf, and finally .1uf. As you increase the size of the capacitor you should notice the treble rolling off and the music getting bassier. By the time you reach .1 the circuit will probably be rolling off *all* audible frequencies; you'll hear almost nothing and probably think the circuit is mis-wired. You will need to patch the preamp into a better amp and bigger speaker than the mini-amp we've been using, if you want to hear the detail of these changes.

Given the extremely bright high end of our square wave oscillators, some high-frequency roll-off might be welcome now and then. Patch any of your oscillators through a preamp set for unity gain (RI = 10k, RF = 10k) and try the capacitor substitutions as above. The waveform should mellow out into something more like a triangle wave or sine wave (for you analog synth aficionados), bringing relief to canine and human cohabitants alike.

Unlike the Low Pass Filter on a synthesizer, the High Frequency Equalizer on a mixer, or even the simple treble control on a home stereo, the amount of roll-off cannot be continuously adjust with a pot in this design. This circuit is best suited for fixed settings, such as softening the oscillators into triangle waves (as described above,) or mellowing a fuzztone (see below). You could add a switch to select between two or three different capacitors if you want some variation (rotary switches can select amongst several different values). Before you sneer at switched EQ, remember that vintage Neve, API, and Pultec equalizers command stratospheric prices despite (or because of) such switching—and a few other factors, admittedly, such as brilliant design, beefy transformers, luscious knobs, rarity, etc.

Remember the Input and Output Capacitors I told you not to worry about? If you still feel like worrying, you can perform similar capacitor substitutions on the Input Capacitor. This time, as you *decrease* its value from the nominal .1uf down to .01uf, .001uf, 100pf, and 10pf, you should notice that the bass frequencies begin to vanish and the sound gets tinnier—we've made a simple "High Pass Filter." With careful selection of the optimum capacitor size, you can make a useful filter for rolling off low frequency wind noise or handling noise and rumble from microphones and contact mikes.

The six inverter sections in the 4049 can be used interchangeably—you can make a six-channel contact mike preamp with one chip, for example. Each preamp can be wired to its own output jack for connection to an external mixer, or you can sum them together with 10k resistors as we did with the multiple oscillators in chapter 18. You can build them into the mixer designs will we introduce later, in chapter 27.

Distortion

Amplifier sections can also be cascaded to produce greater gain: by putting two stages with 10x gain in series you get a net gain of 100. But this simple approach to accumulative amplification is not "perfect," and by adding a lot of gain in series we introduce distortion, the guitarist's friend. The circuit in figure 23.5, based on a venerable design by Craig Anderton (the godfather of musical hacking), is simple, versatile, and sounds great.

Plug in a guitar—always the best instrument for evaluating a distortion circuit—and turn the pot: as the gain increases the sound should move from clean amplification through tube-like "overdrive" into distortion and, eventually, uncontrollable noise and oscillation. Ahh, bliss! As Robert Poss says:

Rule #23: Distortion is Truth (Poss's law).

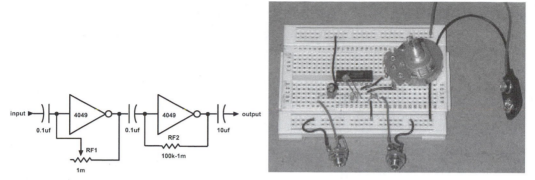

Figure 23.5 Craig Anderton's Distortion circuit.

But truth comes in many flavors. If you are really interested in distortion, you should spend some time substituting different components throughout this circuit until you find perfection. In particular, try:

- Various resistors, from 100k–10mOhm, for RF2.
- Various feedback capacitors, from 10pf to 100pf, for CF1 and CF2, in parallel to RF1 and RF2. These values can be set with fixed values or made switch selectable, as we suggested above for our simple EQ circuit (see figure 23.6).
- Adding an additional gain stage, which makes the distortion more extreme (see figure 23.7).

Figure 23.6 Distortion with feedback capacitors added (schematic only).

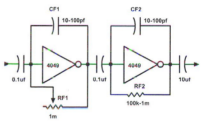

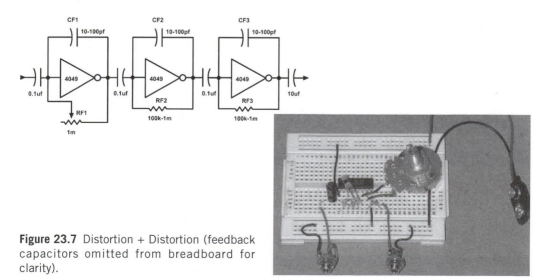

Figure 23.7 Distortion + Distortion (feedback capacitors omitted from breadboard for clarity).

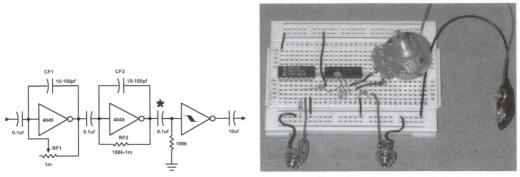

Figure 23.8 Distortion + Fuzz (feedback capacitors omitted from breadboard for clarity).

- Following the circuit with a Schmitt Trigger Inverter from a 74C14, which clips the signal in the style of a classic 1960s fuzztone (see figure 23.8). You may need a resistor of about 100kOhms between the input of the Schmitt Trigger and ground to keep the circuit from making oscillating in the absence of an actual input signal; sometimes removing the capacitor marked with the asterisk and replacing it with a straight wire also improves stability.

This last variation tips us over the line into the subject matter of our next chapter.

Chapter 24

ANALOG TO DIGITAL CONVERSION, SORT OF: MODULATING OTHER AUDIO SOURCES WITH YOUR OSCILLATORS

You will need:

- Something to amplify: an electric guitar is best.
- A breadboard.
- Distortion circuit from the previous chapter.
- CD4093 Quad NAND Gate Schmitt Trigger.
- CD4040 Binary Counter/Divider.
- Assorted resistors, capacitors, and pots.
- Some solid hookup wire.
- Assorted jacks and plugs.
- A 9-volt battery and connector.
- An amplifier.
- Hand tools.

The preamp and distortion circuits in the previous chapter are useful on their own to boost a low level signal or make an electric guitar sound legitimate but also in conjunction with other circuits. An ordinary line-level audio signal (such as the output of a CD player) measures a bit less that 1 volt peak-to-peak, and fluctuates in a curvy, Baroque way; the circuits we've been making with CMOS digital chips put out 9 volts peak-to-peak (if powered by a 9-volt battery) and snap between 0 and 9 volts with Modernist decisiveness. But with enough gain and distortion, any analog audio starts to look like one of our digital square waves. The more it looks like a digital signal, the easier it is to fool other digital circuitry into accepting it as kith and kin. This deception lets us easily interface sounds from the analog real world to our digital circuits for unusual signal processing.

The Fuzzy Dicer

The circuit shown in figure 24.1 is a variation on the gated oscillator in chapter 20. Instead of using one oscillator to modulate another, however, here the pseudo-square wave output

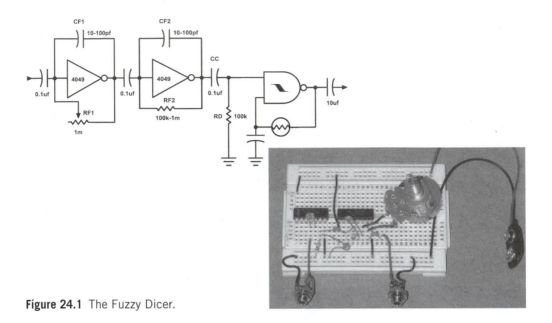

Figure 24.1 The Fuzzy Dicer.

of the distortion circuit gates the oscillator. When the oscillator runs at low speeds (1–10uf timing capacitor) it effectively "chops" the output of the distortion circuit on and off—like the photocell gate in chapter 22, but with a much sharper edge and a complete muting in the off state. At higher speeds (0.01–0.1uf capacitor) the oscillator interacts with the distorted signal to create a "ring-modulator"-type effect.

Try your favorite version of the distortion circuit in chapter 23. The circuit may be more stable with or without the coupling capacitor CC—try both ways. A "pull-down" resistor (Rd) between the 4093 input and ground may be needed to mute the circuit when you are not sending it an input signal (i.e., not playing the guitar). If it seems insensitive, only triggering on very loud signals, you may need to increase the gain of your distortion circuit—try the triple-inverter version shown in figure 23.7 in chapter 23, or the fuzz circuit in figure 23.8.

If it seems too sensitive, and prone to fits of high frequency squealing, try putting larger capacitors in the feedback loops of any or all of the 4049 stages of the distortion circuit. This will roll off the higher frequencies, remove excess noise, and send the subsequent circuits a signal that emphasizes the fundamental pitch. This circuit may take more tweaking than the ones we've made before, but the effort is worth it—and you can't buy one anywhere (yet) (see track 17 on the CD).

The Low Rider

Substitute the output of a distortion circuit for the clock/oscillator driving the clock input of the 4040 divider circuit (pin 10) we used in chapter 21, and the divisor outputs become subharmonics of whatever you play into it—a "Rocktave Box," to use the vulgar industry parlance (see figure 24.2).

You can use switches to select different subharmonics (how about a tilt-switch on the headstock of your Fender Mustang?) or select a fixed mix. Divided down far enough, an

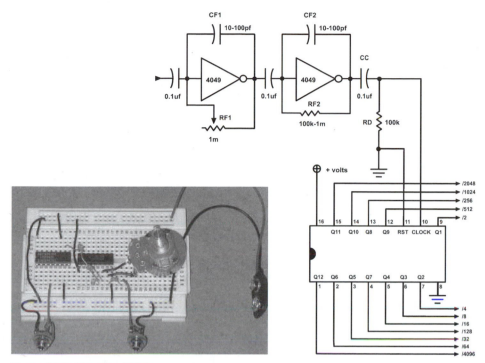

Figure 24.2 The Low Rider.

E-chord becomes a rhythmic pattern, which can be used to blink an LED to control a photocell to gate on and off…whatever.

As with the Fuzzy Dicer, you may need to experiment with the coupling capacitor CC and the pull-down resistor Rd; adding the Schmitt Trigger buffer as we suggested for the Fuzzy Dicer will likely make the pitch tracking more stable. Likewise, larger feedback capacitors in the distortion stages will strengthen the fundamental pitch of the incoming signal and minimize the circuit's tendency to fly off. Tweak tweak!

These designs get us into a very woolly area of circuit conglomeration, never anticipated by the original designers of these chips—trial and error is the best working method. This distortion-based pseudo-analog-to-digital conversion can be coupled with any chips in the CMOS family (time to start downloading those PDFs or order a data book; see Appendix A), some of which will yield exquisite signal transformations. Try using distortion as an interface to inject external signals into your hacked toys or radio. But please observe our No-AC-Power safety practice and use these techniques on battery-powered circuits only.

PART V

LOOKING

Chapter 25

VIDEO MUSIC/MUSIC VIDEO: TRANSLATING VIDEO SIGNALS INTO SOUND, HACKING CHEAP CAMERA CIRCUITS, AND EXTRACTING SOUNDS FROM REMOTE CONTROLS

You will need:

- A video camera or camcorder.
- A video monitor.
- Photoresistor-controllable oscillators.
- A cheap, hackable CCD video camera circuit board (see text).
- A phototransistor.
- A photoresistor.
- An infrared remote control from a TV or other appliance.
- An audio amplifier.
- Some speakers.
- Some small mirrors, a laser pointer or flashlight.

Various ingenious software tools exist for translating pictorial data into sound and vice versa: Soundhack's "Open Any…" turns any computer file into a sound file (i.e., a Photoshop-to-hit-record converter), STEIM's "Big Eye," and Max's "Jitter" track moving objects in a video image and extract MIDI or audio information. But here are a few simple hardware approaches to the same problems that bypass the computer.

Light and Shadow

Several artists have translated images directly to sound by placing photoresistors on video monitors or projection screens (see "Visual Music"). Wire up a few photoresistor-controlled oscillators (see chapter 18). Place the sensitive side of a photoresistor against the screen of a video monitor and use a thin strip of opaque electrical tape across the back to hold it in place; repeat for each photoresistor, distributing them across the screen. Hook up a camera or play back a tape. Action! Instant soundtrack! You can do this on a projection screen as well.

You can also use the photoresistors to adjust the loudness of any audio signal (CD, tape, microphone, etc.) in response to fluctuations in the image, by adapting the gating and panning circuits from chapter 22 to work with photoresistors affixed to a monitor or projection screen.

Frame Rate Music

Connect the analog video output of a camera to an amplifier and speaker—that's right: the *video* output to the *audio* input (the camera puts out a video signal that is about the same level as a CD player). Pan the camera around the room as you listen. You should hear a steady drone whose overtones fluctuate in response to the image content and brightness. The fundamental pitch is a function of the video frame rate (NTSC or PAL-specific), and therefore unwavering if the camera is functioning normally, while the overtone balance directly represents the image data, line by line. Very nice, if you like drones.

Aim the camera through a rotating fan; vary the fan speed and you may hear interference patterns between the frame rate and the fan speed. Focus on a white card off-center on a black turntable mat, and switch between 33 and 45. Aim the camera at the monitor and look and listen as you experiment with video feedback. A video mixer, keyer, or special effects box introduces audible artifacts as well as visible ones. Aim an IR remote at the camera (most video cameras detect infrared light and show it as hot white) and listen to the burst pattern of the encoded data (see Channel Surfing Music below).

The frame rate is fixed, and normally doesn't budge unless you move between NTSC and PAL. But if you invest in a cheap black and white CCD camera circuit board (scrounged from a surveillance camera, or available from most electronic surplus outlets for less than $25.00), you can experiment with tickling the clock frequency by a laying of hands (as we did in chapters 11 and 12) or replace the clock crystal with a variable oscillator (as discussed in chapter 21). The crystal is usually pretty conspicuous on the circuit board—often a metallic silver small cylinder or block (see figure 25.1).

Figure 25.1 Camera board with switch for disconnecting crystal (circled, right) and electrodes for tickling clock frequency (left, visible below switches).

Visual Music

Electronics have pervaded and altered our visual world as profoundly as our sonic one and, furthermore, allowed us to link the two in peculiar, causal ways. In his 1965 work "Magnet TV," Nam June Paik sat a large magnet on top of a television set to distort its image; although technically rather crude, this piece presaged the considerably more "sophisticated" electronic image processing that would come to typify much subsequent video art. "Magnet TV" established a hacker precedent that would remain a consistent presence in Paik's work, as well as in that of many multi-media artists who followed him. Before lightning-fast personal computers with massive amounts of memory made digital video processing as commonplace as word processing, Paik-like hacks were the only affordable way to manipulate visual images in real time, or to create linkages between video and audio. Video feedback was as common a tool for early video artists as audio feedback was for electronic music composers: Bill Viola (USA) made extensive use of it in the 1970s; more recently Billy Roisz (Austria) VJs with video feedback, modifying it through simple video mixers and keyers, and splitting the video signal to feed the PA as well, so that the bursts and jitter of the images are heard in parallel as glitches and hums (see figure below).

"Cloud Music" was a video/music installation developed by David Behrman, Bob Diamond, and Robert Watts between 1974 and 1979. In the earliest version, a camera was pointed at the sky and connected to a video monitor. A number of photoresistors were affixed to the screen. The light values of the passing clouds changed the resistance of the photoresistors, and, in turn, affected the sound score. Yasunao Tone (JP/USA) used a similar approach in his "Molecular Music" (1982–85): photoresistors were taped to the surface of a screen onto which a film was projected; each photoresistor controlled the pitch of an oscillator (similar to

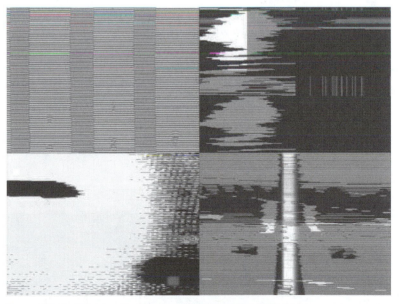

Four stills from video feedback performance by Billy Roisz.

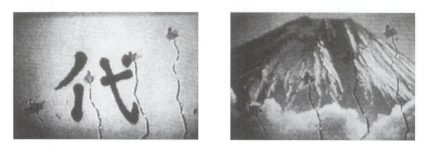

Two stills from "Molecular Music," Yasunao Tone.

those described in chapter 18), and the resulting sound mass responded directly to the change in projected images (see figure above). Today, Tone is best known as the "grandfather of glitch": he began "wounding CDs" in 1985 by applying Scotch Tape punctured by pinholes to the underside of the disks; the resulting frenetic digital error-fest was the first documented music made with intentionally damaged CDs (see track 20 on the CD). The intertwining of light and sound are central to Tone's work: the deflection of lasers through pinholes is a miniaturized, but nonetheless logical, extension of film interrupting the projector's light before it strikes the photoresistors.

In 1969, long before planetarium laser shows, Lowell Cross (USA), a frequent collaborator of John Cage and David Tudor, created the first sound-modulated laser projections for his work "VIDEO/LASER II": the laser (enormous at the time—see figure below and top of next page) was reflected off a mirror mounted on a speaker-like device called a galvanometer, which vibrated in response to sound input to create curving Lissajous patterns on the wall. (Lowell Cross also built a beautiful photoresistor-based matrix mixer embedded in a chessboard for the famous 1968 John Cage/Marcel Duchamp chess-playing performance, "Reunion").

In 1999, when Stephen Vitiello had an artist's studio on the ninety-first floor of the World Trade Center in New York City, he and Bob Bielecki (see "The Luthiers," chapter 29) hooked up a photoresistor to a battery (as shown in figure 25.6), placed it on the eyepiece of a telescope, aimed it down at New Jersey, and

Lowell Cross (L), Eugene Turitz (C), and David Tudor (R) setting up for the first laser light show to use *x-y* scanning, Mills College, Oakland, California, May 9, 1969.

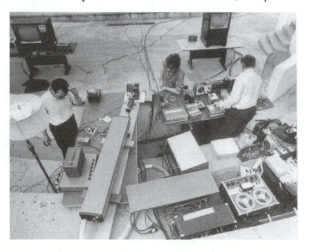

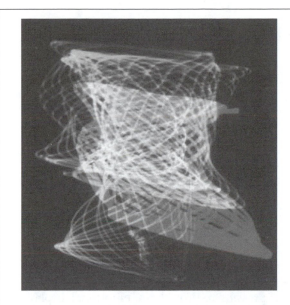

Laser projected image from "VIDEO/LASER II" (December 1969), Lowell Cross.

sat together listening to the flashing lights on a police car across the Hudson. Vitiello has made a beautiful series of recordings using this "audio-telescope" (see track 18 on the CD). Norbert Möslang, ex-Voice Crack (see "Composing Inside Electronics," chapter 14), has used similar circuits to extract surprisingly rich rhythmic and harmonic textures from the light patterns of bicycle flashers and LEDs on toys (see track 19 on the CD).

Computers finally caught up with video, but visual hacking hasn't stopped. The disparity between the $100-portable LCD TV and the $5,000-video projector offended the sensibility of the Dutch electronic performance trio BMBCon (Justin Bennett, Wikke 't Hooft, and Roelf Toxopeus), so in the mid-1990s they took the screens from cheap TVs (which have the same dimensions as 35mm slides) and dropped them into old slide projectors from the flea market—voilá: the home-made, low-budget video projector (see figure below). Jon Satrom (USA) has built his VJ career on transforming a child's "video paint box" into an instrument he calls the "Vitch" (see figure top of next page). By inserting Circuit-Bending-style jumpers between various points on the circuit board, Satrom is able

Homemade LCD projector, BMBCon.

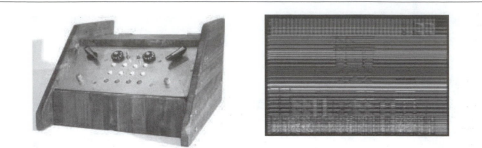

The "Vitch," Jon Satrom (left). Video image from performance with the "Vitch," Jon Satrom (right).

disrupt the toy's functions to produce a remarkable range of fragmented, frozen, superimposed, and digitally warped images (essentially a video equivalent of the keyboard malfunctions described by Phil Archer in "Circuit Bending," chapter 15). And in a pseudo-Victorian twist that would make John Bowers proud, Dutch artists Remko Scha and Arthur Elsenaar attach electrodes to Elsenaar's face and electrically stimulate the muscles of expression to provide an "emotional display" for their computer.

Split the camera output between a video monitor and amplifier, so you can *see* as well as *hear* the affect of your hack. Sometimes lifting one leg of the camera's crystal time base makes it just unstable enough to produce a coherent image when left alone, but jitter like crazy when touched. You may be able to make an oscillator whose pitch is controlled by a pot, photoresistor, etc., and whose timbre is a function of what it sees. The video image produced by a tickled camera is reminiscent of 1960s 8mm film "scratch animation", and the sound is somewhat meatier than the typical hands-upon-radio swoops.

> **USE A BATTERY-POWERED VIDEO MONITOR AND AMPLIFIER IF AT ALL POSSIBLE TO MINIMIZE THE RISK OF ELECTROCUTION. IF THIS IS NOT POSSIBLE, APPROACH THIS EXPERIMENT WITH *EXTREME* CAUTION.**

The hacked camera will not generate a stable sync signal when tickled. Most video monitors will continue to display scratchy video in the absence of a stable sync, but many video projectors are too "smart": they will interpret intermittent sync as a sign that there is no video signal at all, and will display that irritating blue screen with the legend "no video input." Providing a proper sync under scratch video is beyond the scope of this book, sorry—use an old TV instead, or patch your hacked camera through a video mixer or other device that can restore the sync.

As long as we are on the subject of old TVs, I would be remiss if I did not remind you, the reader, of the beautifully liquid image distortion that results from putting a hefty magnet in close proximity to a television picture tube (ineffective on modern LCD screens). Take an old TV. Tune it to any station or even inter-station static. Move a big

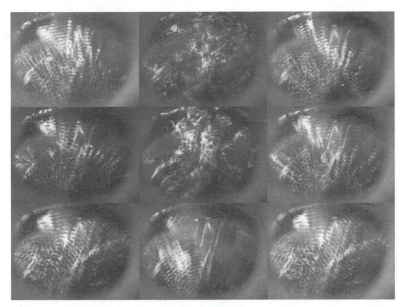

Figure 25.2 Water-filled speaker, showing ripples produced by low-frequency sound.

magnet over the top and sides, and watch the image wiggle—a gift from Nam June Paik (see "Visual Music").

Video-Free Video

Visual display of sound patterns can be accomplished without video cameras and monitors, of course. As we described at the end of chapter 5, you can take a large raw loudspeaker, fill it with sand or talcum powder, connect to an amplifier, play some sound, and watch the dancing dust. Coat the inside of the cone with paint or rubber cement, fill it with water or oil, and repeat the experiment; you can reflect a focused light or laser pointer off the water's surface onto the wall or ceiling (see figure 25.2). A mirror glued to the center of the cone also reflects a laser nicely.

Channel Surfing Music

In chapter 3 we used coils to pick up the electromagnetic signals given off by various appliances and electronic devices. We can also eavesdrop on light signals of various kinds by using a specialized type of photosensor. The "phototransistor" is the heart of any infrared remote control receiver circuit, such as that in your TV. It detects the pulses of infrared light sent by your remote control and converts them into a stream of binary pulse waves that are, in turn, translated back into digital data by the microprocessor in the TV. Earlier in this chapter we detected these data burst using a video camera, but there are cheaper methods.

Aim a remote control at the simple circuit in figure 25.3 (keep it close) and you should hear pulse trains as you press the buttons. If not, reverse which leg of the phototransistor connects to +9 volts and which connects to the load resistor. The differences between one

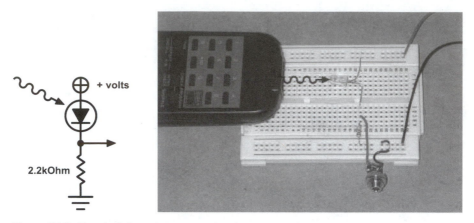

Figure 25.3 Simple infrared detector circuit.

button and another may sound pretty subtle, even though the encoded data is different. Try different remotes—the fundamental frequency and basic timbre may differ from one to another, but it might be a subtle difference, since they're all sending similar pulse trains. You'll notice that the loudness of the signal falls off pretty sharply as you pull the remote farther from the circuit, so you do have some dynamic control over this instrument.

You can substitute an ordinary photoresistor for the phototransistor; you may need to increase the size of the load resistor from 2.2kOhm to 10kOhm or larger, as shown in figure 25.4. Because photoresistors are sensitive to light across the spectrum (not just infrared), you will get much more interference from the power grid's AC frequency present in incandescent and fluorescent lighting (60hz in the United States, 50hz in Europe),resulting in an underlying drone. But you may find this interesting rather than irritating, so try it.

Since the lights on many electronic circuits look steady but are in fact "scanned" by the central processor unit, you can use these circuits to extract unexpected sound patterns from almost any device with LEDs. Try it on bicycle flashers (see track 19 on the CD), toys with blinking lights, the front panels of studio gear, TV screens, computer monitors. Sometimes bicycle lights and blinking toys sound astonishingly much like heavy metal chord progressions.

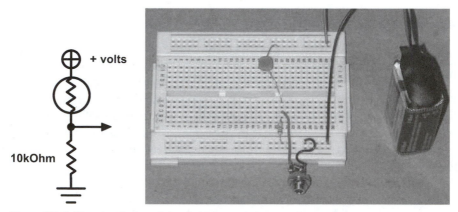

Figure 25.4 Simple photoresistor light-to-sound converter.

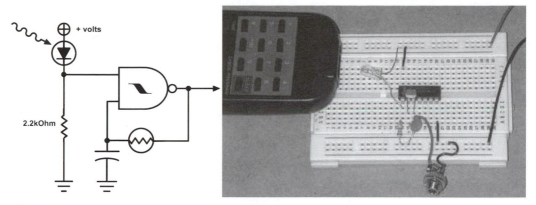

Figure 25.5 Infrared-gated oscillator with photoresistor-controlled frequency.

If these pulsey or hummy sounds get too dull, try using the phototransistor or photoresistor circuit as the control input to the basic 4093 gateable oscillator circuit from chapter 20. If you use a photoresistor for the oscillator's frequency control resistor, you get a pretty expressive "multi-phase" light-to-sound converter that responds to both ambient and modulated light sources (such as remote controls) (see figures 25.5 and 25.6).

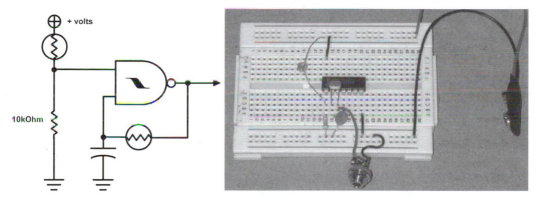

Figure 25.6 Photoresistor-gated oscillator with photoresistor-controlled frequency.

Chapter 26

LCD ART:
MAKING ANIMATED MODERN DAGUERREOTYPES AND
ALTERNATIVE VIDEO PROJECTORS

You will need:

- A toy with an LCD screen.
- Some test leads.
- A 9-volt battery and battery hook-up clip.
- Hookup wire.
- Some straight pins or short needles.
- A basic oscillator circuit from chapter 18 or 20.
- A flashlight and some lenses, or a slide projector.
- Hand tools, soldering iron, and electrical tape.
- If possible, a "video paint-box" toy with video output.
- An amplifier.

Lower Tech

A lot of handheld toys and games incorporate small LCD screens. In general-purpose LCD character displays and video monitors a grid of pixels is *bit-mapped* by a microprocessor that turns individual pixels on and off to "draw" any character or image, etch-a-sketch style. In cheap toys, on the other hand, the screen often contains a handful of "ready-made" graphic components: lips, a nose, and pair of ears are turned on and off against a printed cardboard backdrop to add distinguishing features to Mr. Potato's otherwise generic head, for example. These rebus-like images take on new meaning when the background is removed—leaving the body parts floating like a medium's apparitions—or superimposed on an alternative drawing or photograph that you provide (Mr. Turniphead? Baby Sister rev. 2.0?).

Moreover, when the screen is removed from the circuit its graphic elements can be turned on and off with simple connections of voltages, either directly from a battery or from an oscillator. Start by tinning the tips of the red and black power lines from a 9-volt

Figure 26.1 LCD elements being activated by direct battery connection.

battery clip to give them stiff, sharp points—you can also solder sewing pins to the wires for stronger, finer contacts. Locate the connections to the LCD—usually these are tiny dark points embedded in a rubber strip pressed under either edge of the glass, but sometimes they are larger metal tabs. Poke the "+" lead against a dark point in one strip, and press the ground wire to one in the other strip (see figure 26.1). Keep trying different pairs of points while watching the screen—at some point an LCD element should become visible; if none does, try reversing which wire goes to which side. Make a note of the location of the contact point pairs that enable specific graphic objects, and keep exploring. Once you find a set of images that you like, you can make the connections more stable by wedging and taping wires or pins into or against the contact strips.

If you remove the rubber strips, you can usually make direct contact with the LCD connections by pressing the wire tip directly to the glass where the rubber sat, or by clamping the jaws of a narrow clip lead to the edge of the glass. Look carefully: you should be able to see very fine lines etched on the glass—these are the electrical contacts. Move the probe or jaws along the edge and catalog the hot spots for the individual screen elements.

You can *animate* the images by using the outputs of oscillators to blink the LCD elements instead of setting them "permanently" on with battery leads. Take one lead from the output of an oscillator running at a low speed (metronome range) and one from the circuit ground (battery "−"). Connect the leads to points along the LCD edges that you know enable images (see figure 26.2). Adjust the oscillator speed and watch the LCD element turn on and off. If nothing happens, swap the oscillator output and ground connections to the LCD.

LCDs are kind of spooky—the image often lingers on the screen for several seconds after power is disconnected before fading out. The small screens bear a resemblance to old daguerreotypes, and have a certain charm as modern miniatures, whether superimposed on new backdrops or left in their rather ghostly, mostly transparent state as tiny digital stained glass windows. They are lovely hung in a sun-dappled window.

The current consumption of the LCD device and a low-frequency oscillator is so small that you can leave the object running on a 9-volt battery for weeks before it runs down. You could even power the whole thing with a small solar panel (especially if you *do* choose

Figure 26.2 LCD elements animated by oscillator output.

to hang it in a sunny window). If you go shopping for the latter, look for one that puts out anywhere from 3 to 12 volts, with a current capacity of 5 milliamps or so. Some CMOS and LCD circuits can even be powered by a battery made from an apple or potato (so dust off those childhood science fair notes).

With a decent light source and the appropriate lens you can project your LCD onto a wall. You'll have to experiment with flashlights and magnifying glasses, but it's worth the effort. Invest in one of those "third hand" devices: use the two articulated arms with alligator clips to hold the LCD, and the magnifying glass to focus the image projected by a narrow-beam table lamp. You can also drop the LCD screens from tiny portable "stadium TVs" into older slideprojectors (see "Visual Music," chapter 25). You can do the same with the displays from many cheap hand-held games—the stupidest thumb-driven hockey match looks pretty cool projected huge and slightly fuzzy on a wall.

Don't let the visual charm of LCDs distract you from their sonic potential. Clip the ground half of an audio cable to the battery ground of a working LCD circuit (before you do the hacks described above) and touch the hot lead to the various scan lines of the LCD display: you often hear deep, rich chords.

Higher Tech

Several companies specializing in high-end electronics toys, most notably V-Tech, make "video paint boxes" for children. These devices connect to a television and include a simple graphics tablet and keyboard with which the kid creates drawings and animations. Inside are some very sophisticated graphic chips that can be bamboozled into doing strange things. Following the technique described in the "Almost a Short Circuit" section of chapter 15, use a 1k resistor and a pair of clip leads to interconnect any points on the circuit board. Occasionally you will get lucky and find connections that cause the graphics engine to freeze mid-way through drawing an image, recolor blocks of pixels, superimpose graphics from its memory, etc. And while you're at it don't forget to listen to different points on the board as well. (See section on Jon Satrom in "Visual Music," chapter 25.)

PART VI

FINISHING

Chapter 27

MIXERS, MATRICES, AND PROCESSING: VERY SIMPLE, VERY CHEAP, VERY CLEAN MIXERS, AND WAYS OF CONFIGURING LOTS OF CIRCUITS

You will need:

- An assortment of sound-making and processing circuits, found or made.
- A few pots of the same value (approximately 10KOhm–100kOhm), preferably "audio taper."
- Assorted resistors and photoresistors.
- An unneeded computer keyboard.
- Some solid and stranded hookup wire.
- Assorted jacks and plugs.
- Some clip leads.
- An amplifier or two.
- Soldering iron, solder, and hand tools.

Mixers

Now that your collection of noisemakers is growing, a simple mixer might prove useful. Here are some completely *passive* circuit designs—they use no batteries, no chips or other active components; they need no on/off switches or circuit boards. Even if you already have a "real" mixer, this is a very convenient way to expand its inputs. The basic schematic is shown below in figure 27.1.

The signal (i.e., tip) of each input jack is connected directly to one ear of a pot (the one designated "C" in figure 13.6 in chapter 13). The center tap on the pot (nose or "B") is soldered to a "summing" resistor. The non-pot ends of all the summing resistors are tied together and connected to the signal/tip of the output jack. The grounds/shields of all the jacks are connected together with wire, and soldered to a similar wire linking the other ear ("A") of all the pots—this common ground bus is indicated by the runic ground symbol. As in some of our earlier schematics, the ground connections for the input and output jacks are assumed and, for the sake of clarity, omitted from the drawing.

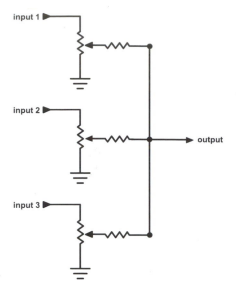

Figure 27.1 Basic three-input mono mixer.

The summing resistors and pots should be about the same value, i.e., for 10k pots use 10k summing resistors, for 50k pots use 50k summing resistors, etc. The pots can be of any value between 10–100kOhm, but it's best if all the pots are the same value. Figure 27.2 shows which ear of the pot to use for input and which for ground if you want a traditional mixer behavior (i.e., turning the knob clockwise raises the level).

You can expand the circuit in figure 27.1 to accommodate any number of inputs, simply by adding another jack, pot, and resistor for each new input signal. By adding some switches and another output jack you can make a stereo version of the same circuit (figure 27.3). Each summing resistor is connected to the switch's Common terminal (C); the Normally Open terminal (NO) is connected to one output jack, and the Normally Closed (NC) to the other. Throwing the switch swaps the signal between the left to right outputs. It's a kind of binary panner, alternating between hard-left and hard-right, with no gradations in between—crude, but much simpler than adding a proper pan-pot.

Pots are specified as "linear taper" (what we've been using so far in this book) and "audio taper," which are optimized for adjusting audio level. You may find that the raising and

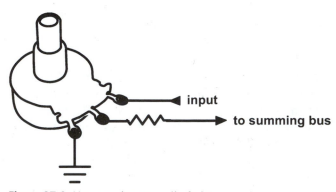

Figure 27.2 How to wire an audio fader.

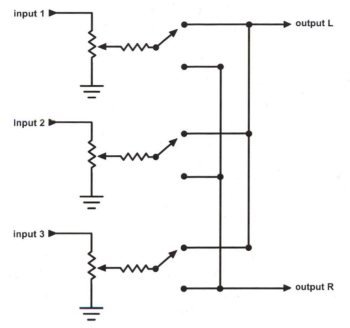

Figure 27.3 Basic three-input stereo mixer.

lowering of volume sounds smoother with an audio taper pot. If you are mixing a lot of stereo signals (like the outputs of CD players) you may want to use "stereo" pots, which are two pots couple to a single shaft; this mechanical design lets you trim two signals in parallel from a single knob (see figure 27.4). One pot in each stereo pair will take the left half of a stereo input and send it to your left bus, while the other will take the right input and send it to the right bus. You wire each section exactly like an ordinary single pot.

Figure 27.4 A stereo potentiometer.

You can use ordinary rotary pots for these mixer circuits, or slide pots (easy to find through online sources), which make your circuit look more like a "real" mixer, but be warned:

Rule #24: It is easier to drill round holes than slots.

Because they contains no amplifiers or other gain circuits, these circuits are best for mixing signals of more or less similar levels (i.e., CD and tape players, oscillators), and are not so useful with low-level signals like microphones. You can incorporate preamplifier circuits, such as those in chapter 23. If you get ambitious, insert them between the input jack and the pot. What these designs lack in gain and EQ they make up for in cost and audio quality—as with the optical gating and panning circuits in chapter 22, passive mixers are quite coveted by certain audio purists.

Matrices

David Tudor, one of the pioneers in the field of live electronic music (see "David Tudor and *Rainforest*," chapter 8), used mixer matrices to combine relatively simple circuits into networks that produced sound of surprising richness and variation. Instead of simply mixing a handful of sound sources down to a stereo signal, Tudor interconnected sound modules with multiple feedback paths and output channels. The recent rise of the "no input mixing" school of internal machine feedback has exposed a new generation of musicians and listeners to the possibilities of matrix feedback. Consider the 3 × 3 matrix mixer shown in figure 27.5.

You will notice that the design is similar to that of our basic mixer in figure 27.1, but here each input signal is connected to three pots instead of one, and we have three output

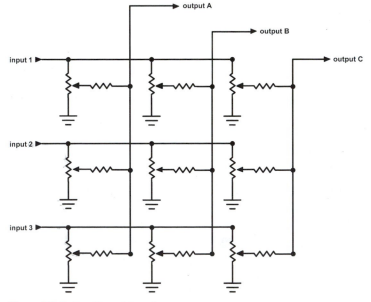

Figure 27.5 3 × 3 matrix mixer.

buses instead of one. You can expand this circuit with as many pots and jacks as you need and can afford.

Connect a few circuits, including both sound *generating* circuits, such as your oscillators or toys, and some *processing* circuits, such as the photoresistor gate, the distortion circuit, or any guitar pedal (such as a delay, wah-wah, or graphic equalizer). Send one output of the matrix to an amplifier for listening, and the others can be sent to the inputs of your circuits. By adjusting the levels of the various pots you can create a pretty straightforward signal path (toy through distortion to speaker) or a more devious one (toy through distortion to speaker, distortion also to delay which goes both to speaker and back into its own input).

The piezo-driver pseudo-reverbs we discussed in chapter 8 work very well in these configurations. Some of the most unassuming rock pedals reveal astonishing musicality when placed in feedback loops. Incorporated into matrices, time based effects (such as delays and flangers) contribute a wonderful instability that transforms a table of commonplace effects into a richly challenging performance instrument (see figure 27.6) .

If you intend to use a matrix to generate feedback you will need some gain, which you can provide with the simple 4049 preamp circuit of chapter 23, or using effect pedals that include a gain stage. Feedback matrices benefit greatly from the inclusion of some kind of equalization, to aid in steering pitch response and nulling out unwanted shrieks—a simple graphic EQ effect pedal provides both the requisite level boost and useful frequency shaping.

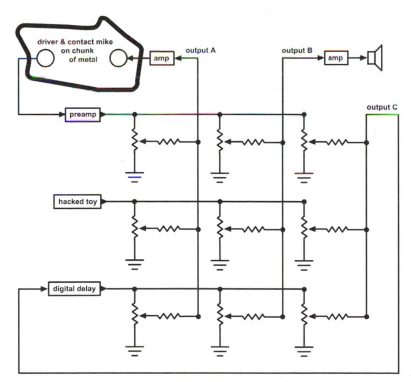

Figure 27.6 Circuits in a matrix.

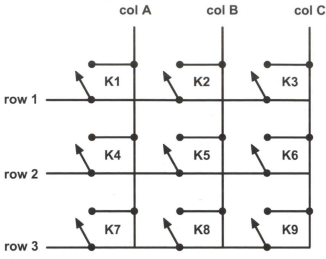

Figure 27.7 A keyboard matrix.

Computer Keyboards

Discarded computer keyboards roam contemporary urban streets like unwanted mutts in Latin America. While bereft of cool wet noses or beseeching brown eyes, these electronic strays can nonetheless prove friendly companions. A computer keyboard consists of a switch matrix: instead of each key closing two discrete contacts, it bridges specific lines in an X–Y grid, as shown in figure 27.7.

Pressing Key 1 connects horizontal row 1 to vertical column A, Key 3 connects row 1 to column C, Key 4 connects row 2 to column A, etc. In a computer keyboard there are enough rows and columns to handle the full alphabet, plus numbers and all those extra function keys. A 10 by 8 matrix, for example, will handle the 80 keys. The computer "scans" the matrix to detect which key is depressed. It sends a pulse down each row and checks which column it comes out of (like an extreme version of Splat the Rat).

If you open up the keyboard and scrutinize the circuit board, you should notice that the traces are arranged in a vague grid (see figure 27.8). Solder a wire between the ground terminals of two female jacks; solder a wire to each of the hot terminals, and strip the loose ends.

Connect a sound source, such as a CD player, to one jack, and connect the other jack to an amplifier. Use a clip lead or solder to connect the wire from the sound source (CD) jack to one of the traces (the traces may be routed to connectors at the edge of the circuit board) (see figure 27.9). Press down a key and touch the amplifier lead to other traces until you hear your sounds; then release the key: if the sound shuts off, you've found a cross point in the matrix—mark it somehow. If it doesn't, you've just touched another point along the trace that the sound source is connected to, so keep testing other points until you find a cross.

By repeating this admittedly arduous process you should be able to decode the matrix into rows and columns. Solder each row and column to the hot terminal of an audio jack. Connect all the shields together. Use all the rows as inputs and all the columns as outputs, or vice versa. By pressing keys you can route any input to any output. You can use this device

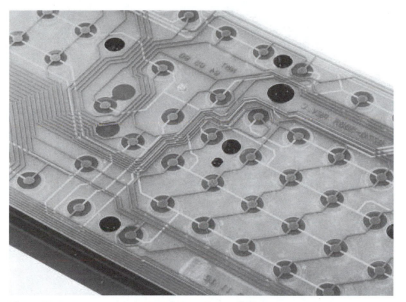

Figure 27.8 Computer keyboard circuit board showing matrix traces.

alone—as a signal router for spatial distribution, for example—or in conjunction with the matrix mixers described above to add switching to matrix-based signal processing.

If the decoding process sounds too daunting, you can find smaller, more easily decodable switch matrices in touch-tone telephones (3 columns x 4 rows) or calculators—two frequently discarded household items. "Raw" matrix keypads of various sizes can also be bought from a number of online retailers (see Appendix A). Membrane switches, commonly used in inexpensive keypads, have the advantage that, in addition to being able to close the switches by direct finger pressure, one can often activate them by "drawing"

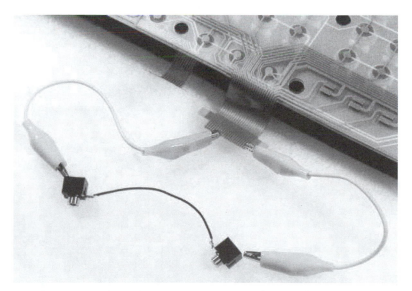

Figure 27.9 Computer keyboard wired for testing audio routing.

out A   out B   out C

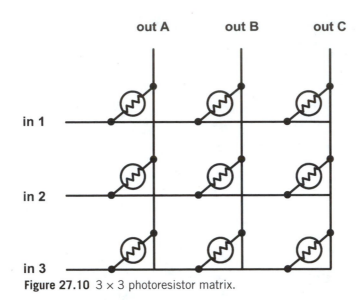

Figure 27.10 3 × 3 photoresistor matrix.

across the surface with a stylus of some sort, or rolling a billiard ball over it—nice gestural options.

Automation

The basic photoresistor gating circuit described in chapter 22 can be expanded into a matrix array as well (see figure 27.10). The photoresistors can be activated by flashlights, ambient light and shadow, video or film projection, or oscillator-driven blinking LEDs, depending on the degree of control or indeterminacy you desire.

Chapter 28

A LITTLE POWER AMPLIFIER: CHEAP AND SIMPLE

You will need:

- Something to amplify: a guitar, a cassette or CD player, etc.
- A breadboard.
- Audio Power Amplifier chip, LM386.
- Assorted resistors, capacitors, and pots.
- Assorted jacks and plugs.
- A small speaker.
- Some solid hookup wire.
- A 9-volt battery and connector, or four AA batteries and a holder.
- Hand tools.

Whether in pursuit of a self-contained electronic instrument or some form of sound sculpture, one day you will tire of choosing between some putty-colored mini-amplifier and a bulkier, more expensive (and potentially more dangerous) amplifier and speaker. There are a number of kits available from online retailers that include the essential Integrated Circuit, associated passive components (resistors, capacitors, etc.), and a printed circuit board (see chapter 1). But if you want to save a few dollars and get some more design experience, consider soldering up your own using the LM386 (see figure 28.1). At less that $1.00 retail, this chip, combined with a few other components in a very simple configuration, makes a cheap but decent low-power audio amplifier. It is the heart of many mini-amps, and—once soldered up—can be substituted accordingly.

The basic configuration shown in figure 28.2 gives a gain of 20 and is best for line-level signals such as CD players, computers, your oscillators, etc. By adding a 10uF capacitor between pins 1 and 8 the gain rises to 200 (see figure 28.3), which is more suitable for contact microphones, coils and guitar pickups. You can add a switch to bring the capacitor in and out of circuit to select high or low gain for different input sources, as shown in figure 28.4.

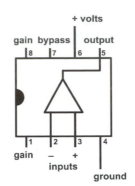

Figure 28.1 LM386 amplifier pinout.

The "+" voltage from the battery connects to pin 6, and the "–"/ground connects to pin 4. You'll want to add a power switch as well, or disconnect the battery from its clip when not in use, since this circuit drains more power than a lot of the others we've made. Pin 1 is also tied to ground, and the input signal goes to pin 3 after passing through a potentiometer used as a volume control. The 0.05uF capacitor and 10 Ohm resistor shown at pin 5, and the .1uF "bypass" capacitor at pin 7 are optional parts, to be added if the circuit oscillates and whines by itself.

This circuit puts out about 1/4 watt of audio power, and can be used to drive small speakers or headphones. It runs nicely off a 9-volt battery or a set of four AA batteries (the latter will last longer). It can drive a piezo disk at pretty high sound levels using the backwards output transformer trick shown in chapter 8. This amplifier can also drive directly a small motor (such as the vibrating motors from cell phones and pagers, also discussed in chapter 8) or a low-power solenoid or relay.

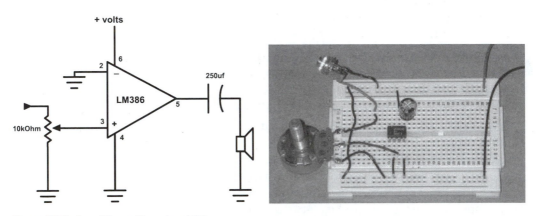

Figure 28.2 Amplifier with gain of 20.

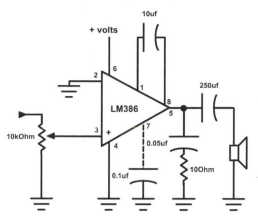
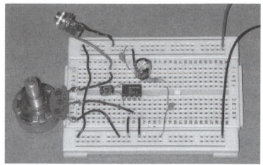

Figure 28.3 Amplifier with gain of 200.

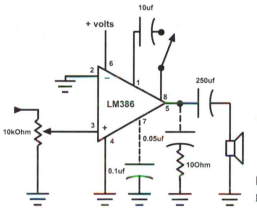

Figure 28.4 Amplifier with switch-selectable gain of 20 (open) or 200 (closed).

Chapter 29

ANALOG TO DIGITAL CONVERSION, REALLY: CONNECTING SENSORS TO COMPUTERS USING GAME CONTROLLERS

You will need:

- A computer running some kind of music software that accepts external control devices—joysticks, game pads, trackballs, etc.
- A MIDI synthesizer, sampler, drum machine, etc., if the software on your computer does not generate sound directly.
- An expendable joystick, game pad, trackball, etc. compatible with your computer.
- Assorted pots, photoresistors, pressure sensors, etc.
- Some hookup wire.
- Soldering iron, solder, a solder-sucker, and hand tools.

Now that the end of the book is in sight I will confess: I am not the raving anti-digital Luddite you might take me for after all these pages. I actually don't mind computers—in fact I've been making music with them since before the Apple was a twinkle in the collective Jobs and Wozniak eye. The issue for me has always been how to *play* them: sometimes an ASCII keyboard and a mouse don't give you enough control, or the right kind of control; sometimes you want to play something that feels less like a typewriter and more like a musical instrument (with apologies to Leroy Anderson). Of course you can use a MIDI interface to connect any commercial MIDI controller to your computer, but your choices are usually limited to piano-like keyboards, mis-triggering guitars, the odd pseudo-saxophone, and a handful of truly alternative controllers created by a few die-hard visionaries (see "The Luthiers").

It would be nice to be able to cobble together a computer instrument out of the sensors we've been working with so far: take a handful switches, pressure sensors, pots, photoresistors, etc.; stick them onto to a tennis racket, mailing tube or nerf ball; connect them to your computer; and play your favorite music software with a sort-of guitar, clarinet or stress reliever. Well, it's possible.

There are a number of interfaces available that link sensors to a computer through the USB or Ethernet ports, or using a MIDI interface. The granddaddy of them all was

The Luthiers

The unsung heroes of electronic music are the engineers who build the instruments but don't necessarily make a career of playing them. While the name "Moog" is almost synonymous with "synthesizer," pioneering designers such as Donald Buchla, Serge Tcherepnin, Tom Oberheim (whose companies bore their names), Alan Pearlman of ARP, and David Cockerell of EMS are virtually unknown outside extremely geeky circles. Although the introduction of MIDI in the early 1980s resulted in explosive growth for the synthesizer industry, these new machines were purposefully generic, the musical equivalent of the putty-colored office PC. But on the sidelines of the industry, inspired and quirky engineers continue to flourish.

Today the late-Robert Moog's company manufactures one of the best Theremins available (ironically, he got his start in business as a teenage entrepreneur selling Theremin kits of his own design), as well as a collection of sound processing devices based on his historic synthesizer modules. Likewise Donald Buchla continues to develop highly personal and expressive electronic musical instruments, such as Lightning, a controller that translates the position and movement of handheld wands into MIDI data. In 1975 Craig Anderton wrote what probably was the first book on musical circuits that could be understood by nonengineers, and he has been publishing how-to articles in musicians' magazines for years.

And in a world of off-the-rack musical tools, there still remains a special place for bespoke tailoring from the hands of the clever, personal luthier, such as Bob Bielecki, Bert Bongers or Sukandar Kartadinata. Based in New York, Bielecki helped Laurie Anderson realize many of her idiosyncratic instruments, including the "Tape Bow Violin" (see "Tape," chapter 9) and her first "masculating" pitch shifter. Later he built drone circuits for LaMonte Young (USA), precision sine wave oscillators for Alvin Lucier (USA), a light-to-sound interface for Stephen Vitiello (see "Visual Music," chapter 25), and other personalized electronic devices for artists such as Charles Curtis (USA), Arnold Dreyblatt (USA), Annea Lockwood (USA), Linda Montana (USA), and Bill Viola (USA).

Bert Bongers (Netherlands) studied computer science and ergonomics before finding his calling as an instrument builder, initially for STEIM (Amsterdam) and The Institute of Sonology in The Hague. He later founded his own reseach labs in Barcelona and Maastricht, where he now runs the MaasLab with artist Yolande Harris. He built exquisite instruments for numerous artists, including Laetitia Sonami's (France/USA) "Lady's Glove," an evening wear take on virtual reality controllers (see figure top, next page); Jonathan Impett's (UK) "Meta-Trumpet," a trumpet extended with ultra-sound position sensors, valve movement detectors, and additional switches; and Michel Waisvisz's (Netherlands) "Hands II" free-air gestural controller for computer music.

Sukandar Kartadinata (Germany) has been developing hardware and software tools for numerous artists since the early-1990s, including a hacked greeting card anklet for violinist Jane Henry (USA) (see figure bottom, next page and track 16 on the CD), computer-controlled ratchet noise-makers for German installation

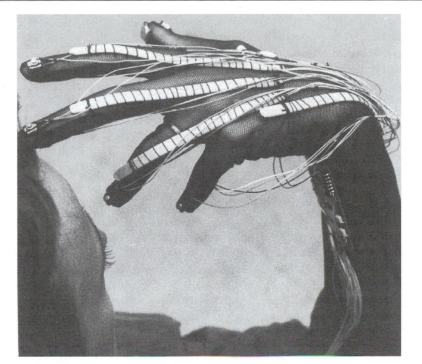

Laetitia Sonami, "Lady's Glove, v. 4," gestural computer music controller, built by Bert Bongers after a prototype by Laetitia Sonami.

artist Jens Brand, and software/hardware hybrid instruments for Richard Barrett (UK/Germany), Annette Begerow (Germany), Steve Coleman (USA), Axel Dörner (Germany), Walter Fabeck (UK), Sabine Schaefer (Germany). In 2004 he designed the "Gluion," a general purpose, configurable interface between sensors and computers (see figure 29.3).

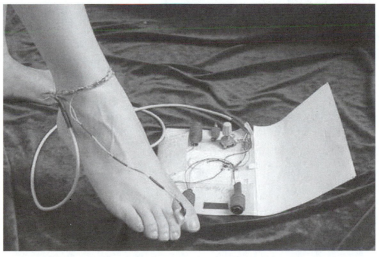

"Chipsaw," hacked musical greeting card anklet bracelet, designed for Jane Henry by Sukandar Kartadinata.

Bielecki, Bongers and Kartadinata are virtuosos of "glue" technology—the seamless integration of hardware and software to solve problems that slip between the cracks of commercially available solutions. As with master printers, these designers are true collaborators, whose technical expertise and imagination result not only in workable solutions, but also in new inspirations and directions for the artists with whom they work.

No list of resources for the befuddled artist would be complete without mention of STEIM—the Studio for Electro-Instrumental Music (or, in Dutch, Stichting voor Elektro-Instrumentale Muziek). Founded in 1968, STEIM (in Amsterdam), remains a spiritual retreat and think tank for musical innovation; through its residency program hundreds of artists have been helped to realize ambitious, heartfelt, and often impractical projects.

STEIM's SensorLab (see figure 29.1), which translated sensor data directly into MIDI, and also let you program sophisticated interpretations of that data in a C-like language—a complete run-time computer music instrument, sadly no longer in production at the time of writing.

The I-Cube from Infusion Systems and Eric Singer's MidiTron are less expensive, computer-configurable, sensor-to-MIDI interfaces that can control MIDI devices directly or can connect to a computer for further processing of the raw sensor data. CH Products manufactures an inexpensive joystick development circuit board that lets you read thirty-two switches and ten analog channels through your USB port (see figure 29.2). Sukandar Kartadinata's "Gluion" is a high-speed Ethernet interface that can be configured for a wide range of sensors (see figure 29.3). Similar systems are available from a number of other sources. Prices range from under one hundred dollars to several thousand dollars. Some of these interfaces are bi-directional, allowing you to send control information through them to external relays, motors, etc., as well as receive data from various sensors.

But there is a cheaper (if tackier) solution that should appeal to someone who's made it through this book: hack a game pad.

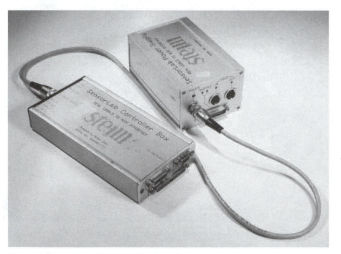

Figure 29.1 The STEIM SensorLab.

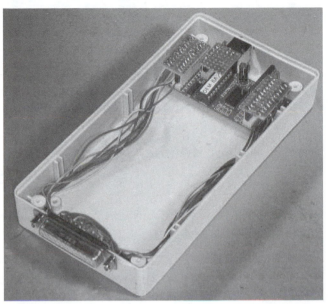

Figure 29.2 Sensor-to-USB interface built with CH Products interface board (open).

Oh Joy!

Most controllers for computer games—joysticks, game pads, etc.—consist of a microprocessor that translates the state of various switches and analog sensors into data that is sent to the computer via the USB interface. Some of these devices make excellent musical controllers in their own right—a good joystick gives several axes of motion that can be mapped to various aspects of your sound (pitch bend, modulation, filtering, etc.); this can be used by itself or in conjunction with a standard MIDI device (such as a keyboard) for very expressive musical control. A wireless game controller liberates you from sitting in front of your laptop like an accountant. And joysticks and game pads are cheap: they can be had for under $20 new (wireless ones cost a bit more).

All you need is software that accepts USB data from an external device. Programming languages such as Max, SuperCollider, and PD have objects or routines that receive USB data and configure it to control any aspect of your program. "JunXion," STEIM's elegant little utility, maps any USB data directly to MIDI; this MIDI output can then be used to

Figure 29.3 The Gluion.

Figure 29.4 Open game pad showing rubberized switch pads.

control a synthesizer or sampler directly, or can be patched within the computer to any music software that accepts MIDI control.

When you get tired of the fighter pilot imagery of joystick-controlled electronic music, it's time to get out the screwdriver and get down to work. As with the toys we hacked earlier in the book, it is the work of but a moment to remove any of the switches or joysticks and replace them with external variants. Sometimes simply rearranging the layout of switches and other controls changes the way you play them: replacing the cluster of trigger buttons with a line of switches can transform a Top Gun weapon into a musical instrument; substituting photoresistors or pressure pads for the pots in the joystick opens up new gestural options.

The first step is to boot up a program that can be controlled by the stock game pad *before* you start to hack it. Make sure all switches, joysticks, and other sensors are working, and familiarize yourself with what each one does. This way after you make component substitutions you have a reference for the correct functioning of the interface.

Now open the game pad (see figure 29.4). The hacks themselves are pretty simple. Most switches on game pads are the kind you're probably familiar with from toys: conductive rubber "hats" that press down against gold interlocking traces on the circuit board (see figure 29.5).

Figure 29.5 Switch pads removed to reveal switch traces on circuit board.

Figure 29.6 Switch pad traces with wires soldered on for remote switch.

To attach a different kind of switch simply solder one end of a thin flexible insulated wire to each half of the trace network (see figure 29.6), and solder the other ends to the contacts on your new switch (as we did with photoresistors in chapter 22). Sometimes you can find a hole through the switch trace somewhere nearby—it's easier to solder to one of these, if available.

As we observed in chapter 18, a joystick consists of two pots positioned so that when you move the stick front-to-back it rotates the shaft of one pot, while movement side-to-side rotates the other; complex movements are parsed into x–y data from the two pots interacting. If you look at the circuit board under the joystick, you should notice three solder pads in a line under each of the pots (see figure 29.7).

The "ears" of the pot (A and C) are soldered to the end pads, and the "nose" (B) to the center pad. Typically the pot is configured as a "voltage divider": one end pad is connected to ground, one to a positive voltage. As the pot rotates, the center tap puts out a voltage that varies between ground and the positive reference. This voltage is read by the

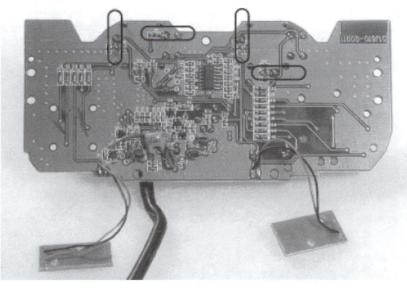

Figure 29.7 Joystick solder pads (outlined with black oval).

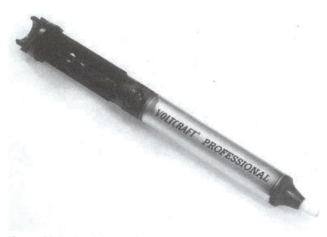

Figure 29.8 A solder sucker.

microprocessor and sent down the USB cable as a numeric value. To hook up an external pot or other analog sensor you first need to remove the joystick. A "solder sucker" is a useful tool here (see figure 29.8): melt the solder at each pot pad with your soldering iron and use the vacuum of the solder sucker to extract as much of the solder as possible from around the connection (see figure 29.9). There may be additional solder joints between the mechanical framework of the joystick and the circuit board; clear these out as well.

When all the pads have been cleared of solder gently pry the joystick off the board (see figure 29.10). You may need to apply the tip of the soldering iron to various connections to melt last traces of solder as you wiggle the joystick free—this is not a pretty job. Once the joystick is removed, solder flexible insulated wire to each hole in the pot triple-sets (see figure 29.11).

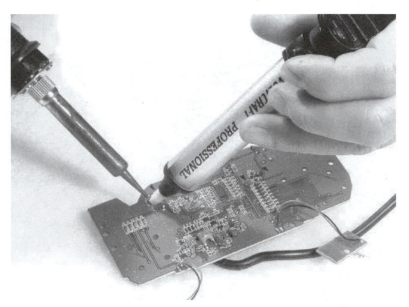

Figure 29.9 Sucking solder.

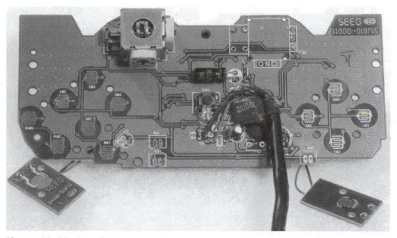

Figure 29.10 Joystick removed.

These wires can now be connected to any electronic component that can either function as a "voltage divider," or generate its own output voltage in the range between ground and the "+" voltage present at the solder pad of the other ear of the removed pot. For example, figure 29.12 shows a simple photoresistor-based voltage divider that you can swap into any place occupied by a pot.

Solder the points labeled "A," "B," and "C" to the pads on the circuit board previously occupied by same terminals on the joystick pot you removed. The photoresistor changes resistance as light level fluctuates (you know this already). The replacement pot sets the operating range of the voltage divider—start with a 1mOhm pot. Run your test program (see above) and vary the light on the photoresistor. Adjust the pot until light variation produces the same range of values in your program that the corresponding axis of the original joystick did. You may need to substitute a larger or smaller pot for the 1mOhm one shown in figure 29.12. When you find a setting of the pot that gives you a good range

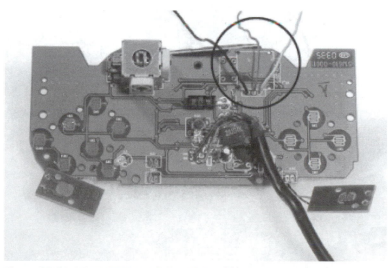

Figure 29.11 Wires attached to joystick solder pads.

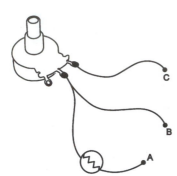

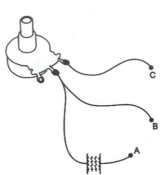

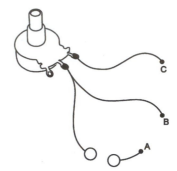

Figure 29.12 Photoresistor voltage divider.

Figure 29.13 Pressure-sensor voltage divider.

Figure 29.14 Electrode voltage divider.

of response you can remove it from the circuit, measure the resistance between the two terminals used (with a multimeter), and substitute a fixed resistor; alternatively, you can keep the pot in circuit, so you can trim the range to suit different light conditions.

To make a squeezable instrument substitute one of our homemade pressure sensors from chapter 15 for the photoresistor in the same basic configuration (see figure 29.13). You can also use this approach to interface electrodes for direct skin control (see figure 29.14). As with the light sensor, adjust the pot to set the range; you can replace the pot with a fixed value resistor (if desired) after determining its value experimentally.

Once you tried various sensor substitutes for the original joystick, the next task is to design an ergonometrically appropriate mechanical configuration for them—i.e., a physical instrument. If you've ever played air guitar on a tennis racket, now is your time to shine. On the other hand, if you're indecisive, slap a bunch of Velcro onto some switches, pots, pressure pads, photoresistors, and add chunks of Styrofoam or wood—voilá—musical Lego! Figure 29.15 shows a stretched wireless game pad.

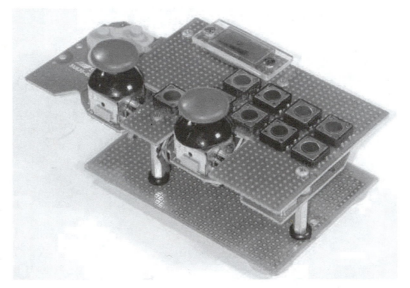

Figure 29.15 A hacked wireless game pad, Nicolas Collins.

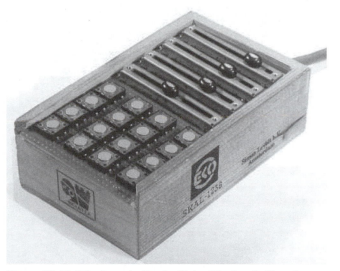

Figure 29.16 Wind controller built by Nicolas Collins from a USB interface, with four slide pots, sixteen switches, and an air pressure sensor.

Beep Beep

Feeling adventurous? A Web search under "sensors" or "robotics" will turn up a dazzling array of gizmos capable of measuring temperature, humidity, distance, weight, air pressure, compass direction, acceleration, gas mixture—you name it. Air pressure sensors make great breath controls for digital wind instruments: the tea box in figure 29.16 combines a breath control (blow into the lady's ear), a few slide pots and sixteen switches to make a sort of usb-melodica. Accelerometers map the movement of hands and bodies. Many pretty sophisticated sensors are surprisingly cheap. In the early days of homemade electronic instruments, all our components seemed to be guilt-laden by-products of the dreaded military-industrial complex. Now, we lap up trickle-down from the automobile industry: pressure sensors control fuel injection systems, accelerometers trigger airbags, compasses keep us on the straight and narrow.

Look for sensors described as having a "voltage output" (as opposed to serial digital data or timed pulses). Download the documentation before you buy anything. You'll typically have to provide power (a battery will usually do, but some sensors are fussy about requiring 5 volts, which means a 9-volt battery will fry them), as well as a ground connection between the sensor and the game pad. Wire the sensor's output to the middle pad of one of the joystick's pots. With luck you'll be in the right range; if not, it's probably easier to trim the data values in software rather than fiddling with resistor values.

Of course you needn't use your new digital instrument exclusively to control sound: digital data is digital data, and can just as easily be used to manipulate video, control the speed of motors, or steer your RC car. It's only a question of software.

Chapter 30

POWER SUPPLIES:
IF YOU MUST, HERE'S HOW TO PLUG INTO THE WALL
WITH MINIMAL RISK

You will need:

- A DC wall-wart plug-in power supply.
- A diode, 1N4004 or equivalent.
- Some capacitors, 0.1 and 100uf or so.
- An 8- or 9-volt positive regulator (LM7808 or 7809).
- Hand tools, test meter, and soldering iron.
- A breadboard on which to test your circuit.
- A solderable circuit board on which to assemble your circuit.
- Some solid and stranded hookup wire.

Oh dear, I feel like a father enrolling his son in a driver education class or explaining safe sex: I wish we could stop here, but one day you will leave home and must be prepared for the big world. This is truly the last chapter of this book.

Although the Second Rule of Hacking barred you from touching an AC power cord, the time will come when batteries will not suffice. You will tire of the cost of replacing them, and the accompanying environmental guilt (although these concerns can be minimized by rechargeable batteries), or you will build a circuit that draws so much current that it drains the battery flat before you can say "Union Carbide." As a stopgap solution to exposing your hands (and heart) to lethal voltages, you can advance to the ubiquitous "wall-wart" that powers so many domestic appliances these days (see figure 30.1).

The power grid in North America delivers to your outlet a sine wave that fluctuates between 0 and 120 volts 60 times per second (in Europe, 240 volts at 50 cycles per second). If you plugged a very strong speaker directly into the wall (not recommended, by the way), you would hear a loud, low pitch around 2 octaves below middle C. The wall-wart consists of a transformer encased in plastic and wired directly to an AC plug. The transformer takes the 120 volts of alternating current (AC) and steps it down to the nonlethal range suitable for powering electronic circuitry. The advantage of the wall-wart supply is that the dangerous voltages remain (in theory) within the plastic lump, and the ends of

Figure 30.1 A typical wall-wart power supply.

the wires present a mild, relatively safe, battery-like voltage. The traditional power supply found inside your TV or guitar amplifier, on the other hand, brings the wall voltage right into the chassis, where it can easily be touched (ouch!) as you tinker. So, if you *must* use a power supply, let the wall-wart be your condom.

There are two kinds of wall-wart. An AC wall-wart consists solely of a step-down transformer; it puts out a low voltage 60 or 50hz signal, which must be further conditioned to make it useful for powering circuitry. A DC wall-wart contains some additional circuitry (a few diodes and a big capacitor, to be specific) required to smooth out the fluctuating signal into a voltage that more closely resembles the steady DC output of a battery.

The wall-wart should be marked with the following information:

- The *primary voltage* that the wall-wart can be plugged into, i.e., 120 (North America) or 240 (Europe) volts AC (VAC). Some modern, "premium" wall-warts handle any input voltage between 100 and 240 volts. Choose the appropriate primary voltage for your country.
- The *secondary voltage* that appears at the loose end of the long dangling wire, i.e., something in the range of 3–24 volts. We need a secondary voltage between 6–18 volts.
- Whether it has an AC or DC output. We need DC.
- The amount of power the transformer can provide, usually measured in watts (W), amps (A or MA), or volt-amps (VA). We want a transformer that puts out a minimum of 100 milliamps (ma), which may be indicated as 0.1 amps or 5–10 watts.

For example, a wall-wart might be labeled "120vac input, 12vdc output, 200 ma." You can find wall-warts everywhere (often cheap) with a zillion slightly different types of connectors. Some offer switchable output voltages and/or interchangeable connectors on the secondary side.

When adapting a battery-powered circuit to a wall-wart you must observe two critical factors:

- The voltage must be within two limits (i.e., greater than 6 volts but less than 18 volts), but the current capability can be anything higher than the minimum need to power the circuit (i.e., a circuit requiring 20 ma can be powered by a supply producing 20 ma, 100 ma, or 1000 ma.)

- Note the polarity of the secondary connector or wires: you must know which is "+" and which is "−" before connecting the wall-wart to your circuit, or fatal pyrotechnics may result.

Sometimes the wall-wart will indicate which wire or which part of the connector is "+" and which is "−," but it is always safer to test using a multimeter. Set the meter to measure "DC Voltage." One probe plugs into the meter's "ground" or "−" input, while the other connects to something probably marked "voltage" in red. Touch one probe to the end of one of the power supply's wires or one part of the connector, and the other to the other. If the meter reads out a voltage with no prefix (i.e., "13.6"), then the wire/connector touching the ground probe is the "−" output, and the other is the "+." But if the meter puts a "−" before the number (i.e., "− 13.6"), you know that the connections are reversed, that the wire touching the minus probe of the meter is actually the "+" output and the other is "−." Confused? Try this test on a nice familiar 9-volt battery. Then test the wall-wart again.

Once you figure out which wire is which, mark them carefully. If the output voltage of your wall-wart measures *less* that 15 volts DC you can connect it directly to your circuit as shown in figure 30.2. You can either find a matching connector to whatever plug is attached to the wall-wart's cord, or you can cut off the plug and solder the wires directly to the board. Double-check the polarity before you plug it in! As a safety precaution against frying your circuit with a backwards power supply, you can connect a diode across the power supply as shown in the figure.

Cheap wall-warts will usually have some "AC ripple" in their voltage output—a sign of skimping on parts in the conversion from AC to DC (you don't get what you don't pay for). A circuit powered with such a supply may hum slightly. Until you get good at designing or finding better power supplies, a battery will usually sound cleaner. One easy fix that sometimes helps is to add a big capacitor, say between 100–10,000uF, between "+" and "−" supply on your circuit board. As mentioned in chapter 18, big electrolytic capacitors have polarity, like a battery, which is marked on the body. Make sure you connect "−" to the ground bus, "+" to "+" supply. Placing an additional 0.1uF capacitor between the "+" and ground supply pins of a chip also helps lower noise and reduce "crosstalk" between different parts of your circuit. Both these capacitors can be seen in figure 30.2.

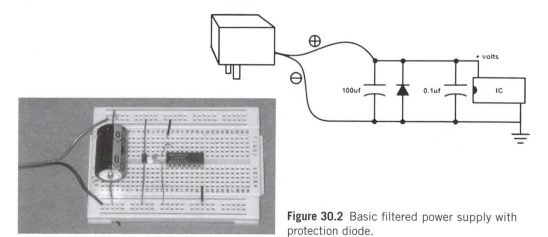

Figure 30.2 Basic filtered power supply with protection diode.

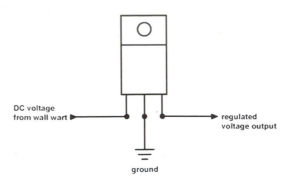

DC voltage
from wall wart ▶

regulated
voltage output

ground

Figure 30.3 Voltage regulator pinout.

Finally, for a really clean supply you should add a simple integrated circuit called a "regulator" (see figure 30.3). A regulator filters out the last of the ripple and sets the voltage to a precise level, which you specify when you select the chip: 7812 = 12 volts, 7805 = 5 volts, etc. A 7809 will accept an input voltage as high as 25 volts or so, and puts out a stable 9 volts, just like the battery we've been using for our circuits. It must have an input voltage at least 3 volts higher than it is expected to put out (i.e., 12 volts in for 9 volts out), so measure the output of your wall-wart with your meter to make sure it is high enough. You can get regulators for a wide range of voltages, should you need them for future projects, but these basic design principles remain the same (see figure 30.4). It's normal for the regulator to get a bit hot—bolt the tab to a piece of metal to dissipate the heat.

The regulator chip not only keeps the supply voltage free of spurious hum and noise, but it lets you be sure of the exact voltage being used to power your circuit. A simple measurement with a meter will show that even though a wall-wart might be marked "12 volts DC" in bright white letters, it could put out anything from 10 to 20 volts. The CMOS chips used in most of our circuits were chosen in part for their forgiving nature, but they have limits—upper limits: they can run on power supplies from 3 volts to about 18 volts, but above 18 volts they can expire quite dramatically. A 9-volt battery sits comfortably between these two extremes, and a 9-volt regulator substitutes neatly for that battery.

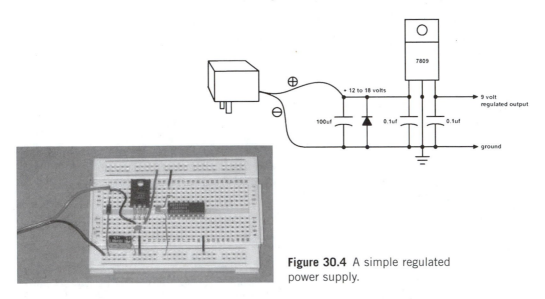

Figure 30.4 A simple regulated power supply.

If you choose to use a wall-wart-based supply that is merely filtered (by capacitors) and not regulated, always measure its actual output voltage and polarity *before* connecting your circuit—don't rely on the markings on its case.

Rule #25: Never trust the writing on the wall-wart.

If the voltage of your wall-wart is greater than 15 volts DC you *must* use a regulator to drop the voltage into a safe range, whether you care about hum or not. Otherwise go out and find one that puts out a lower voltage.

APPENDICES

Appendix A

RESOURCES

The Web

A few years ago I walked into the office of a technically minded colleague at my school to ask for a reference manual in which I could look up the pinout and schematic of an unfamiliar chip. Clamping a large, Chicago-style hand to my shoulder, Ed replied, "Nic, I *could* loan you the book, but let me ask you this: give a man a fish and he's fed for one day, teach him how to fish and he...?" "...wastes all his time fishing when he should be helping out around the house?" I continued. "No," sighed a disappointed Ed. "Type the part number into Google and you will find the data sheet in the first hit," he muttered as he closed the door. The point I missed in his parable: it's never been easier to hack.

In the early days of homemade electronic music, schematics and suggestions were exchanged by word of mouth and sleight of hand, like cures for colicky babies. Then a few dumbed-down circuits crawled out of engineering journals into magazines for electronic hobbyists and aspiring electric guitarists; one or two books appeared, written in something vaguely like English rather than Technese. Finally Tim Berners-Lee birthed the World Wide Web and a hundred fuzztones flowered.

Anything you want to know is out there; all you need to do is find it and understand it. Finding it is easy—understanding it may take some work. You will have to teach yourself a bit more of the vocabulary of electronics than was demanded by this book—you'll need to start reading schematics. As Ed suggested, typing a part number or name of a component will usually retrieve a PDF of a manufacturer's data sheet—here you'll find all the basic information you'll need to start working with it: what pins are connected to power, which are inputs, which are outputs, etc. Enter a descriptive phrase instead ("'Phase Shifter'+schematic") and you'll be directed to any number of wacky Web sites hosted by people who seem to have nothing better to do than compile vast collections of circuit diagrams and provide links to like-minded fanatics. All you need to do is figure out how to translate the schematic onto the breadboard. A little trial and error, persistence, patience, and an occasional glance back at this book should get you there.

Books

PDF data sheets can be downloaded as you need them, but thick data books are still available from the major chip manufacturers—they're expensive, but worth it if you get in deep. Often they include schematics of suggested basic circuits using specific chips, or more detailed "application notes."

There are a several books that can help fill in theoretical gaps between this handbook and the more engineer-oriented data you will find on the Web or in the data books. Don Lancaster's *CMOS Cookbook* (Indianapolis: SAMS Publications, 1977) provides a thorough introduction to the chip family we have misused throughout my book. Walter Jung's *OpAmp Cookbook* (Indianapolis: SAMS Publications, 1974) will introduce you to the component out of which most audio circuits are built, but which I have avoided completely in our designs. Craig Anderton, the grandfather of electronic hacking for musicians, published *Electronic Projects for Musicians* back in 1975 (New York: Amsco Publications) and it's still an excellent guide to basic musical circuits and general principles of design and construction, written in large, reassuring, musician-friendly letters. For super low-tech, "foxhole technology," *Sneaky Uses for Everyday Things* by Cy Tymony (Kansas City: Andrews McMeel Publishing, 2003) is a wonderful source of circuit designs built from little more than stationary supplies, salt, spare change, and wet paper towel. Reed Ghazala, the patron saint of Circuit Bending, has recently put out a book that is an excellent companion to the one you are reading now: Reed Ghazala, *Circuit Bending: Build Your Own Alien Instruments*. New York: Wiley Publications, 2005.

Stuff

What holds true for information also goes for material resources. Although the Big Apple's Canal Street no longer teems with the warrens of weird electronic and mechanical surplus shops that enthralled me throughout my childhood, the Web has become a virtual medina of the misplaced and unwanted. Add "+price" to the search field after anything you desire—plugs, piezo disks, tape heads, tilt-switches—and you'll soon find a place to buy it. Since you're not manufacturing missiles or airbags in quantity, you'll need to find a source that will sell to the common man or woman. For ICs, resistors, capacitors, and other small components a straightforward electronic retailer is probably the best bet. As of the time of writing some good sources that stock a wide range of parts include Digikey (www.digikey.com) and Jameco (www.jameco.com).

For hackable gizmos, used equipment, pots, jacks, boxes and general inspiration, however, you must try the "surplus" outlets. Here are a few reputable sources that have been around for a while selling cool stuff:

All Electronics: www.allelectronics.com
Marlin P. Jones: www.mpja.com
Electronic Goldmine: www.goldmine-elec.com
B.G. Micro: www.bgmicro.com
Surplus Shed: www.surplusshed.com

Paia is a longstanding manufacturer of kits for building everything from modular synthesizers to an electronic wind-chimes: www.paia.com. Velleman (www.velleman. be) and a few other companies (mostly European) make kits for a wide range of circuits, from amplifiers to zappers-of-bugs. A convenient source in North America is Quality Kits in Kingston, Ontario: www.qkits.com. Another useful kit outlet is Ramsey Electronics: www.Ramseykits.com.

The Web knows no national boundaries, but the U.S. Post Office does. The above U.S. sources will charge a premium for shipping abroad. In England Maplin (www.maplin.co.uk) carries a wide range of components. In Germany, Conrad Electronics is a good bet (and they have retails shops in Berlin and several other cities): www.conrad.de. RS Components is a full range dealer of new parts that delivers across Europe: http://rswww.com.

For impulse shopping in Yourtown, USA there's always Radio Shack, which is also available online (www.radioshack.com).

Finally, I am pleased to report that the authentic, old-fashioned "electronic junkyard" is not entirely extinct. As I write this I have just returned from a delirious crawl through Apex Surplus at 8909 San Fernando Road in Sun Valley, California. Their overstuffed shelves and murky corridors abound with fifty years of electronic technology and just plain weird stuff. The Web address is www.apexelectronic.com but this is no time for a virtual experience—having read this book you owe it to yourself to visit Apex once before you (or it) die—even if you never get to Mecca, Jerusalem, or St. Peters. Weird Stuff Warehouse (www.weirdstuff.com) in Sunnyvale, California, is the elephant graveyard of obsolete computers and computer accessories—just the place to pick up a fully functional Fat Mac. American Science and Surplus in Chicago (www.sciplus.com) has provided my students with a wide range of excellent materials. The Axeman, with several locations in the Minneapolis/St. Paul area, includes a fair amount of electronic parts amongst a wide range of general surplus material (such as East German crossing guard blinking braces). There are many other wonderful stores around the country, I've been told, but these are ones I have visited and can personally vouch for.

Cultural Artifacts

The music made by the artists mentioned in this book is, with few exceptions, not only unavailable on major labels, but unlikely to be found on most file sharing sites. Individual artist Web sites are a good start, and I've included as many as possible in Appendices B and E. An excellent, non-Amazon source for CDs, books and periodicals of fringe music is CDemusic (http://www.cdemusic.org).

Two good general histories of electronic music, featuring many of the artists discussed in this book, are:

Joel Chadabe, *Electric Sound — The Past and Promise of Electronic Music*. New York, Prentice Hall, 1997.
Thom Holmes, *Electronic And Experimental Music* (second edition). New York: Routledge, 2002.

Leonardo Music Journal (http://mitpress2.mit.edu/Leonardo/lmj/) has for many years published writings by experimental musicians and sound artists, and is a rare source of first person accounts of struggles with circuits.

Appendix B

REFERENCES AND NOTES:
WHO'S WHO AND WHAT'S WHAT

The following Web sites, books, periodicals, and recordings are relevant to specific chapters. For many of the people and things referenced in the text Web sites are the fastest, most economical first step towards learning more.

Forward
David Behrman: www.lovely.com/bios/behrman.html
Henry Cowell: http://www.schirmer.com/composers/cowell_bio.html
Conlon Nancarrow: http://www.tomate.com.mx/nancarrow/
Harry Partch: http://www.corporeal.com/
David Tudor: see "David Tudor and 'Rainforest'", chapter 8.
Gordon Mumma: www.brainwashed.com/mumma/
    www.lovely.com/bios/mumma.html
Max/MSP: http://www.cycling74.com/

Introduction
John Cage: see "John Cage", chapter 7.
Don Buchla: see "The Luthiers", chapter 29.
STEIM: see "The Cracklebox", chapter 11, and "The Luthiers", chapter 29.

Chapter 1: Getting Started
Weller soldering irons are the choice of the serious hacker: http://www.cooperhandtools.com/brands/weller/

Chapter 3: Circuit Sniffing
Irdial records (http://www.irdial.com) has been involved in some of the more arcane aspects of radio culture—the
    "Conet Project" CD set documents the bizarre phenomenon of shortwave "number readers."

Mortal Coils
Leon Theremin: there are hundreds of Web sites devoted to Thermin and his instruments, but this one, by his niece,
    is a good place to start: http://www.lydiakavina.com/therem.html
    Another, with a good bibliography: http://www.thereminworld.com/pubs.asp
    And Steven Martin's film is wonderful and available on video: "Theremin: An Electronic Odyssey" (1994).
Gert-Jan Prins: http://www.gjp.info/

Alvin Lucier: http://alucier.web.wesleyan.edu/
> A recording of "Sferics" can be found on *Sferics*, Lovely Music, Ltd. VR 1017, 1988.
> A collection of interviews, writings, and scores by Alvin Lucier: Alvin Lucier, *Reflections. Interviews, Scores, Writings (Reflexionen, Interviews, Notationen, Texte)*, English-German Edition, MusikTexte, Köln, 1995.

Karlheinz Stockhausen: http://www.stockhausen.org/
Disinformation: http://www.irislight.demon.co.uk/
> http://www.ashinternational.com/

Joyce Hinterding: http://www.sunvalleyresearch.com/Luminoska/index2.htm
Haco: http://www.japanimprov.com/haco/
> Haco. *Stereo Bugscope 00*. Improvised Music from Japan, IMJ-523, 2004.

David First: http://www.davidfirst.com/
> "TellTale 2.1," *A Call for Silence*. London: Sonic Arts Network CD/book, 2004.

Andy Keep. "My Laptop Colony, Colony In My Laptop" *A Call for Silence*. London: Sonic Arts Network CD/book, 2004.
Jérôme Noetinger: http://www.metamkine.com/
Lorin Parker: http://music.calarts.edu/~lorinp/

Chapter 5: The Celebrated Jumping Speaker of Bowers County
For information on John Bowers see "Circuit Bending", chapter 15.

Chapter 7: How to Make a Contact Mike
A good history of piezoelectricity: http://www.piezo.com/history.html
Information on Plastidip: http://www.plastidip.com/consumer/index.html

John Cage—The Father of Invention
Some good Cage Web sites:
> http://www.music.princeton.edu/~jwp/texts/worklist.html
> http://www.johncage.info/
> https://www.edition-peters.com/
> http://212.96.130.213/CSS%20Files/composers/JCage%20bio.htm

Read this: John Cage, *Silence: Lectures and Writing*, Wesleyan University Press, 1961.
Lou Harrison: http://www.newalbion.com/artists/harrisonl/

Piezo Music
Hugh Davies, *Sounds Heard*, Soundword, Chelmsford, UK, 2002.
Richard Lerman: http://www.west.asu.edu/rlerman/
Peter Cusack, *Baikal Ice*, ReR CD, 2004.
Collin Olan, *Rec01, Listen 001*, Apestraartjje CD, 2002.
Eric Leonardson: http://pages.ripco.net/~eleon/

Chapter 8: Turn You Tiny Wall Into a Speaker
An informative history of the spring reverb: http://www.accutronicsreverb.com/history.htm
Rolen Star Audio Transducer: http://www.rolen-star.com/
Bass Shakers: http://www.aurasound.com/
Soundbug: http://www.feonic.com/fr.asp?section=products

David Tudor and Rainforest
The David Tudor quote is from "From Piano to Electronics," *Music and Musicians* V.20, August 1972, interview with Victor Schonfeld.
Tudor Web sites: http://www.emf.org/tudor/
> http://www.getty.edu/research/conducting_research/digitized_collections/davidtudor/
"Composers Inside Electronics—Music After David Tudor," *Leonardo Music Journal* Vol. 14, 2004.

Drivers
For information on Alvin Lucier see "Mortal Coils" chapter 3.
Alvin Lucier, "Music For Solo Performer." Lovely Music, Ltd. VR 1014, 1982.

Ute Wassermann with Windy Gong: "Improvised Music From Solitude in Eleven Parts," CD, animato acd 6008-3, Germany. 1994.

Nicolas Collins: www.NicolasCollins.com

> Collins' backwards electric guitar can be heard on:
>> *Sound Without Picture, Periplum Records, 1999.*
>> *It Was A Dark And Stormy Night, Trace Elements Records, 1992.*

E-bow: (http://www.ebow.com/)

Felix Hess, *Light As Air*. Heidelberg, Germany: Stadgalerie Saarbrücken, Kehrer Verlag, 2001.

Chapter 9: Tape Heads
Tape

Alvin Lucier, *I am sitting in a room*, Lovely Music, Ltd., 1981/1990.

Steve Reich, "Come Out", on *Steve Reich: Early Works*, Nonesuch Records, 1987.

Pauline Oliveros, "I of IV" on *New Sounds in Electronic Music: works of Oliveros, Reich, Maxfield*; Odyssey Records, 1967.

Terry Riley, *A Rainbow in Curved Air*, CBS Masterworks, 1969/1990.

Nam June Paik, Random Access: http://www.nydigitalsalon.org/10/artwork.php?nav=artists&artwork=13

Laurie Anderson: http://www.laurieanderson.com/

> The Tape Bow Violin can be heard on:
>> "*Three Walking Songs (for Tape Bow Violin)" from United States Pt. 1.*
>> "*Sax Solo (for Tape Bow Violin)" from United States Pt. 1.*
>> "*I Dreamed I Had To Take a Test..." from United States Pt. 3.*

> The quote is from: Laurie Anderson. *The Record of the Time*. Lyon: Musée Art Contemporain Lyon, 2002.

Mark Trayle: http://shoko.calarts.edu/~met

> Mark Trayle, "Free Enterprise: Virtual Capital and Counterfeit Music at the End of the Century", in *Leonardo Music Journal* vol. 9, 1999.

Chapter 10: A Simple Air Mike

Rob Danielson has done extensive experiments with electret microphone elements. His Web site lists many resources for mike builders: http://www.uwm.edu/~type/

An excellent guide to amplifying *any* instrument (on a small budget) is: Bart Hopkin, *Getting a Bigger Sound: Pickups and Microphones for Your Musical Instrument*. Tucson, AZ: Sharp Press, 2003. Hopkin covers making and using coil pickups, contact mikes and air mikes.

A great resource for budget-bound audio experimenters is the *Tape Op—The Creative Music Recording Magazine* (http://www.tapeop.com). They review gear, publish how-to articles, interview independent music engineers and artists, and provide an excellent useful resource for alternative recording practice.

Chapter 11: Laying of Hands
The Crackle Box

For a detailed history of the Cracklebox go to: http://www.crackle.org/CrackleBox.htm

To purchase a Cracklebox go to: http://www.steim.org/steim/cracklebox.php

Chapter 14: Ohm's Law For Dummies
Composing Inside Electronics

An excellent resource on the history of the San Francisco Bay area music scene can be found at: http://o-art.org/history/index.html

Center for Contemporary Music at Mills College: http://www.mills.edu/academics/undergraduate/mus/center_contemporary_music.php

Robert Ashley: http://www.lovely.com/bios/ashley.html

> "Music With Roots in the Aether" (1976), Ashley's video portrait of seven American composers, provides an excellent insight into the Zeitgeist of the post-Cagean culture of "seat of the pants" electronic music.

Kenneth Atchley: http://www.katch.com/

John Bischoff: http://www.johnbischoff.net/

> Douglas Kahn, "A Musical Technography of John Bischoff", in *Leonardo Music Journal*, vol. 14, 2004.

Chris Brown: http://www.cbmuse.com/

Laetitia de Compiegne Sonami: http://www.sonami.net/

Scott Gresham-Lancaster: http://www.o-art.org/Scot/
Frankie Mann: http://www.lovely.com/bios/mann.html
Tim Perkis: http://www.perkis.com
Mark Trayle: see "Tape", chapter 9.
Nicolas Collins: see "Drivers", chapter 8.
Ron Kuivila: http://framework.v2.nl/archive/archive/node/actor/default.xslt/nodenr-65793
Serge Tcherepnin: http://www.serge-fans.com/history.htm
Paul De Marinis: http://www.well.com/~demarini/
Voice Crack: http://homepage.hispeed.ch/bots/
        http://www.moeslang.com
Jim Horton: http://mitpress2.mit.edu/e-journals/Leonardo/lmj/horton.html
The Kim 1: http://www.kim-1.com/
        An excellent insider's history of the emergence of early microcomputer music from the Bay area home-made
        circuitry scene can be found at: http://crossfade.walkerart.org/brownbischoff/introduction_main.html

Chapter 15: Beyond the Pot
Suggestions for making batteries from fruits, vegetables, spare change, salt, and wet paper towel can be found in: Cy
        Tymony, *Sneaky Uses for Everyday Things*. Kansas City: Andrews McMeel Publishing, 2003.

Circuit Bending
Reed Ghazala: http://www.anti-theory.com
        Reed Ghazala, *Circuit Bending: Build Your Own Alien Instruments*. New York: Wiley Publications, USA,
        2005.
Experimental Musical Instruments: http://www.windworld.com/
Bent 2004: http://www.thetanknyc.org/bent2004/
The Phil Archer quotation is from personal correspondence.
Phil Archer: http://www.studios.uea.ac.uk/people/staff/archer
John Bowers: http://www.n2nr.net
Bowers, J., and Archer, P. "Not Hyper, Not Meta, Not Cyber but Infra-Instruments." In Proceedings of NIME,05
        (New Interfaces for Musical Expression), May 26–28, 2005, Vancouver, BC, Canada. Downloadable from
        http://hct.ece.ubc.ca/nime/2005.
The Sarah Washington quotation is from personal correspondence.
A good web site for information on the British Circuit Bending scene is: http://www.lektrolab.com/

Chapter 17: Jack, Pack and Batt
Peter Zummo: http://www.frogpeak.org/fpartists/fpzummo.htm

Chapter 18: World's Simplest Oscillator
For general information on the CMOS family of Integrated Circuits, suggested applications, and a hands-on primer
        in binary logic get a copy of:
        Donald Lancaster, *CMOS Cookbook*. Indianapolis, IN: SAMS Publications, 1977.
For a great example of early photoresistor-controlled oscillators, listen to:
        David Behrman, "Runthrough," on *Wave Train*, Alga Marghen CD, 1998.

Chapter 22: On/Off
Numerous discussions on the virtues of optical gates, compressors and the like can be found in *Tape Op Magazine*
        (see references for chapter 10).
Lowell Cross: see "Visual Music", chapter 25.
"Bruit Secret": http://arthist.binghamton.edu/duchamp/Hidden%20Noise.html

Chapter 23: Amplification and Distortion
Craig Anderton: see "The Luthiers", chapter 29, and Appendix A.
Robert Poss: http://www.distortionistruth.com/
Robert Poss. "Distortion is Truth." *Leonardo Music Journal*. Vol. 8, 1998.

Chapter 25: Video Music/Music Video

Soundhack: http://www.soundhack.com/
Big Eye: http://www.steim.org/steim/bigeye.html
Jitter: http://www.cycling74.com/products/jitter.html

Visual Music

Nam June Paik, "Magnet TV": http://www.nydigitalsalon.org/10/artwork.php?artwork=27
Bill Viola: http://www.billviola.com/
Billy Roisz: http://gnu.klingt.org/
Watts/Behrman/Diamond, "Cloud Music": http://www.vasulka.org/Kitchen/PDF_Eigenwelt/pdf/152-154.pdf
Yasunao Tone: http://www.lovely.com/bios/tone.html
> *Yasunao Tone* (Asphodel Ltd., Asphodel 2011), 2003.
> *Solo for Wounded CD* (Tzadik, TZ-7212), 1997.
Lowell Cross: http://www.LowellCross.com
> http://www.8ung.at/fzmw/2001/2001T1.htm
Lowell Cross, "'Reunion': John Cage, Marcel Duchamp, Electronic Music and Chess." *Leonardo Music Journal*, Vol. 9, 1999.
Stephen Vitiello: http://www.stephenvitiello.com/
> http://www.ubu.com/sound/vitiello.html
For Norbert Möslang see "Composing Inside Electronics", chapter 14.
BMBCon: http://www.bmbcon.demon.nl/con/
Jon Satrom: http://infosuperweb.info/jon/satrom/projects/-/vitch/
Arthur Elsenaar and Remko Scha, "Electric Body Manipulation as Performance Art: A Historical Perspective." *Leonardo Music Journal*, Vol. 12, 2002.

Chapter 26: LCD Art

For more information on making batteries from fruit and vegetables see notes to chapter 15.

Chapter 29: Analog to Digital Conversion, Really

Leroy Anderson: see "The Typewriter" on http://www.leroy-anderson.com/html/hearthemusic.htm
SensorLab: http:/www.steim.org/ steim/products.htmlwww.steim.org/steim/sensor.html
I-Cube: http://infusionsystems.com/
MidiTron: http://www.ericsinger.com/
CH Products: http://www.chproducts.com/oem_flash/misc_usbkit.html
Gluion: http://www.glui.de/prod/gluion.html
JunXion: http://www.steim.org/steim/junxion.html
As long as you're hacking game controllers you might read up on their history: J. C. Herz, *Joystick Nation*, Abacus (Little and Brown), 1997.
An excellent overview of the general theory of the design of physical interfaces for computers can be found in: Bert Bongers, "Interaction with Our Electronic Environment – an E-cological Approach to Physical Interface Design", Cahier 34, Academie voor Digitale Comunicatie, Hogeschool van Utrecht, Utrecht (NL), 2004.

The Luthiers

Robert Moog: http://www.moogmusic.com
Donald Buchla: http://www.buchla.com
Serge Tcherepnin: http://www.serge-fans.com/history.htm
Craig Anderton: http://www.craiganderton.com/
Craig Anderton, *Electronic Projects for Musicians*. New York: AMSCO Publications, 1975.
Bob Bielecki: http://www.bard.edu/academics/faculty/faculty.php?action=details&id=120
Bert Bongers: http://www.xs4all.nl/~bertbon/
Laetitia Sonami: see "Composing Inside Electronics", chapter 14.
Jonathan Impett: http://www.uea.ac.uk/mus/staff/academic/impett.html
Michel Waisvisz: see "The Cracklebox", chapter 11.
> http://www.crackle.org/
Sukandar Kartadinata: http://www.glui.de
STEIM: http://www.steim.org/steim/
Jane Henry: www.janehenry.com

Appendix C

TOOLS AND MATERIALS NEEDED

This is a list of the essential supplies needed to do the projects in this book. Most can be obtained from a variety of sources. I have listed online outlets that stocked the parts at reasonable prices as of December 2005 Be advised that the stock of "surplus" retailers can fluctuate wildly; when the specified part vanishes, however, there's often an acceptable alternative available from the same vendor. Most of the designs are forgiving of a wide range of component variation and substitution; those few items that are critical and should not be substituted without due care and attention have been noted in the list. You should be able to pick up all the needed parts for under $50; tools might set you back another $25–$50.

I have not specified in this list all the scrounged objects, such as tape heads, and loudspeakers, as these are best hunted locally, following the advice in specific chapters.

Source Key

The four major sources for the materials needed are indicated as follows:

AE = www.allelectronics.com (All Electronics)
J = www.jameco.com (Jameco)
RS = www.radioshack.com (Radio Shack)
MPJA = www.mpja.com (Marlin P. Jones)

Within Europe the major source is:

RS Components = http://rswww.com

Tools

The tools needed to do the projects in this book are:

Good soldering iron, with as fine a tip as possible; 15–60 Watts.
Roll of "rosin-core" electrical solder (not "acid core" solder, which is used for plumbing and metalwork).
Battery-powered amplifier
RS: 277-1008, $12.99

Or an amplifier kit, with a scrounged speaker added:
 MPJA: Kit 17, #6017KT, $4.06
 MPJA: Kit 27, #6027KT, $4.69
Assorted patchcords to connect to amplifier from various jacks.
Prototyping breadboard:
 AE: PB-400, $3.00
Inexpensive digital multimeter (voltage, resistance, current).
Small diagonal wire cutters, suitable for light gauge wire.
Simple wire strippers, suitable for light gauge wire.
Set of small screwdrivers (sometimes called "jeweler's screwdrivers"), flat and Phillips
 tips, suitable for opening electronic toys, portable radios, etc.
"Sharpie" style fine-tipped permanent marker.
Roll of insulating electrical tape.
Flashlight.
Small saw for plastic and metal.
Double-stick tape.
Files.
Electric drill and bits.
Small spring clamps or clothespins (nonconductive: plastic or wood, not metal).
Scissors.
Utility knife.
Swiss Army knife—always useful.

Parts and Supplies

Additional parts and supplies needed to work on projects in this book are listed below.
Just to be on the safe side, always pick up a spare or two especially if the part is cheap. All
costs are approximate and are listed in US dollars.

Pcs = pieces (each number of pieces needed will be specified). Where two prices are
separated by a "/" the first number equals the cost for 1–10 pieces; the second equals the
cost for 10–100 pieces (i.e., $0.35/0.30).

Insulated wire, 22–24 gauge, stranded, approximately 20 feet.
Insulated wire, 22–24 gauge, solid, approximately 20 feet.
Shielded audio cable, 1 conductor + shield, lightweight (as thin as possible), approxi-
 mately 20 feet.
Can of "Plasti-Dip" tool handle insulation paint; $13.00.
Plastic terminal barrier strip, 1 piece.
 AE: TB-20, $2.10
 RSUK: 725-061
Sheet of antistatic foam (used for packaging Integrated Circuits).
 J: 13864, $7.95 (1pc 24"x 12"x 1/4")
5: 1/8" (3.5mm) male plugs (if you are using an amplifier with 1/8" input and output
 jacks—otherwise select appropriate jacks for your amplifier).
 AE: PMP, $0.35/$0.30
 RSUK: 449-994

5: 1/8" (3.5mm) female jacks (or 1/4" female jacks if you are working with that standard)
  AE: MJW-8, $0.30/$0.20
  RSUK: 454-249
2: piezo disks (1.36")
  AE: PE-35, $0.75/$0.50
4: 9-volt battery connector clips
  AE: BST-3, $0.25/$0.15
  RSUK: 489-021
10: test leads with alligator clips at each end
  AE: MTL-10, $2.50/10 pcs
1: telephone pickup coil
  AE: TPX-1, $1.50
1: audio output transformer
  RS: 273-1380, $2.99 (this part is difficult to find from any other vendor)
6: 1.0 megOhm linear taper potentiometers
  J: 29065, $0.99/$0.79
4: audio taper potentiometers
  10kOhm: AE: ATP-10K, $0.50
  or 20kOhm: AE: AP-20K, $0.50
6: photocells
  J: 120310, $1.20/$1.09 (this is a very good, wide range part, preferable to most others I've found)
Resistor Assortment, common values (most important values are 1k, 2.2k, 10k, 100k, and 1meg—if you wish to buy them something less than a full set get 10 of each of these).
  RS: 271-308, $5.99 (100 pcs)
Capacitor assortment; most values are not critical. Any general purpose capacitor assortment that covers this range will do:
  monolithic ceramic caps
      10: 10pf; J: 15333, $0.07/$0.06
      10: 100pf; J: 15341, $0.05/$0.035
      10: 0.01uf; J: 25507, $0.09/$0.06; RSUK: 829-586
      10: 0.1uf,; J: 25523, $0.07/$0.06; RSUK: 829-615
  electrolytic caps
      10: 1.0uf; J: 29832, $0.057/$0.048; RSUK: 324-5543
      10: 10.0uf, J:198838, $0.045/$0.03, RSUK: 324-5593
      10: 47uf, J:31114, $0.06/$0.05, RSUK: 324-5492
6: LEDs
  J: 152864EF, $0.24/$0.19
6: small signal diodes (1N914 or equiv.)
1: phototransistor
  J: 112168, $0.30/$0..24
3: 74C14 Hex Schmitt Trigger Integrated Circuit (all Integrated Circuits should be "dual in-line package," not "surface mount").
  These MUST NOT BE 74AC14 or R HC14, ONLY 74C14!
  J: 44257, $0.35/$0.31

3: CD4093 Quad NAND Schmitt Trigger Integrated Circuit
    J: 13400, $0.25/$0.19
    RSUK: 345-5728
2: CD4040 Binary Divider Integrated Circuit
    J: 12950, $0.29/$0.19
    RSUK: 345-5475
2: CD4049 Hex Inverter Integrated Circuit
    J: 13055, $0.24/$0.21
1: LM386N-3 Power Amplifier Integrated Circuit
    J: 24133, $0.59/$0.49
    RSUK: 414-6318
1: 8 pin DIP IC socket
    J: 51570, $0.07/$0.06
4: 14 pin DIP IC socket
    J: 112213EF, $0.10/$0.075
RSUK: 402-765
2: 16 pin DIP IC socket
    J: 112221EF, $0.13/$0.115
    RSUK: 402-771
1: PC board
    R: 276-0170, $2.99
2: 9-volt batteries for circuit breadboarding
A portable radio (see chapter 11).
An electronic toy (see chapter 12).
Batteries for radio and toys, as needed.

THE RULES OF HACKING

Rule #1: Fear not (chapter 2)!

Rule #2: Don't take apart anything that plugs directly into the wall (chapter 2).

Rule #3: It is easier to take something apart than put it back together (chapter 2).

Rule #4: Make notes of what you are doing as you go along, not after (chapter 2).

Rule #5: Avoid connecting the battery backwards (chapter 2).

Rule #6: Many hacks are like butterflies: beautiful but short-lived (chapter 2).

Rule #7: In general try to avoid short circuits (chapter 2).

Rule #8: In electronics some things are reversible with interesting results, but some things are reversible only with irreversible results (chapter 4).

Rule #9: Use shielded cable to make all audio connections longer than 8," unless they go between an amplifier and a speaker (chapter 7).

Rule #10: Every audio connection consists of two parts: the signal and a ground reference (chapter 7).

Rule #11: Don't drink and solder (chapter 7).

Rule #12: After a hacked circuit crashes you may need to disconnect and reconnect the batteries before it will run again (chapter 13).

Rule #13: The net value of two resistors connected in parallel is a little bit less than the smaller of the two resistors; the net value of two resistors connected in series is the sum of the two resistors (Ohm's Law for Dummies; chapter 14).

Rule #14: Kick me off if I stick (Zummo's rule; chapter 17).

Rule #15: You can always substitute a larger 1.5-volt battery for a smaller one, just make sure you use the same number of batteries, in the same configuration (chapter 17).

Rule #16: It's always safer to use separate batteries for separate circuits (chapter 17).

Rule #17: If it sounds good and doesn't smoke, don't worry if you don't understand it (chapter 18).

Rule #18: Start simple and confirm that the circuit still works after every addition you make (chapter 18).

Rule #19: Always leave you original breadboard design intact and functional until you can prove that the soldered-up version works (chapter 19).

Rule #20: All chips may look alike on the outside without being the same on the inside—read the fine print (chapter 20)!

Rule #21: All chips expect "+" and "−" power connections to their designated power supply pins, even if these voltages are *also* connected to other pins for other reasons—withhold them at your own risk (or entertainment; chapter 20).

Rule #22: Always use a resistor when powering an LED, otherwise the circuit and/or LED might blow out (chapter 22).

Rule #23: Distortion is Truth. (Poss's law; chapter 23).

Rule #24: It is easier to drill round holes than slots (chapter 27).

Rule #25: Never trust the writing on the wall-wart (chapter 30).

The Laws of the Avant-Garde

Law #1: Do it backwards (chapter 4).

Law #2: Make it louder, a lot (chapter 7).

Law #3: Slow it down, a lot (chapter 13).

Appendix E

NOTES ON THE AUDIO CD

In assembling the CD that accompanies this book, I chose existing works by musicians and sound artists which connect to the topics, techniques, and aesthetics discussed in the text. The intent was to place the technical details of the book in a musical context, and to preserve for the experimenter the surprise and satisfaction of hearing a circuit for the first time without a preconceived notion of what it should sound like. Most of the tracks are excerpted from longer pieces; a few were produced especially for this CD.

Track Notes
Circuit Sniffing

1. Andy Keep, "My Laptop Colony—Colony in My Laptop," 3'11"
2. Nicolas Collins, "El Loop" (excerpt) 2'17"
3. David First, "Tell Tale 2.1," 1'6"

The three tracks listed above all use electromagnetic signals as their primary sound material (see chapter 3 and "Mortal Coils" in chapter 3). For "My Laptop Colony—Colony in My Laptop," Andy Keep placed a telephone pickup (see figure 3.1) on his laptop and recorded while he booted the computer and began running his concert software. "El Loop" is an excerpt from a ride on a Chicago Transit Authority elevated train, recorded through stereo telephone pickups. The sounds in "Tell Tale 2.1" result from the Theremin-like interference between two portable radios placed next to each other.

Jumping Speakers

4. John Bowers, "Study One for Victorian Synthesizer," 4'34"

John Bowers created the sounds in this piece using only batteries, clip leads, and scrap metal (see chapter 5).

Piezo Music

5. Collin Olan, "rec01" (excerpt), 3'10"
6. Peter Cusack, "Baikal Ice" (excerpt), 2'39"
7. Richard Lerman, "Changing States 6" (excerpt), 3'38"

These tracks reveal the range of micro-sounds produced by melting and heating that can be heard through inexpensive contact mikes (see chapter 7). Collin Olan froze two Plasti Dip-encased piezos in a block of ice and recorded as it melted. Peter Cusack used similar homemade hydrophones to record the breakup of ice flows during the spring thaw in Lake Baikal. In "Changing States 7" Richard Lerman uses a butane torch to "bow" metal whiskers solder to the edge of piezo disks (see "Piezo Music" in chapter 7).

Drivers

8.   Ute Wassermann, "Improvisation" (excerpt), 3'03"
9.   Nicolas Collins, "It Was A Dark And Stormy Night" (excerpt), 1'10"

These two tracks demonstrate the ethereal effects of resonating materials with sound (see chapter 8 and "David Tudor and *Rainforest*" and "Drivers," both in chapter 8) Ute Was-sermann sings through a "corked" speaker (see chapter 8, figure 8.3 and "Drivers") held against a gong, in an improvised trio with Vladimir Tarasov and Manos Tsangaris on percussion. Nicolas Collins' voice drives electromagnetic coils placed above guitar strings (see figure in "Drivers") and triggers percussion samples, accompanied by Guy Klucevsek on accordion. In both tracks the voices are filtered, resonated, and reverberated by tuned metal to produce sounds akin to an old plate-reverb, or shouting into a piano with the sustain pedal down.

Laying of Hands

10.   Josh Winters, "Radio Study #4," 2002, 2'14"

An AM radio is played with damp fingers (see chapter 11).

Composers Inside Electronics

11.   David Behrman, "Players With Circuits," 6'00"
12.   Christian Terstegge, "Ohrenbrennen" ("Ear-burn,") 13'38"

In "Players with Circuits," David Behrman and Gordon Mumma, pioneers in the field of hardware hacking, mix oscillators (see chapter 18) and acoustic piano into homemade ring modulators to produce unstable, sideband-intensive sound explosions. In "Ohrenbren-nen" ("Ear-burn") four oscillators are controlled by photocells inside small altar-like boxes containing candles; the pitches of the oscillators rise in imperfect unison, punctuated by swoops that trace the sputtering of the candles as they burn down (see "Composing Inside Electronics" in chapter 14).

Circuit Bending

13.   Phil Archer, "'Yamaha PSS-380" 4'37"
14.   P. Sing Cho, "Long Nosed," 5'10"
15.   Maestros, "Electricity and its Double," 2'54"
16.   Jane Henry, "The Chip is Down: Jerry Goes to Glory" (excerpt) part 2 of "In Jerry's Wake," 2'01"

Here come the Benders! All four of these tracks were made with bent electronic toys and other simple hacked circuits (see chapters 12–17, and "Circuit Bending" in chapter 15). Phil Archer makes arbitrary connections between components on the circuit board of a Yamaha keyboard with a piece of wire, triggering notes, bursts of noise and warped "auto-accompaniment" sequences (see figure 15.11). "Long Nosed" is a live performance by the all-bending quintet, P. Sing Cho; their sounds are born of tables strewn with electronic ephemera. In "Electricity and its Double" the Maestros (David Novak and James Fei) pair a bassoon with a toy that plays barnyard sounds. "The Chip is Down" is Jane Henry's duet for violin and hacked greeting card, excerpted from a larger work dedicated to the maverick Texas composer, Jerry Hunt (see figure in "The Luthiers" in chapter 29).

Distortion

17.   Robert Poss, "Dicer," 2'35"

Robert Poss' guitar is chopped and channeled by two "Fuzzy Dicers" (see chapter 24, figure 24.1).

Optical Music

18.   Stephen Vitiello, "World Trade Center Recordings," 2'05"
19.   Norbert Möslang, "Blinking Lights," 4'00"
20.   Yasunao Tone, "Imperfection Theorem of Silence," 2'05"

These three pieces link light and sound (see chapter 25 and "Visual Music" in chapter 25). Stephen Vitiello placed a photocell on the eyepiece of a telescope (see figure 25.3) and focused it on nighttime traffic far below his studio on the ninety-first floor of the World Trade Center. Norbert Möslang's similar circuits extract rhythmic patterns from blinking bicycle lights. Yasunao Tone uses Scotch tape to disturb the laser reading a CD, resulting in a plethora of glitches.

Biographies

Andy Keep is a performer/composer, who researches behavioral models and timbrel languages of audio feedback set-ups through responsive strategies in improvisation and composition. He works in Bath, UK.

Nicolas Collins, the author, has been hacking and designing musical circuits since he was eighteen years old. He was also one of the first artists to use microcomputers in live performance (1978). New York born and raised, he currently lives in Chicago. Additional information on his work is available at http://www.NicolasCollins.com.

New Yorker David First has long been interested in the secret worlds of minimal gestures, hyper-sensual tuning relationships, and ritual phenomena. Additional information on his work is available at http://www.davidfirst.com.

John Bowers is a composer, performer, computer scientist, and researcher of early electrical instruments. He currently works in Norwich, UK. Additional information on his work is available at http://www.nw.net.

Collin Olan is a New York-based artist and performer working with computers and recording technology to create alternate visions of everyday phenomena.

Peter Cusack's work combines his long-standing interests in improvisation, live electronic performance, and environmental recording. London-based, he travels extensively in pursuit of sound.

Richard Lerman has been working with piezo disks since the late 1970s, integrating them into performance instruments, audio installations, and recordings. He lives in Phoenix, Arizona. Additional information on his work is available at http://www.west.asu.edu/rlerman.

Ute Wassermann is a singer, sound artist, and instrument designer based in Berlin. She has collaborated with numerous composers and improvisers. Her multiphonic singing brings the various resonant spaces of the body into vibration, and generates resonant phenomena in space.

Josh Winters is a visual artist and performer working in Chicago and Urbana, Illinois.

New Yorker David Behrman was one of the first composers to build his own electronic instruments in the 1960s. He has also been at the forefront of live computer music since the advent of the Kim 1 microcomputer (see Foreward).

Since the mid-1980s, Hamburg-based sound artist Christian Terstegge has specialized in elegant, minimal installations incorporating homemade circuitry.

Phil Archer's work revolves largely around the creative modification of consumer electronic devices, altering their sound production capabilities to generate previously impossible results. He is based in Norwich, England. Additional information on his work is available at http://www.studios.uea.ac.uk/people/staff/archer.

P Sing Cho is an all circuit-bending band of five London artists: Knut Aufermann, Moshi Honen, Sarah Washington, Chris Weaver, and Dan Wilson.

The Maestros (James Fei and David Novak) perform live with acoustic instruments, hacked toys, contact mikes, and vintage analog synthesizer modules. They are loosely based in New York City. Additional information on their work is available at http://www/jamesfei.com.

Jane Henry performs free improvisations and original compositions as a solo violinist, and sometimes with low-tech electronic devices, and/or human partners. She is currently active in presenting international new music improvisers in Texas venues. Additional information on her work is available at www.janehenry.com.

Robert Poss was a founding member of Band Of Susans. He has performed and recorded with Nicolas Collins, Rhys Chatham, Ben Neill, Phill Niblock, David Dramm, and Bruce Gilbert and recently began working with choreographers Alexandra Beller and Sally Gross. A New Yorker, he continues to perform his innovative guitar and electronics pieces in the United States and Europe. Additional information on his work is available at http://www.distortionistruth.com.

Stephen Vitiello is an electronic musician and media artist. His sound installations, photographs, and sculptures have been exhibited internationally. He currently resides in Richmond, Virginia where he is an assistant professor in the Department of Kinetic Imaging at Virginia Commonwealth University. Additional information on his work is available at http://www.ubu.com/sound/vitiello.html.

Norbert Möslang co-founded the legendary Swiss electronic duo Voice Crack in 1972. He and currently performs solo and in collaboration with many musicians around the world. He is a master of "cracking everyday electronics" and a virtuoso of circuit-based performance. Additional information on his work is available at http://homepage.hispeed.ch/bots/ and at http://www.moeslang.com.

Yasunao Tone was raised and educated in Japan, but has long been a fixture on the New York avant-garde music scene. He is the first person to have made music out of intentionally-induced CD malfunctions.

Credits

Artists retain full copyright on their submitted tracks.

1. Andy Keep, "My Laptop Colony—Colony in My Laptop" was previously released on *A Call For Silence*, Sonic Arts Network, 2004. Used by permission of Andy Keep.
2. Nicolas Collins, "El Loop" was commissioned by Chris Cutler for broadcast on Resonance FM, London, 2002. Used by permission of Nicolas Collins.
3. David First, "Tell Tale 2.1" was previously released on *A Call For Silence*, Sonic Arts Network, 2004. Used by permission of David First.
4. John Bowers, "Study One for Victorian Synthesizer" was recorded expressly for this CD. Used by permission of John Bowers.
5. Collin Olan, "rec01" was released in full on *rec01*, Apestaartje CD, 2002. Used by permission of Colin Olan and Apestaartje.
6. Peter Cusack, "Baikal Ice" was released in full on *Baikal Ice (Spring 2003)*, ReR CD. Used by permission of Peter Cusack.
7. Richard Lerman, "Changing States 6" was recorded in concert at the Audio Arts Festival in Krakow, Poland, 1999. Used by permission of Richard Lerman.
8. Ute Wassermann, "Improvisation" was recorded in concert at Akademie Schloss Solitude in 1995, and was released in full on *Improvised Music From Solitude in Eleven Parts* (Vladimir Tarasov, artistic director,) Akademie Schloss Solitude CD, 1995. Used by permission of Jean-Baptiste Joly, artistic director, Akademie Schloss Solitude, Manos Tsangaris, Vladimir Tarasov and Ute Wassermann.
9. Nicolas Collins, "It Was A Dark And Stormy Night" was released in full on *It Was A Dark And Stormy Night*, Trace Elements CD, 1992. Used by permission of Nicolas Collins.
10. Josh Winters, "Radio Study #4" is used by permission of Josh Winters.
11. David Behrman, "Players With Circuits" was recorded in concert at Lincoln Center Library, New York City, in 1966, and was previously released on *Wave Train*, Alga Marghen CD, 1999. Used by permission of David Behrman.
12. Christian Terstegge, "Ohrenbrennen" was recorded in concert at Künstlerhaus Hamburg, Hamburg, Germany, 1988. Used by permission of Christian Terstegge.
13. Phil Archer, "Yamaha PSS-380" is used by permission of Phil Archer.
14. P. Sing Cho, "Long Nosed" was recorded live at the 12 Bar Club, London, England, 2005. Used by permission of Sarah Washington.
15. Maestros, "Electricity and its Double" was previously released on *Precision Electro-Acoustics*, Organized Sound Recordings, 2001. Used by permission of James Fei.
16. Jane Henry, "The Chip is Down: Jerry Goes to Glory" was recorded in concert at Roulette, New York City, by Jim Staley, 1996. Used by permission of Jane Henry.
17. Robert Poss, "Dicer" was recorded expressly for this CD. Used by permission of Robert Poss.
18. Stephen Vitiello, "World Trade Center Recordings" (1999) was previously released on *A Call For Silence*, Sonic Arts Network, 2004. Used by permission of Stephen Vitiello.

19.   Norbert Möslang, "Blinking Lights" was recorded expressly for this CD. Used by permission of Norbert Möslang.
20.   Yasunao Tone, "Imperfection Theorem of Silence" was previously released on *A Call For Silence*, Sonic Arts Network, 2004. Used by permission of Yasunao Tone.

CD Mastering: Robert Poss.

ILLUSTRATION CREDITS

All photographs and illustrations by Simon Lonergan except:

Figure 1.3, 5.4, 7.7, 8.2, 15.6c, 15.12, 17.4, 18.11, 19.5 © Nicolas Collins.

Figure 11.1 photos © Nicolas Collins, design by Simon Lonergan.

Figure 15.11, 17.1, and "Circuit Bender," page 92 © Phil Archer, used by permission.

Figure 17.5 © David Behrman, used by permission.

Figure in "Mortal Coils," page 12 copyright © Gert-Jan Prins, used by permission.

Figure in "Piezo Music," page 35 by Andrzej Kramarz, used by permission of Richard Lerman and Andrzej Kramarz. © Andrzej Kramarz

Figure in "Piezo Music," page 35 © Eric Leonardson, used by permission.

Figure in "David Tudor and *Rainforest*," page 40 drawing by David Tudor, used by permission of Jean Rigg and the David Tudor Trust. © David Tudor Trust

Figure in "Drivers," page 44 © Ted Blanco, used by permission.

Figure in "Drivers," page 44 © Ute Wassermann, used by permission.

Figure in "Drivers," page 45 © André Hoekzema, used by permission of Nicolas Collins.

Figure in "Drivers," page 46 © Gert Jan van Rooij, used by permission of Nicolas Collins.

Figure in "Tape," page 50 drawing by Laurie Anderson © Laurie Anderson, used by permission of Laurie Anderson/Canal Street Communications.

Figure in "Tape," page 51 © César Eugenio Dávila-Irizarry, used by permission.

Figure in "Composing Inside Electronics," page 80 © Paul De Marinis, used by permission.

Figure in "Composing Inside Electronics," page 81 © Norbert Möslang, used by permission.

Figure in "Composing Inside Electronics," page 81 © Christian Terstegge, used by permission.

Figure in "Circuit Bending," page 93 © John Bowers, used by permission.

Figure in "Circuit Bending," page 93 © Sarah Washington, used by permission.

Figure in "Visual Music," page 165 © Billy Roisz, used by permission.

Figure in "Visual Music," page 166 © Yasunao Tone, used by permission.

Figure in "Visual Music," page 166 © Baron Wollman for the Tape Music Center, used by permission of Lowell Cross.

Figure in "Visual Music," page 167 © Lowell Cross, used by permission.

Figure in "Visual Music," page 167 © BMBCon, used by permission.

Figure in "Visual Music," page 168 © Jon Satrom, used by permission.

Figure in "The Luthiers," page 193 by André Hoekzema, © André Hoekzema, used by permission of Laetitia Sonami.

Figure in "The Luthiers," page 193 © Istvan Szilasi, used by permission of Jane Henry.

INDEX

Page numbers in italic refer to figures.